Dame Celia Johnson is p[ ]
as Laura Jesson in Davi[ ]
In fact her acting career spanned more than fifty years until
her death in 1982. She began her film career during the Second
World War when she was chosen by Noel Coward to play
his wife in *In Which We Serve*. *This Happy Breed* followed
and then *Brief Encounter*, the final few days filming of which
was interrupted by VE Day celebrations.

Now, Celia Johnson's daughter, Kate Fleming, draws on
her parents' letters, reminiscences of friends and her own
memories to produce a touching and poignant portrait of one
of Britain's best-loved stars.

Kate Fleming is the elder daughter of Celia Johnson. She read Russian at Oxford University and has written a book on the Churchill family. She is married to John Grimond and they have three daughters.

Also by Kate Fleming

The Churchills

CELIA JOHNSON
A Biography

Kate Fleming

ORION

AN ORION PAPERBACK

First published in Great Britain by
George Weidenfeld and Nicolson Ltd in 1991
This paperback edition published in 1993 by Orion Books Ltd,
Orion House, 5 Upper St Martin's Lane, London WC2H 9EA

A CIP catalogue record for this book is available from
the British Library.

ISBN: 1 85797 162 0

Typeset at Create Publishing Services Ltd, Bath, Avon

Printed in England by Clays Ltd, St Ives plc

Contents

Illustrations

The author and publishers are most grateful to the copyright holders for permission to reproduce their photographs.

Introduction

A publisher approached my mother, Celia Johnson, in 1979 and asked her if she would consider writing her memoirs. She refused. 'I told them that I won't write my autobiography because I never had an affair with Frank Sinatra, and if I had had, I wouldn't tell anyone.' This book, though not salacious, would not have had her blessing. In spite of the reservations she would have had, it nevertheless seemed to me to be a story worth telling. It is an English story, very much of its time, shaped by two world wars.

Celia was on the stage for over fifty years. The sort of career that she had, fashioned at the outset on the West End stage, no longer exists. A performer now darts – if he or she is lucky – between London theatre, regional theatre, television, commercials, voice-overs, video promotions, cinema and radio. In the 1920s, when Celia began acting, an actor or actress looked forward to working on the open stage, no more, no less.

Celia belonged to the generation of Laurence Olivier, John Gielgud, Ralph Richardson and Peggy Ashcroft – to a glorious age of British acting. Celia gave herself less to her profession than did her distinguished colleagues. She once said to a fellow-actor, Robert Harris, that she didn't know why she acted – she simply found herself in plays and she wasn't sure why. Her touch, however, was true.

During the war, when she lived in the country with her widowed sister and widowed sister-in-law and eight small children, she was unable to commit herself to the run of a West End play. By chance she began her work in films. She made three films then with Noel Coward and David Lean, culminating, in the last year of the war, with *Brief Encounter*, a classic of British cinema and her enduring monument.

Her association with and marriage to Peter Fleming was of very long standing. He was a brilliant travel writer before

the war, a landowner and urbane essayist after. I was surprised
to find, after Celia's death, almost all Peter's letters to her
from their earliest days together, in 1932, to the end of the
war – surprised because Celia was scatty, untidy, kept no
records and lost many things. I also found her letters to him
in a box at the back of a cupboard. Peter's letters are immacula-
tely written; hers show her natural, unaffected character, and
those written during the war give a clear picture of her life
in the country, small domestic considerations being inter-
spersed with accounts of her work in the Women's Auxiliary
Police Corps and calls from, say, Noel Coward or the producer,
Binkie Beaumont, with offers of parts.

My sister and I were born after the war when Celia was
nearly forty, and so, by the time we were of an age to reason
and reflect, Celia was well into middle age. She rarely talked
of the past, being of a disposition to look forward rather than
back. Therefore only the last part of her life was familiar to
me; the earlier years have involved research and discovery. Not
many now remember her performances in the 1930s, so I have
been obliged to rely on the critics of the time; in particular I
have quoted from James Agate of the *Sunday Times*, Charles
Morgan of *The Times*, W.A.Darlington of the *Daily Telegraph*,
Ivor Brown of the *Observer* and J.C.Trewin, who over the years
wrote for various papers, all of whom were in their posts for
many years and wrote of the theatre with perception.

Many people have helped and encouraged me in this work.
In particular, I would like to thank my brother, Nichol, and
my sister, Lucy; unwittingly we were responsible for keeping
Celia from the theatre during her prime. I would not have
been able to write about the very early years without the help
of my aunt, Pamela Dennis, Celia's older sister, nor about
the early thirties without the help of Lady Mary Clive, whose
memory is first class, and Sir Rupert Hart-Davis. I am most
grateful to them. I would like to thank Mrs James Thomson
for recalling the war years spent with Celia at Merrimoles.
I also thank my brother-in-law, Simon Williams, who let me
use him as a theatrical encyclopaedia, Frith Banbury, who
saw nearly all of Celia's stage performances and was able to
put them into perspective, and Duff Hart-Davis, who wrote

a thorough biography of my father, Peter Fleming, in 1974, when all the friends and relations were still alive. Celia's brother, John Johnson, was keen for me to write this book but sadly did not live to see me get down to it. Thanks, too, to my husband, Johnny, whose editing, schooled by many years at *The Economist*, was sharp and to the point.

I would also like to thank Andrew Alford, Mark Amory, Lindsay Anderson, Mrs J. Anderson, the late Dame Peggy Ashcroft, Lady Helen Asquith, Mrs Philip Astley, Christopher Balfour, Eirene Beck, Tony Britton, Stuart Burge, Simon Cadell, Judy Campbell, Joyce Carey, Jacquie Childs, librarian at St Paul's Girls' School, Bryan Coleman, Peter Copley, Caroline Cornish at the BBC Written Archive Centre, Michael Denison, the late Ralph Dennis, William Douglas-Home and Lady Dacre, Robert Eddison, Emma Fisher, Amaryllis Fleming, Charm Fleming, Lord and Lady Glendevon, Sir Alec Guinness, Kendall Hailey, Verena Hanbury, Robert Harris, Mrs Alan Hartley, Sir Anthony Havelock-Allan, Patricia Hayes, the late Raymond Huntley, Angela Huth, Ann Hutton, C.R.Jakes at the Central Library, Cambridge, Mrs Oscar Johnson, Peter Johnson, Alan Keith, Lady Keswick, Mrs Maisie Landale, the late Sir David Lean, Marjorie Linklater, Patricia McNaughton, Anna Massey, Mrs Barbara Miall, Sir John Mills, Philip Mitford, Caroline Moorehead, Sheridan Morley, Ronald Neame, Lady Nugent, Mr and Mrs Stan Nowak, Brian Oulton, Eva Parslow, the late Bill Pound, Tristram Powell, Alvin Rakoff, Mr and Mrs Frank Regent, Margaretta Scott, Alexander Schouvaloff, Lorna Schuster, Irene Shubik, David Taylor at the Central Library, Manchester, the staff at the Theatre Museum, London, Mrs Anthony Thesiger, James Thomson, Barbara Todd at RADA, Dorothy Upton, Michael White, Margaret Williams, Judy Wilson and Mary Wood.

Weidenfeld and Nicolson maintained a blind faith in the unwritten book and their editor, Rosemary Legge, subjected the written text to a patient scrutiny; I am most grateful.

I apologise for any inaccuracies or omissions and trust that my mother will forgive me.

Kate Fleming
JUNE 1991

1

Cotton and cloth

The beginning was very ordinary. Celia Elizabeth Johnson was born on 18 December 1908 in Richmond in Surrey, where her father, Robert Johnson, was a doctor. She was his second child. Pamela, her older sister, had been born in 1906, and John, her brother was born in 1912. Ethel Johnson, their mother, was a handsome, nervous woman from Lancashire. The household in Ellerker Gate on Richmond Hill had two maids, Ellen and Charlotte.

It was a comfortable, respectable, Edwardian, English middle-class family – almost the epitome of such a family. Go back a generation into the nineteenth century to Robert's and Ethel's parents, Celia's grandparents, and you confront a phalanx of worthy members of the Victorian middle class; yet look a little closer at them and the differences begin to show; nuances of region, of belief, of character. Attitudes diverge, temperaments clash, disapproval is shown.

The Johnsons, Celia's father's family, came from Cambridge and Essex, from the east of England. The Griffiths, her mother Ethel's family, came from the North-west, from Lancashire and from Cumberland and, as the name suggests, from Wales. Surprisingly, though on the face of it they were so similar, the two families saw things differently. The Johnsons owned a shop in Cambridge – Johnson, Son and Nephew – suppliers and outfitters to the colleges, and were prominent in local Liberal politics, aldermen and city councillors. The Griffiths, typical beneficiaries of nineteenth-century free enterprise, owned and ran three cotton mills in the North in the heart of the Victorian textile country. Both families were prosperous and well respected. Both provided their children with good education: Robert Johnson, Celia's father, attended one of the best schools in Cambridge – the Perse School – and her mother, Ethel Griffiths, one of the best in Manchester – Pendleton High School. The same Christian names, often a social pointer, occur in both families: there was an Ethel and an Oscar in each.

Therefore, when Robert Johnson's proposal of marriage was accepted by Ethel Griffiths, it seemed a good match, and, it would appear, well balanced on the social scale. Thomas Arthur Griffiths, Ethel's father, the cotton manufacturer, as a businessman and with his daughter's interest at heart, wrote to Robert, his prospective son-in-law, to ask whether he had taken out life insurance or some similar provision. Robert replied in a flippant fashion, and in so doing caused offence and infuriated Thomas Griffiths who attempted to call off the wedding. 'The row ruined the summer,' Winifred, Ethel's younger sister, later recalled. Poor Ethel went to London to find Robert's brother, Percy Johnson (who worked at Leggatts, the fine art dealers), to ask if he knew whether Robert would marry her or not.

In the event they were married and the wedding took place in Worsley outside Manchester on 1 October 1904. Robert spent the night before in the Midland Hotel in Manchester (and always said that he was so nervous that he put mustard in his porridge at breakfast). In the church he was made to kneel on a marrow which had been positioned for harvest festival. Ethel wore a sealskin coat and hat which she had bought at Kendalls in Manchester over a pale blue suit and lace blouse. Her parents did attend, but with bad grace. Not until Pamela was born two years later were they reconciled to the marriage.

Ethel was the only one of Thomas Griffiths' five daughters to marry; her older sister died as a child and none of her younger sisters – Dora, Amy and Winifred – married; they remained at home and after their parents had died the three of them continued to live together for the rest of their lives. The girls had two brothers, Edgar and Oscar; Edgar went blind and died young, and Oscar in time inherited the cotton mills. Their father had started and built up three cotton mills in Preston and Accrington and was very proud when the moment came that his business was quoted on the Manchester Stock Exchange. Celia's sister, Pamela, remembers being taken by her Aunt Amy to one of the mills, and climbing high up a narrow stair on the wall of the mill and looking down over the large clanking machinery. She also remembers hearing the clogs of the workers as they walked to the mills.

Thomas Griffiths was a typical figure of the Industrial Revolution. In appearance, he was a tall strong-looking man with a small beard. He was formal in manner, and as an employer was thought to be considerate. He played the piano well, until in old age his fingers seized up and he bought a pianola. His wife, Emma Snape, came from the Lake District. Her pronounced eyebrows and quizzical expression show a woman of character. Her grandchildren found her a little intimidating. Her household was beautifully organised and she ran it with iron efficiency, a skill not passed on to her daughter, Ethel, or in due course to her granddaughter, Celia. Ethel and her sisters, Dora, Amy, and Winifred, had to turn out their rooms once a week; Winifred usually paid Amy or Dora to do hers for her. Ethel and Winifred were the stronger characters; Amy and Dora were quiet and obliging.

The family first lived in a house called Devonshire Villa in Ellesmere Park in Eccles, just outside Manchester. Later they moved a little further out to The Gables in Broad Oak Park, Worsley. This last was a large house with a spacious and well-kept garden at the end of which was a pergola. The garden adjoined Worsley golf course and Thomas Griffiths would put mugs of water for the caddies on the wall by the pergola. In the distance beyond the golf course, the chimneys of the textile mills could be seen.

Ethel Griffiths had, in fact, been sent away from the family as a small child to stay with her aunt and uncle, Hannah and Judson Berry, in Manchester. The Berrys had had a child who had died young, and Ethel was sent for two or three years to take its place. When this odd arrangement came to an end, she had great difficulty settling back into her own family, and from then on was always something of a rebel. This may explain why, ultimately, she was able to escape from her pious, claustrophobic family, something her sisters never achieved.

After the death of Thomas Griffiths towards the end of the First World War, Emma Griffiths sold The Gables and moved – with Amy, Dora and Winifred – to Lytham St Anne's (near the golf course). When she died a few years later, the spinster daughters upped and went to Menton in France because of Winifred's supposed delicate health. No doubt finding foreign ways not to their liking, they returned north and settled in Ilkley in Yorkshire because of its hydro. There they remained for the rest of their days, never ceasing, as Lancastrians, to find fault with the ways of Yorkshire people.

There was nothing whatsoever wrong with Winifred's health. During the war she had much enjoyed working in the office of the cotton mills and ever afterwards hankered after some similar employment. She was restricted by the era in which she lived. She did do some work, part time, for a doctor in Ilkley and the sisters' house was organised to suit her hours. She was also a golfer of county standard. Dora was her slave and did as she was told. Amy had wanted to be a nun, but contented herself with going to church a lot and working with the poor and destitute in Leeds. Once, when she was ill, Winifred went in her place to make her usual visits but found the work was not at all to her taste – 'It nearly killed us,' she said. Ethel used to call on the kindhearted Amy to help her out when there were crises in Richmond. But when anyone ever suggested a visit to the aunts in Ilkley, Winifred would say: 'Write to them, Dora, and say it's not feasible.'

The Griffiths were conventional, God-fearing, sensible and a little solemn. They were good games players and enjoyed golf, tennis and bridge. They were tall and athletic. The Johnsons, Celia's father's family, were squatter and rounder and played cricket. They were more easy-going than the Griffiths, more artistic and less churchy. On the whole they were rather clever.

The outfitter's shop that Robert's father ran in Cambridge had been started by a forebear, John Johnson, around 1800. It passed, through the nineteenth century, from him to a Susannah Johnson, to William Johnson, to another John (Robert's father) in the 1890s. By the time Celia came to know it, it had been established for over a hundred years. John Johnson, her grandfather, was a small man with a long white beard. You would find him at the back of the shop wearing a black velvet jacket with a parrot as companion. He had a cabinet there filled with many precious stones, all labelled; he would allow his grandchildren to take them out and hold them up to the light. His wife, Elizabeth Carter, of broad face and pleasant disposition, died in 1909 (when Celia was one). She came from a large family of furniture dealers based in the Minories in the City of London; she was an accomplished landscape painter.

John and Elizabeth Johnson had five children who survived infancy: Robert (Celia's father); Percy, who met Ernest Leggatt at a children's party given by his aunt, Mrs Robert Carter, in 1883 and subsequently joined him as a partner in Leggatt Brothers, the fine art dealers (Percy's son, Oscar, left Leggatts and, with his son, started Oscar and Peter Johnson, also picture dealers); Edward, a public-spirited fellow who championed, in particular, the cause of disabled ex-servicemen and their families after the great war; he inherited the shop in Cambridge, which, after his early death in 1922, was sold, but continued under different ownership until 1981; Bessie, who kept house first for her father and then for her brother, Edward; and Ethel, who married Will Dyson, headmaster of Ripon Grammar School. Robert had a talent for verse, Percy painted birds and flowers, and Bessie and Ethel did superb needlepoint; a wing chair covered in the finest tapestry by Bessie was sent to America, after photographs had been taken of it and sent to all the family.

Robert, who was clever at school, wanted to be a doctor but his father said that he could not support him during his studies, so he went as an apprentice pharmacist to Liverpool Royal Infirmary and studied to be a doctor at the same time. It was while he was there that he was introduced to the Griffiths and met Ethel. He would join her family on trips to Windermere and other places. He also found time to write, usually in verse, humorous sketches for the other medical students to perform. He had a great facility for amusing rhymes and limericks and could write page after page of verse. While he was there he published a book of poems called *The*

Parachute and Other Bad Shots, a typical pun, which was illustrated by a friend from Cambridge, C.E.Brock. This is what
he proposed to write in the fly-leaf:

> When your friend takes this book as may happen some time
> And begins from the height of culture sublime
>> To launch critical curses
>> At some of the verses
>
> Bid him look to the drawings – and not to the rhyme.

He patented a somewhat dangerous trick which involved putting a hat pin into a toy hat. He had a gentle wit and was
a popular fellow. He was also able, and when he came to
the end of his medical studies, his examiners suggested that
he work for a further qualification. Probably for financial
reasons at the time, but to his lifelong regret, he did not take
up their suggestion. Instead, after a couple of years (1896 and
1897) as a ship's doctor sailing first to South America and
then to Australia, he looked around for a practice to buy.
In those days, as a doctor, you bought a house and practice
together. It was the very good furniture, no doubt appraised
by his cousins the Carters, in the house in Ellerker Gate in
Richmond that decided him in favour of that particular practice. His sister, Bessie, bicycled round Cambridgeshire and
found two maids for him, Ellen and Charlotte. He was therefore well established by the time he married Ethel and brought
her back to the house in Richmond in 1904.

Such was the family into which Celia was born; it was
very plain, very much of its time and very very English –
with a dash of Welsh. Take her four grandparents – John
Johnson, Elizabeth Carter, Thomas Griffiths, Emma Snape
– you could scarcely find more ordinary, English names. From
the Johnsons she got her round face and her large eyes, and
from the Griffiths, her tall, slim figure and her athleticism.
From the Johnsons she inherited a sense of fun and a sense
of humour, an easy-going attitude, some creative flair and
an aesthetic sensibility; from the Griffiths, thrift, stoicism,
and a sense of moral duty, and a degree of northern toughness;

to some extent these two strains, the creative and the conventional, were at war within her throughout her life. It was an inheritance with scant trace of any feeling for the theatre.

Richmond, lying round a little hill on the banks of the Thames, a few miles from the centre of London, has always been a handsome town. It still has many well-proportioned Regency and Georgian houses. At the turn of the century with even more of those houses still standing, and not ravaged by traffic, it had great charm. With its elegant architecture, a beautiful sweep of the river Thames running through it, and the vast and glorious Richmond Park with its herds of red and fallow deer, it is the best of suburbia. Suburban now, in 1900 it felt more detached from London. Not until you crossed Hammersmith Bridge did you feel that you were entering London. It was a lovely place for a family to live and Pamela, Celia, and John had a settled, happy childhood there in Ellerker Gate on Richmond Hill.

Dr Johnson was a popular general practitioner with many loyal patients. After the First World War he was doctor to the Star and Garter Home, and for a while he was physician to the Duke and Duchess of York (the future King George VI and Queen Elizabeth) when they lived at White Lodge in Richmond Park in the early days of their marriage. His children inherited no interest in medicine. They remember sitting on the stairs and listening to him give his customary advice over the telephone: 'Well, I should keep him warm and let him inhale.' He was a passionate early motorist and kept for many years a much-loved de Dion Bouton. It had two pedals, one for the clutch and one which served as accelerator and brake combined. When, in the end, he had to replace this car, he was unable to cope with the three pedals in his new one and had several minor accidents in Richmond. He would always ask anyone arriving by car to see him: 'Did you get through?' – as if motoring were an exciting adventure. He could always be teased.

Ethel, his wife, had a less equable temperament. She ran a mildly chaotic house and would often get into a nervous state about things. She was more of a fusser. There was a little bit of Welsh fire in her, and she was less amenable to being teased.

Pamela was round-faced and pretty and a little plump, uncomplicated in nature and a favourite of her father. Once, as a small child when her father was ill, she had been sent to stay with her grandmother, Emma Griffiths, in Lancashire. Instructions for what she should eat had been sent with her; these had been ripped up by her grandmother who had then fed her largely on Horlicks, or so it was believed. Pamela's tendency to plumpness as a child was always blamed on this visit. Celia (who was known as Betty when she was small) was a thin child, with enormous eyes and prominent teeth and limbs not fully under control – neither plain nor pretty. Her father was rather frightened of her, and her mother at her command. John, a weakling, was much cosseted, or so the sturdier Pam felt. He was a quiet, clever boy with an easy-going character and bookish leanings; he became in later life a respected literary agent.

Holidays were sometimes spent with the Griffiths in North Wales. Thomas Griffiths would take a house which belonged to Lloyd George at Criccieth. He would walk his grandchildren to the chapel there and sit on the grass outside and listen to the Welsh singing inside. He would take a little silver knife on a chain out of his pocket and cut an apple into pieces for them. The aunts would take them to the sea.

Summer holidays with the Johnsons were spent on the east coast, at Hunstanton in Norfolk. These were larger family gatherings, for there were more Johnson cousins. Robert's brother, Percy, had five children (Oscar, who joined Leggatts, Alec, who was killed in the last week of the First World War, Margaret, who remained in Cambridge, and Mary and Cynthia, who both became architects and went to live in Africa); they would all stay with a landlady in Old Hunstanton. Robert's sister, Ethel Dyson, had one son, Alec, and they would stay with Bessie Johnson who had a modern house on the sea-front. Robert and Ethel and the children took a house in the village of Holme nearby. The cousins would join up and play on the beach or organise games of cricket which were taken seriously and which Robert would umpire.

Christmas was often spent with the Dysons in their school at Ripon in Yorkshire. There too there were games and charades and Celia would sometimes try and get her cousins to join her in putting on little plays. Her father would entertain the children with displays of magic; he would go behind a screen in the school hall and then reappear in a cloak and hat and red nose and would pretend to mix a huge Christmas pudding which would then explode, to the children's horror and delight. He was a charming and amusing man, a favourite uncle.

When the girls were six and eight, the First World War began. Before long, a camp for wounded soldiers was put up in Richmond Park. Soldiers in blue uniform with bandages and with crutches were seen around and were attended by Dr Johnson. Perhaps moved by the sight of them, or for some other reason, Celia and Pam decided to put on a performance to raise money for the Red Cross. To an audience of their parents' friends they recited some poems and performed a little play, *King Cophetua and the Beggar Maid*. Celia gave a touching performance as the beggar maid making full use of her stick-like arms and legs and her round staring eyes. Pamela was a solid king. They raised 22s. 6d. and took it to the headquarters of the Red Cross which were in an elegant house on Richmond Green. There they solemnly presented the money to a large woman in Red Cross uniform who kept a straight face. To their delight the occasion was reported in the *Richmond and Twickenham Times*.

During the war, Celia and Pamela were sent to do lessons with a Miss Richmond, who had fallen on hard times and was taking in a few pupils. Towards the end of the war, they were both taken very ill with measles; Celia always attributed her poor eyesight to this illness. About the same time as this Ellen, the housemaid, and Nanny, who mostly looked after their delicate little brother, John, never on the best of terms, fell out irreconcilably, and Ellen left; this put Ethel Johnson into a nervous state. So to restore the girls' health and no doubt to help bring back calm to the house, Celia and Pamela were sent for the summer of 1918 to a farm near Pagham in Sussex. A tutor was engaged to teach them geography;

he bicycled out from Bognor every day, and at his approach they hid in the haystacks. They had a heavenly time running free in the countryside, and both remembered the weeks spent there with great affection.

When they returned to Richmond they took the entrance test for St Paul's Girls' School in Hammersmith – and failed. However, Miss Gray, the High Mistress, suggested that they take some lessons with a lady who lived across Brook Green from St Paul's. Thus tutored, they were accepted by the school, and in April 1919, Celia entered Miss Fraser's class (Form III) and Pamela, Miss Wigg's (Upper IV).

St Paul's Girls' School

St Paul's Girls' School has always enjoyed a high reputation. Founded in 1904 by the Mercers' Company as a sister school to the long-established St Paul's Boys' School, from the outset it prepared girls for all sorts of professions – such as medicine, teaching and the civil service. At a time when women's education in Britain was, on the whole, poor – indeed many middle- and upper-class children never went to school at all, but had a smattering of European culture imparted to them by a governess – St Paul's was sending its abler girls to Oxford and other universities. Many of the women who were educated there in its early days had reason to be grateful to it. Certainly it made a profound impression on them all, and in particular they remember with awe and respect Miss Frances Gray, its first High Mistress (as the principal has always been called).

Miss Gray was immensely august. Part Irish and part American, she was small and erect, her white hair swept most efficiently back into a bun. She wore long grey silk dresses with black net tied round her neck, and on St Patrick's Day she sported an enormous shamrock. She dominated the school, but with a 'beneficent despotism' – very much a force for the good. You listened to what she had to say and felt the better for it. She had strong moral principles, but also a keen understanding of her girls so that her expectations of their behaviour were never unrealistic. She picked her staff well and generally ran an excellent school, putting into practice her theories about education, some of which were advanced for the day. The necessary minimum in education, she considered, was geography and obedience, but few girls, if any, left St Paul's having learnt only those.

Music gave her great pleasure, and she considered herself fortunate to have Gustav Holst as head of music at the school. He was a small quiet man with a gentle nature and a rather surprised expression, much loved by the girls, and the music at the school was spectacular. Celia played the oboe just well enough to be in the orchestra, which was of high calibre. She later said that Holst must have realised that she had little aptitude but he had still taken great trouble and encouraged her. Pamela preferred art to music, so, taking her courage in her hands, asked Miss Gray if she could give up music in favour of drawing. Miss Gray promptly guided her along a passage to a room in which there was a piano, played a note and asked her to sing it. By chance Pamela hit the right note, so Miss Gray said that as she could sing she should not miss the opportunity of being taught by Mr Holst. 'Music cultivates the brain,' she wrote in her autobiography, 'just as Latin or Mathematics cultivate it, only not, perhaps, the same bit of brain.'

Miss Gray also set great store by physical fitness and gymnastics. The school doctor inspected the girls every term, looking in particular for any sign of curvature of the spine – Miss Gray's especial horror. Celia early on was found to be shortsighted, and had to wear glasses for the rest of her life. However she was very good at gym and she soon gained the narrow white girdle which, provided their character was stainless, girls were awarded once they had reached a certain standard. Later, if they showed distinct ability, they were given a broad white girdle. This was much prized. And, in due course, Celia received it too but not before the less athletic Pam – to her surprise and somewhat to her consternation for the news had to be broken tactfully to Celia – had earned one. The school had an early indoor swimming bath with a Heath Robinson system of pipes along the roof for blowing hot air. Girls learned to swim at the end of a long pole. Lacrosse, hockey, netball and cricket were played. Eminence in games, Miss Gray noted, gave you greater status at school than intellect or birth. Celia, as she grew, was marked as a promising netball player, also a good cricket player, and at the top of the school she was in the first lacrosse team. 'C. Johnson is a most promising attack, with a good speed. Her stick work and tackling need continuous practice.' She was very keen.

Miss Gray believed in the use of conversation for learning French, and once a year a French week was held when

Each day throughout the school was heard
La langue parisienne.

Celia enjoyed this and remembered a lot of 'Voulez-vous m'en voyer le sel'. The excellent teaching of Mlle Rivoire, the French teacher, was in fact to pay unexpected dividends later. A play was sometimes performed at the end of the French week, and these were the only plays that were put on at the school, for drama did not rate highly with Miss Gray — although reading aloud did. Her mother had read beautifully to her as a child in Ireland: 'It made me intolerant of much that passes for fine reading,' Miss Gray wrote, 'and it gave me a very hearty desire that every one of my pupils should read aloud with simplicity and intelligence. A beautiful voice is a gift and cannot be had for the asking or even for the working; but no one is obliged to read badly.' One particular bugbear of pronunciation was an inserted 'r' between words, i.e. an idea-r-of, a cedilla-r-under the 'c'; 'Few Southern ears can hear, and no Irish or Scottish ears can tolerate, the intrusive "r".' This irritation stayed with Celia and she would try and correct it in her children.

When Celia and Pam arrived at the school, the First World War had just ended. It was a strange time. Families had suffered devastating losses. Armistice Day was an important date in the school calendar; Miss Gray usually held a fancy dress party. There were Eastern houris, jesters, Red Indians, Grecian goddesses. The party would end with the girls dancing Sir Roger de Coverley and singing 'God Save the King'; one year there was a prevalence of influenza germs, and another year everyone was sent home early because of the dense fog, which often used to suffocate London in those days (indeed the school kept a special dynamo for clearing thick fog). Prizes were presented one year by Princess Mary, and the next by Princess Alice of Athlone. In 1921 Miss Gray had words about the wave of frivolity: 'I think the frivolity is very much on the surface,' she concluded, 'and perhaps rather aggressive where it is found.' The roaring twenties perhaps were on their way.

During the General Strike in 1926 the girls were very much exhorted to get to school as a matter of principle. A contemporary of Celia's, Helen Asquith, remembers feeling that she was letting the side down when she was unable to make the journey. Celia and the other girls from Richmond arrived by boat, passing under Hammersmith Bridge instead of over it.

For Celia, it was a happy time. She was clever, she was athletic, and she was musical enough – she flourished at the school; she was always competitive. Having, like her father, a facility for rhyme, she started writing verse and early on won a nursery rhyme competition:

> *Jack Gentleman*
> Little Jack Gentleman
> Sits among the rushes,
> All around his caravan
> Sing blackbirds and thrushes.
>
> There he'll sell you pots and pans
> Candlesticks and brushes,
> While his pretty little wife
> Curtseys and blushes.

She enjoyed games; she was the best high-jumper. She was busy. She was invited to join La Société Ash; this was a French club of great prestige which occasionally put on plays. In 1924 they staged a tedious production of *L'Oiseau Bleu* by Maeterlinck. Celia took the part of Tyltil, and her friend, Comfort Turner, was Mytyl. Although rather sombre in feel, it was quite an occasion, and the school magazine, the *Paulina*, had this to say:

The Singing Hall was literally full up to the roof and throughout the performance the atmosphere was electrified with interest ... Perhaps it was the dusky robes of 'La Nuit', perhaps the 'sangfroid' of Tyltil, or perhaps the 'wise sad eyes' of La Lumière that filled us with foreboding, and made the Palais de la Nuit a fearful shadow-haunted place.

Celia had found there was something else she enjoyed doing. None of the later efforts of La Société Ash were on such a scale but Celia took part in the few things there were. The Literary and Classical Society read *The Rivals*, with Celia as

Captain Absolute. 'The Society is fortunate in possessing a number of good actresses this year,' the *Paulina* noted. This was followed by an Elizabethan verse-play with songs, *The Knight of the Burning Pestle*, in which Holst's daughter, Imogen, played the heroine. Generally there was little encouragement for acting, and little knowledge of the theatre.

It was rather a surprise therefore that Sybil Thorndike should have visited the Literary Society; this she did in 1924 during her final rehearsals for Shaw's *St Joan*. Later the girls went to see the play at the New Theatre. It was a famous production in which Sybil Thorndike gave a fiery heroic performance of great influence and magnificence.

Celia's main friend at school was Comfort Turner. Rather unusually for that time, Comfort's parents were divorced; her mother was an American novelist called Mary Borden (who later married General Spears) and her father was governor of Exeter prison. Celia sometimes spent part of the holidays with Comfort and her father in Devon. On one occasion she and Comfort were playing by the sea, when Celia jumped from a pier on to a pebbly beach, landed badly and hit her mouth with her knees. Her front teeth were knocked out. In pain and in panic, she rang home, from where the advice came to try and find the teeth. She and Comfort returned to the beach and searched – to no avail. Celia was to have false front teeth for the rest of her life. She was very stoical about the accident at the time.

Around this time, when Celia was about fifteen, her family moved from the house in Ellerker Gate to a larger and very handsome Queen Anne house, Marshgate House, on the Sheen Road in Richmond. Dr Johnson moved his surgery there, and Ethel soon created an untidy old-fashioned cosiness. She had decided, somewhat to Pam's disgust, that the journey from Richmond to St Paul's was too tiring for Celia. So Celia became a boarder at Bute House, a boarding-house run by the school just nearby. Although at first she found the restrictions rather irksome, she came to like and admire Miss Janet Cunningham, who ran it. Janet Cunningham, like Miss Gray, had been brought up in Ireland. On coming to England, she had taken a job running the household of the widowed Sir

John Simon, a former Home Secretary. When this came to an end, she accepted the post at St Paul's. Tall and rather frumpish in appearance, she nevertheless brought to the house a breath of the outside world. She knew many interesting people, she loved the theatre; she covered the walls of Bute House with hessian – a most advanced taste – and on them she hung her good collection of pictures. She held dinner parties. In short, she introduced the girls to a more grown-up life. Plays were occasionally performed in the house. In the one play in which Celia took part, Janet Cunningham recognised a small talent. Celia became very fond of Cunnie (as she was known) and, later, after Celia had left school, Cunnie encouraged and helped her in her career. Celia was never one to put much effort into keeping up with old friends, but she always remained in touch with Janet Cunningham, writing to her regularly in Ireland after her retirement.

Celia left St Paul's in July 1926, after a memorable prize-giving during which 'Lord Who Hast Made Us For Thine Own' was sung by the whole school to Holst's inspiring setting for voices, organs and strings. Without question, the school had given her a good education, and had made a deep impression. When she left that summer, she had her General School Certificate, friends, thick round glasses and new front teeth. She was eager, naive and somewhat unpolished. Miss Gray suggested that she teach – the one true profession to her mind – but Celia replied, so it is said, that she didn't want to because she had noticed that most teachers did not marry and she thought that she would rather like to. Although it sounded insolent, her view was not at odds with Miss Gray's. 'Whatever success attends my old pupils in the careers that they choose for themselves I am always ready to believe that greater happiness and a fuller life awaits those whose destiny it is to become wives and mothers.' However at some time during those seven years, Celia had decided that she would like to act. In a rare interview, given two days before she died, she said, when asked if she had always had ambitions to act, 'I thought I'd rather like it. It was the only thing I was good at. And I thought it might be rather wicked.' She applied to the Royal Academy of Dramatic Art.

3

Alice Gachet and Nigel Playfair

'The object of the Academy is to provide, as is done in other countries, a thorough general training for the Dramatic Stage in England; and to encourage those who show sufficient talent, and to discourage those who do not, from taking up the stage as a profession.' Thus ran the prospectus for the Royal Academy of Dramatic Art in 1927. As far as that stricture went it could have gone either way with Celia.

When she auditioned in November 1926, she did so with no great ambition, but because she thought she rather enjoyed acting. 'As the candidates entered,' wrote the principal Kenneth Barnes of the selection of students, 'we gauged their degree of nervousness; then what kind of coaching – if any – they had had; the quality of voice tone, the sense of spontaneity, facial expression, bodily and intellectual reactions, and deportment.' Celia was accepted. The fees were fifteen guineas a term and two extra if you did French. She continued to live with her parents at Marshgate House from where she travelled to Gower Street, still very much the eager schoolgirl. Margaretta Scott, who although younger was there at the same time, remembers Celia in a short skirt, long brown stockings, her rather dank mouse-coloured hair parted on one side, and iron-rimmed glasses. She also remembers students doing a piece from *St Joan*, possibly for the audition, or possibly soon after, and most producing a rumbustious land-girl in the manner of Sybil Thorndike; Celia, however, played down Joan's militancy and strove instead to bring out her inner spirituality, the force of which inspired an army. Her quiet sensitive reading was thought effective and original by her fellow-students.

By the second term, she and Margaretta Scott had gained enough points from their classes to share a scholarship (seven guineas a term). The subjects taught included voice production, speech phonetics, the art of expression by gesture, acting, dancing, deportment, fencing, the history of drama and – a new subject – training in broadcasting. Also you could take the extra subject of acting in French 'for those who already know something of the language'. Celia's excellent French from St Paul's meant that she was able to join the French class, and thereby benefit from the teaching of Alice Gachet, who was probably the outstanding teacher at the Academy at that time.

The Royal Academy was the first and also the foremost school of acting in the country (although Elsie Fogerty at the Central School of Speech and Drama gave excellent training). Its principal was Kenneth Barnes; indeed he ran it from 1909 to the early 1950s. The brother of Irene and Violet Vanbrugh, leading actresses of their day, he was very much part of the theatrical establishment, and was able to persuade many of the giants of the profession to sit on the council or to award the prizes at the Academy's public show (the students' final performance), or simply to take an interest. Dame Madge Kendal and Sir Johnston Forbes-Robertson would look in. George Bernard Shaw became involved in 1912; he sat on the Academy's council and took a great interest, always attending the public show. In his will he left a third of his royalties to the Academy, a windfall that has endowed it to this day and will continue to do until the copyright runs out in the year 2000. Most of the students got on well enough with Kenneth Barnes, although many complained of his snobbishness, and others found him insensitive in a breezy sort of way. Towards the end of the twenties there was a tendency, which grew stronger later, to take in débutantes who treated it more as a finishing school. Kenneth Barnes did not see a great future for Celia and said as much to her parents, an opinion they kept to themselves. For Celia had by now had enough taste of the theatre to recognise that it was what she wanted to do; although her father did not wholly approve, he and her mother supported her, taking what she later considered to have been a sensible line, neither over-encouraging her, nor discouraging her from at least having a try. She also had a supporter in Mlle Gachet who was known for her acumen in discerning talent and fostering it. According to Brian Oulton, a student with Celia, Alice Gachet was ahead of everyone else in perceiving Celia's talent, and showed great sensitivity and understanding in developing it. Mlle Gachet had red hair, a flamboyant presence (she would powder her nose with a flourish), spoke English well with the odd quirk of pronunciation such as 'stupenduous', and was by all accounts a most inspiring teacher whose classes were known for their liveliness. Celia was extremely fortunate to have caught her attention. Her previous favourite had been Charles Laughton (who had won the Bancroft Gold Medal there in 1926). Celia could not have been more different from Laughton, but she, like he, had shown a tiny capacity in her acting to move people, and this had been seized on by Mlle Gachet.

Apart from Margaretta Scott and Brian Oulton, her contemporaries in 1927 and 1928 included Patricia Hayes, Ingaret Giffard (later Lady van der Post), Alan Keith (then Alex Kossoff, an LCC scholarship boy, who became a superb broadcaster) and many more. Joyce Grenfell spent one term at RADA in 1927, and found herself in Mlle Gachet's class. She thought Celia most talented, and remembered her in particular for not wanting to be an actress, but for wanting to act. Celia and Joyce shared a similar sense of humour and outlook and remained friends throughout their lives. Teachers included Kate Rorke, Robert Atkins, his wife Dorothy Green who taught Shakespeare in the older style, Norman Page who taught voice and phonetics and who could tell immediately which part of the country a student came from, Rosina Filippi, a foremost teacher of drama and a half sister of Eleanora Duse – she in particular emphasised the importance of full vowels and sharp consonants, Helen Haye, a great personality, and Theodore Komisarjevsky who brought new ideas from Russia. The old histrionic theatrical acting of the Edwardian era had passed; the casual off-hand delivery of which Sir Gerald du Maurier was the prime exponent was all the rage. It was a style whose inadequate imitators – languid soft-spoken young men – were much criticised. The Academy, though abreast of the times, did give a thorough grounding in old-fashioned speech and diction – accents were a long way from being encouraged and what was known as standard British speech was fostered. People who trained there at that time still speak with supreme clarity, no letter in any word is ignored or swallowed. Students had a chance to try the classics, and some new plays by writers such as Lonsdale, even an early Coward. Still in the shadow of the First World War, girls outnumbered boys four to one. Celia therefore found herself playing a comic waiter at one time and Quince with a long grey beard at another.

The public show, performed by the students each year, at which the medals and prizes were awarded, was a most important and awesome event. Nine or ten pieces were put on before a large audience and distinguished judges in the old St James's Theatre. From your performance on the occasion, your future might be assured. However not every student who was coming to the end of his or her training was guaranteed a part; the casting for the public show was therefore crucial. Celia to her great dismay learnt that she had not been given a part for the public show in her year. Distraught and in tears, she rang her mother. The family story is that her mother got in touch with Alice Gachet who had been away in Paris, and that Alice Gachet stormed into the Academy furious that her best pupil had not been included, and promptly gave her the lead part in the French production that she was directing. Contemporaries however say that this is an unlikely story, and that Celia was always bound to be in the French play. In any event she played Sylvette to Brian Oulton's Percinet in Act 1 of *Les Romanesques* by Rostand ('Delicious piece' according to one review). However the fact that she was not in any of the English language pieces did mean that she was out of the running for any of the Academy's medals. The show took place on 27 March 1928. *Era*, the theatrical journal of the time, described the occasion:

The programme, which is of necessity an ample one in order to give an opportunity to exhibit the various sides of the Academy's curriculum, was longer than ever. For four and a half hours, Sir Gerald du Maurier, Miss Edith Evans and Mr Frank Cellier sat in judgment, and a large audience was kept interested by the nine items that were presented.

After the ordeal, the Bancroft Gold Medal was awarded to Patricia Hayes, and the Silver to Alex Kossoff. Celia was given a French prize. H.M.Walbrook in the *Daily Telegraph* the next day said: 'Miss Celia Johnson in the part of Sylvette, not only spoke French as it should be spoken, but also showed every sort of delicacy of art and personality. Here undoubtedly the Academy has a pupil of rare promise.'

The following month, arranged by Alice Gachet, she went to Paris to study under Pierre Fresnay at the Comédie Française. Aunt Amy was drafted down from Ilkley to accompany and chaperon her. It was certainly a great honour to be coached by such an eminent French actor, and for Celia, who although nineteen had hardly ever left home before, it must have been rather exciting. The advice that he gave her was that if she was not known within the theatre by the time she was twenty-two, then it would not be worth going on.

She returned for the final term at RADA, and then found herself at a loss. How was that promise that the *Telegraph* had noticed to be fulfilled? She had no theatrical connections at all, no obvious entrée. She needed at this stage a good slice of luck – and an agent. She found, as an agent, a small dark man called Aubrey Blackburn. A kind, rather Edwardian character, he proved a more reliable agent than she ever gave him credit for. Treated peremptorily in later life by Celia, who complained that he never did anything and never once sent her flowers for a first night, he knew her ways better than she thought, and when he died in 1974 she was at a loss.

In 1928, Aubrey Blackburn knew a lady, Miss Madge McIntosh, who was taking a company for a repertory season at the Theatre Royal in Huddersfield in Yorkshire, and he suggested that she might take Celia and Ingaret Giffard with her. She agreed to do so. The season was to mark Alfred Wareing's tenth year as director of the Theatre Royal. He was a distinguished pioneer of repertory theatre and the founder of the League of Audiences, an early precursor of the Arts Council. This northern theatre then where Celia officially made her début was no provincial backwater, but a pretty theatre with an admirable record. She opened in Huddersfield on 23 July 1928 as Sarah Undershaft in Shaw's *Major Barbara*.

Celia's mother fussed about where she might live, and learnt with horror that the landlord of Celia's and Ingaret's first digs was drunk all the time. They moved to a more satisfactory billet. Their pay was £3 a week, of which 1s. 4d. was taken off for insurance; on this wage they lived quite easily and even managed to save. Her aunts, Amy, Winifred and Dora, came over from Ilkley no doubt to applaud her début. The next play in the repertory season was *Outward Bound* by Sutton Vane, then *The Thunderbolt* by Pinero. These were followed by *RUR* by Karel Capek and *To Have the Honour* by A.A.Milne, a popular playwright of the twenties who is now remembered only for his creation of Winnie the Pooh.

Celia played a flapper in this last play. 'The outstanding performance of the evening was undoubtedly that of Miss Celia Johnson as the jolly flapper.' She then, no doubt to her parents' relief, returned to Richmond – and waited. She went to see some of her old friends from RADA who had now found jobs in the theatre and told them how lucky they were and how envious she was. It is quite possible that without certain bits of good fortune, her career as an actress might have ended there; it would only have taken a few reverses for her to have thrown it in. She had no particular drive, no tradition to uphold and no great confidence in herself. She was still very unsophisticated and merely having fun.

She confided her worries to Janet Cunningham, her old house mistress at St Paul's, whereupon Cunnie gave a party at which Celia was to recite some poems. One of the guests was to be Sir Nigel Playfair, a charming man and a clever actor who had rescued and had run for years to great acclaim the Lyric Theatre in Hammersmith, just round the corner from St Paul's. He was a sort of theatrical amateur with excellent taste. His productions were often compared favourably with those in the West End, and he was able to recruit the best actors. Young aspiring actors all wanted to work for him. Celia recited the poems, but there was no sign of Sir Nigel. At the last moment he turned up, and she was obliged to recite again after everybody had left. He was sufficiently impressed to consider taking her on.

He was about to put on at the Lyric, Hammersmith, a Spanish play, *A Hundred Years Old*, by the Quintero brothers translated by Helen and Harley Granville Barker (doyens of the theatre at that time). The play is about an old Spanish paterfamilias gathering his family around him to celebrate his hundredth birthday. Currita is his bright romantic great-granddaughter who falls in love with a rolling stone of a cousin, who has turned up for the party. Currita was the part to go for. Another young actress, just a year older than Celia, Peggy Ashcroft, had been told by Nigel Playfair that she might be in the running for it. Her hopes were dashed. 'No,' he said: 'I've found the most wonderful young actress – Celia Johnson – but you can be Eulalia.' But Celia fooled around and was considered too young and the part was given to Angela Baddeley, with Celia as her understudy. One day she had a chance to play the part, and she did it well. So, in January 1929 she took over from Angela Baddeley as Currita and played it from 29 January to 9 March. The part with its gay innocence must have suited Celia well. The play which now seems very treacly was then considered delightful and pleased its audience; the *Morning Post* called it 'a fragrant and beautiful thing'. The cast included Nigel Playfair himself, Mabel Terry Lewis and Peggy Ashcroft – as Eulalia.

Celia now felt perhaps that she had her foot in the door, as must have her father, whose apprehension at her chosen career was turning to pride. He had the programme and script of *A Hundred Years Old* bound in calf with the inscription 'CEJ from JRJ' embossed on it.

4

Triumph in two flops

On 27 January 1929, two days before Celia took over from Angela Baddeley in *A Hundred Years Old*, she went to a party at the Lyric Theatre given by the Playfairs. There she met a young actor of twenty-one, who was working at the Old Vic under Lilian Baylis. His name was Rupert Hart-Davis, and he fell for Celia. For the next three months or so, he saw her constantly and wrote to her almost every day. She was flattered by his attentions, enjoyed his company but revealed no passion. Their romance was conducted for the large part in his Morris two-seater; he gallantly drove her to and from Marshgate House in Richmond, took her to appointments, escorted her to films. He went to see *A Hundred Years Old* several times and admired her performance more each time. He himself had a part in *The Rumour* by C.K.Munro at the Court Theatre. (C.K.Munro, a writer of fashionable but verbose political plays of the time, became an admirer of Celia's and wrote her wordy letters for many years.)

She finished her play in March and then she and Rupert went to more films and the theatre, including such things as the memorial matinée for Ellen Terry, a production of *Measure for Measure* with Jean Forbes-Robertson, a play by Molly Keane (*The Requital*), and a concert by Paul Robeson at the Albert Hall (her older sister Pamela and younger brother John were included in this). They met for tea at Gunter's tea-shop, a smart rendezvous which served delicious ice-creams, or at the even more fashionable Rumpelmayer's. They watched the Boat Race from A.P.Herbert's garden in Hammersmith. He gave her books and flowers; they would read aloud to each other. That summer they sometimes drove to the country (on one occasion visiting the farm at Pagham where Celia and Pam had stayed as children) and lay among haystacks reading poetry (Meredith, Brooke, Yeats). It was an innocent and happy time, and Rupert was a most long-suffering chauffeur;

Mrs Johnson was often on board the Morris too, or if not her, Celia's little brother, John.

On 1 April 1929, Rupert invited Celia to lunch together with his old school friend from Eton, Peter Fleming, and Peter's girlfriend, Sybil Mayor. The four of them then went to a Cochran review, *Wake Up and Dream*.

When *The Rumour* came to an end, Rupert began rehearsing for a tour of *She Stoops to Conquer*, the cast of which included Peggy Ashcroft. Rupert began taking Peggy out to lunch. One day after lunching with both Peggy and Celia, he and Celia, having dropped Peggy off, escaped injury after a collision in Davies Street. On 26 May, a Sunday night, Rupert and Celia and Rupert's friend, Rupert Harvey, put on their own production of the aptly named play *The First and the Last*, by Galsworthy, at a club. It was reported to have gone well. Peggy was in the audience.

The following week *She Stoops to Conquer* with Rupert and Peggy reached Oxford on its tour, by which time Rupert had decided that his affections now lay with Peggy. However, keeping to an old promise, he fetched Celia from Richmond and drove her to Oxford to see the matinée; passing through Maidenhead Thicket he told her of his change of heart. She was upset; he was confused and did not know what to do with her. By chance they ran into Peter Fleming in Oxford and Rupert asked him to look after Celia for the afternoon, take her to the matinée and put her on the train to London, all of which Peter did.

However, when Rupert returned to London, he continued to see Celia, driving her (and no doubt members of her family) hither and yon, eventually saying goodbye at the end of June after an afternoon watching tennis at Wimbledon. The following month he drove with Peter (in Peter's open Morris two-seater) to France and Corsica, telling Peggy and Celia that he would make up his mind between them before he came back. On his return in August he wrote to Celia informing her that he was going to marry Peggy, which he did in December that year.

Celia received the letter on the 13th August while on tour in Manchester in *Typhoon* (a Hungarian play about a Japanese diplomat who commits hara-kiri after betraying his country and murdering his mistress) with Dennis Neilson-Terry, Fred Terry's son, as the diplomat. She replied the next day, dismayed, professing love for the first time, but wishing him happiness.

I was saying at the theatre that it was the 13th and I had a feeling something dreadful was going to happen – whereupon I heard that most of my very small part is to be cut as the play is far too long and then I came back to these digs and found your letter – it was quite five minutes before I had the courage to open it – you see I knew – and I wanted to keep my hopes till the last minute.

That autumn must have been a little depressing – a reversal in love and, after *Typhoon*, no parts coming her way. However she was young – twenty – and naturally high spirited, so it is unlikely that she was cast down for long. Rupert later became a great friend again and after his divorce from Peggy in 1933 married Comfort Turner, Celia's friend at St Paul's.

Celia was impatient. She wrote to someone she knew at the BBC asking for audition time: 'You may perhaps remember seeing me in *A Hundred Years Old* at the Lyric Hammersmith when you came with Barbara.' Nothing came of this approach. It was Alice Gachet who early in 1930 came to the rescue of her sluggish career, directing her in two French plays, one at the RADA theatre, and the other (*Phèdre* with Sybil Thorndike) at the Arts Theatre Club. Theatre Clubs in the thirties were often used on Sunday nights for trying out plays or putting on one-off productions – they had the advantage of being beyond the scope of the censor; the Arts Theatre Club was perhaps the most renowned.

Then came the break Celia needed – just. She was given a part, probably on Alice Gachet's recommendation, in a play called *The Artist and The Shadow*, described in the programme as 'A New Play of Bohemian Life in Paris'. It was by a young man called George Dunning Gribble and it was pretty good rubbish. Celia had the part of the artist's model, who spoke broken English, bared her back, and only appeared in the last act. The critics on the first night, making for the exit before the end, were restrained by the producer and persuaded to stay and see the young actress in the final act. 'Actress wins Fame in a Day' said the *Daily Express*; 'Redeems a poor play' was the sub-heading in the *Daily Mail*; 'and Miss Celia Johnson,' wrote *The Times* critic, 'who speaks broken English like a Frenchwoman, whose gaiety is unforced, and whose sentiment rings true, gives in a subsidiary part the most persuasive performance of the evening.' The *Express* went on to discuss the implications of instant success: 'Yes, but where does a young actress arrive when she makes a sudden hit in the West End? It all sounds so promising ... The truth is there are never more than thirty actresses employed in straight plays in London at the same time who earn more than £20 a week. A new one only pushes one of these thirty out ...' The writer concluded: 'Mr George Dunning Gribble has no sense of the theatre. Still, I hope Miss Celia Johnson will have cause to thank him.' She did – and she felt sorry for Mr Gribble, thinking him harshly treated. The play lasted a week.

No sooner had it ended, than Frank Vosper (a well-known actor who lived hard) invited her to join him at the Lyric Theatre in Shaftesbury Avenue in *Debonair*, a dramatisation by himself of a novel by Miss G.B.Stern. It was a comedy in which the action, amid handsome settings, moved in a succession of small scenes (an unsatisfactory structure thought to have been copied from the cinema) from Italy to Gray's Inn to Budapest. Celia's part as the mean and wayward girl who flits from one place to another was eighty-eight pages long. The play lasted over three hours, a length not merited by the content; but the gallery on the first night were enthusiastic and called for a speech, not from Frank Vosper who was coming forward to make one, but from Celia. One can only guess at her confusion. She stammered: 'What can I say except to thank you all very much.'

'First Big Part', 'Miss Celia Johnson's Triumph', 'Clever Young Actress', 'Play saved by young actress', ran the headlines. The play generally was slated, and all the reviews recommended cuts. Again a poor play enabled her to shine; she 'cloaked its ennui with her own brilliance'. 'This performance,' wrote W.A.Darlington of the *Telegraph*, 'puts Miss Johnson in the first flight of our youngest generation of actresses.' 'Well, Celia Johnson's performance was so polished and natural that she even managed to make us believe some extravagant lines which compared life first to sardines then to an aquarium, and next, I believe, to a knight in shining armour ...' said the *Sunday Dispatch*. But there were words of caution following the subsequent fuss, interviews and photographs. 'Now if Celia Johnson is a wise young woman she will not attach too much importance to any of this.' James Agate in the *Sunday Times* spoke of her 'uncalculated grace and calculated art' and advised:

This very young actress shows considerable signs of talent, and has the extraordinary advantage of features which partake of interest rather than the normal soul-searing prettiness. My advice to Miss Johnson is to forsake the West End at once and join any touring companies, if such exist, where she may play Celia, and Hero, and Nerissa, and Sweet Lavender, and so learn her business as an actress.

'Her only drawback at present,' said another, 'is a slight immaturity of voice.' 'More like a liberated schoolgirl,' said another.

A glimpse of Celia's dressing-room on that triumphant first night was provided by the *Daily Mirror*:

She had made a quick change to receive the friends who soon crowded into her dressing-room. One of them lit a cigarette for her – her own hands were trembling – another called out 'Your horse won this afternoon' ('A good omen that,' someone interjected) and added 'You've won five shillings.' ... Soon the watchful mother went round saying, 'The child is tired out, so we mustn't overtire her with too much talking and excitement.' And everyone was herded out ...

After this éclat, her name was put up in lights. The play was cut, so much so that Frank Vosper had the strange idea of inserting into the evening as a curtain-raiser, while people were taking their seats, the balcony scene of *Romeo and Juliet* with him as Romeo and Celia as Juliet; no doubt he was hoping to capitalise on Celia's instant popularity. Their costumes and wigs were ugly, and one commentator compared the effect to Puss-in-Boots.

Debonair, in spite of the amendments, did not run for long, but Celia found herself much fêted on the strength of two flops. Later that summer, she was taken on at the Playhouse by Gladys Cooper and Sir Gerald du Maurier in *Cynara* by H.M. Harwood and R. Gore Browne. That was well and truly the West End; Sir Gerald, a casual but consummate actor, was the leading leading man of the day; Gladys Cooper, tough and beautiful, had a remarkable career and had run the Playhouse for many years. But dazzling in West End terms as the set-up was, the finances of the Playhouse were always precarious and economies were encouraged. In one scene Celia had to enter, drenched, in a raincoat and hat; and instead of dousing the raincoat in some sort of special paint to make it look wet but which would spoil the coat, someone poured a bucket of water over her every night just before her entrance. The hat belonged to Pam.

Celia played Doris, a young shopgirl, who enjoys a brief dalliance with a staid middle-aged barrister, Sir Gerald du Maurier, while his wife is away. When she returns, he extricates himself from the affair and Doris commits suicide (to put the plot at its briefest). James Agate, the clever, influential but capricious critic of the *Sunday Times*, had strong words about the structure of the play, complaining of 'stragglesome episodes', and the 'complete absence of dramatic carpentry and workmanship'. He found it 'an odd little piece which can never make up its mind between exquisiteness and banality'. However he thought the play not without merit, and, in particular, it provided the audience with some 'capital acting'.

Sir Gerald has never been less emphatic ... Miss Gladys Cooper moves through the play in languor and superbity ... But the gem of the evening is Miss Johnson's performance of Doris, a performance without a false note, entirely natural, exceedingly pathetic, and crammed with interest from start to finish. That this young player can advance from her jerky harum-scarum playing in *Debonair* to quiet and delicate playing of this order proves how sensitive she is to first-class production.

Another paper headed its notice wearily, 'Celia Johnson again'.

That was rather hard as it was only three months (from March to June 1930) since she had first set foot upon the

West End stage. She was playing opposite Sir Gerald du Maurier and receiving as good if not better notices. It was a sort of dream and she never really believed it. In Sir Gerald she found a fan and a teacher; she benefited enormously from acting with him and always regarded his encouragement, his direction, and his advice as invaluable. Was there perhaps some flirtation between them, the mentor and the pupil?

Cynara in fact ran for seven months and no doubt to Miss Cooper's relief made £5,500. (The title, *Cynara*, had been taken from the poem of that name by Ernest Dowson, which contains the refrain: 'I have been faithful to thee, Cynara! in my fashion.' The poem also has the lines:

> I have forgot much, Cynara! Gone with the wind,
> Flung roses, roses, riotously with the throng,
> Dancing, to put thy pale, lost lilies out of mind.

from which Margaret Mitchell took the title of her famous book.)

These three undistinguished plays, *The Artist and the Shadow*, *Debonair* and *Cynara*, all showed aspects of Celia's acting that were to characterise her work throughout her career – a freshness (almost overpowering then), a lack of sentimentality, an absence of technical trickiness, a feeling for comedy, intelligence, sensitivity, and a weakness in the voice; this last was always to be a limitation. It was not the last time that she showed the power to redeem a bad play – and she was never to give up smoking.

That summer, during her new-found celebrity, she gave an interview to the *Era*. She seldom ever spoke about acting as such, but what she revealed then at twenty-one, and sounding very worldly wise, probably held true for the rest of her life. They talked of *Cynara* first:

'I simply love the part,' she said, 'and think that it is beautifully written. But it is terribly difficult, much more difficult than *Debonair* and the first night was an agonising experience, one of the very worst I remember.'

'Why is it more difficult than *Debonair*, one of the longest parts a young actress ever had to play?' [the interviewer asked.]

'It is cut up into small scenes, which means one has to get one's effect in half a second. In *Debonair* I was there the whole time; if I missed anything, I could pick it up again later. It is so much easier to compose a character on broad lines. One cannot lose the correct mood if one is always on stage.'

'Can you, after a time, get your effects mechanically, without any genuine feeling?'

'Personally, I cannot act mechanically. I have to live my part through at every performance. Some parts, I imagine, might tend to become mechanical if one played them for a long time. But I have never yet been able to get through a performance without keeping myself keyed up to the correct pitch all the time. Acting is always a bit of a strain for me.'

'In your final scene in *Cynara* you give the impression of suffering intensely. Are your feelings real to you then; where do they come from?'

'It isn't exactly feeling. I don't know what it is; can't explain it at all. I don't get wrought up; yet before I go on stage I have to get into a solemn mood. I couldn't rush giggling out of my dressing-room.'

'How do you manage to put yourself so completely into the situations of your characters?'

'By imagination. But when I say that, don't think I'm being grand. It stands to reason that an actress, like everyone else, only lives one *real* life, her own; into the characters she creates she can, of course, put little bits of herself, but for the most part she has to draw on her own imagination and powers of observation. I think books are a great incentive to the imagination. I read a great deal, but without any particular plan or plot. At the moment I am reading Mary Webb's *Precious Bane* for the second time.' ...

'What sort of parts do you want to play in the future?'

'As many different kinds as possible. By the way, my present part is the first one I've played with no comedy in it at all. It seemed so strange at first to hear others getting laughs, and not get any laughs myself. I seemed out of it, and wanted to join in the comedy.'

'Do you go on developing a character during the run of a play?'

'A part grows a bit more after the first night. One has to modify a little bit here and there. It seems to me that a character is not complete until one has played it in front of an audience. When that has been done, it takes on an existence of its own.'

One of the people who attended the first night of *Cynara* on 27 June was Norman Forbes-Robertson, an old actor, the brother of Johnston Forbes-Robertson. He wrote to Celia the following day:

Dear Miss Johnson

I feel that I owe you an apology for my temerity in having pressed in to your crowded room last night to offer among your many admirers my congratulations on your beautiful performance of Doris. My excuse can only be my having been on the stage for 55 years, whereby I have seen and acted with all the greatest of my profession and that I thought your performance one of the most touching I have seen among this long list of artists. A great deal of your performance reminded me of Ellen Terry when she was twenty-four, and I know of no English actress of my time comparable with her work as an artist, so please forgive me, and except [sic] my hearty congratulations on your touching performance. You have indeed a great future before you.

Yours sincerely
Norman Forbes-Robertson

Celia kept very few letters and papers, but this one she clearly treasured. It was a thrilling accolade for a young and unsophisticated girl.

5

West End fare

In an article in the *Daily Telegraph* that summer of 1930, Sydney Carroll assessed the future of three new young actresses – Diana Wynyard, Peggy Ashcroft and Celia Johnson. Diana Wynyard was beautiful, chic and much acclaimed. Would she 'become just a little too plump to retain her atmosphere of romance? At the present moment she is exquisite.' Of Peggy Ashcroft (who was about to open as Desdemona to Paul Robeson's Othello) he said: 'The least praise of the three has, perhaps, come to Peggy Ashcroft yet many declare that the future holds more for her than either of the others.' 'As for Celia Johnson, she seems at the present moment to suffer from her beautiful saucer-like eyes, and from her own high spirits. The latter make her a very intense, but somewhat uncomfortable, person to have around.' It was for her that he prophesied the greatest future.

Peggy and Celia took different paths through the thirties: Peggy towards the newly emergent classical theatre, and Celia towards the West End with its obligatory French windows and cigarette boxes. Celia's direction was the more typical of the time. Classical theatre had been all but confined to the Old Vic during the twenties; for an actor who was comfortable in period dress and who could speak poetry, it was the only place. Now, with John Gielgud's *Hamlet* having moved to the Queen's Theatre in 1930 and more classics moving into the West End, there were new openings and a new interest. But the dominant names in the theatre during the twenties – Sir Gerald du Maurier, Frank Vosper, Gladys Cooper, etc. – kept almost exclusively to the lighter fare of the West End. Celia, who was never to be very happy in costume, continued in that tradition. (Forty years on, it would be a change for Peggy to try light comedy, and the same for Celia to attempt a classical part.) For the next three years, however, from 1931 to 1933, Celia had parts in plays which mean little to anyone now, but which were entirely typical of their time; she shared the stage in them with all the distinguished older actors of the time. While the brilliant new actors of her generation – Laurence Olivier, John Gielgud and Peggy – were trying new things, taking risks, she was going with the mainstream.

Journey's End, a play by R.C. Sherriff about the First World War, had opened in December 1928; (Celia had attended the first night with a friend from Richmond, Andrew Alford). The play had struck an emotional chord, and until it was put on, it had been thought impossible to stage a serious play about the Great War; its success therefore marked a recovery – ten years on – from the war, and helped people to put it behind them. What then was to characterise the new theatre of the thirties? The old melodramas, remnants of Edwardian theatre, had all but disappeared; light comedies, thrillers, whodunnits, lightly written serious plays, musicals and revues filled the theatres. The cigarette box that tinkles a tune when it is opened was the principal stage property of the time. Shaw had had his moment for the time being, Maugham too, Lonsdale was fading; Coward (whose first play was put on in 1920 when he was twenty-one) was in his stride; James Bridie, Dodie Smith, Clemence Dane (whose real name was Winifred Ashton, her pseudonym being taken from the church of St Clement Danes in the Strand), J.B. Priestley, John van Druten, were becoming popular names. It was not to be a particularly distinguished decade for plays, but it did generate some first-class acting. The older actresses – Sybil Thorndike, Edith Evans – still liked to let themselves go a bit, especially Sybil Thorndike, of whom one theatre manager said: 'Yes, Sybil always was a magnificent actress – if you could keep her arms beneath her shoulders.' The younger generation copied Sir Gerald, gave an easy flick and, if they had any technique, hid it.

Other changes in the theatre were nearly complete; the old-fashioned actor-manager had disappeared (with the possible exceptions of Gladys Cooper at the Playhouse and Nigel Playfair at the Lyric, Hammersmith, but their reigns were to come to an end in the early thirties); the tradition that certain theatres put on certain sorts of plays had ended. Actors

were not quite the grand stars they had been, though the
great names were still applauded on their first entrance in
a play, a custom that continues though now considered rather
infra dig. Producers were becoming more important, as were
designers (Nigel Playfair was ahead of his time in using interesting designers such as Doris Zinkeisen and Claude Lovat
Fraser at the Lyric, Hammersmith). And of course the cinema
was confusing matters, dividing loyalties, taking audiences,
shaking things up. The theatre, always on the look-out for
a scapegoat for its shortcomings, found one in the talkies.
Nevertheless, it was an exciting, optimistic time in the theatre,
though it remained a small cosy world.

Celia, in 1930, had made a start; she was twenty-two and
she had fulfilled Pierre Fresnay's criterion – she was known
in the theatre. She had had the good fortune to have been
taken up by Sir Nigel Playfair, Sir Gerald du Maurier and
Frank Vosper, all of whom had wide experience and knew
the theatre as few others, and all of whose careers were in
their final phase and who were to live but a few more years:
Sir Nigel and Sir Gerald both died in 1934, and Frank Vosper
was drowned in 1937.

1930 had been a crucial year for Celia, and from then on
offers of work came in steadily – they were not always very
tempting but there was no shortage of them. That, for an
actress, is most fortunate – and no small tribute – for there
are so many ages she has to go through: the young ingénue
when looks are important, the wife (usually wronged), the
middle-aged woman, the older character parts. The transitions
from phase to phase are not easy, added to which is the fact
that for an actress there is only a fraction of the parts that
there are for actors, and even fewer good parts. Celia had
the luxury of being able to pick and choose; she was not
always the best picker.

After *Cynara*, in 1931 she played Elisabeth in *The Circle*
by Somerset Maugham at the Vaudeville. Thought to be his
wittiest play, it had first been put on in 1921 when, treating
the question of what in those days was known as 'bolting',
it had mildly shocked its audience. This revival was beset
with 'stars': Raymond Massey produced it, Laurence Irving

designed it; Sir Nigel Playfair and Athene Seyler played a couple who had run off together years before and who provided a not very edifying example for Elisabeth (Celia) who was tempted to do the same thing and abandon her husband, a priggish MP (Frank Vosper) for a young planter (Peter Hannen – an excellent young actor who died tragically at twenty-six). It was a feast of acting and the critics relished it. 'Brilliant comedy, brilliantly played,' was *The Times*'s verdict. W.A.Darlington of the *Telegraph* said of Celia: 'No young actress on the stage has a better natural gift for suggesting emotion. She should, however, avoid a trick of staring glassily out into the audience; this might develop into a rather unhappy mannerism.' One complained of her diction, and another said she was too young. Ivor Brown in the *Observer*, ever sensible, elucidated the difference between the two generations in the play:

Mr Raymond Massey, the producer, has had to face a problem which crops up now wherever the older and younger generation are at grips in the same play. Those players who learned their craft before the war use the major key; the post-war people use the minor. The latter, with their muted method, can, of course, achieve an air of natural sincerity; Miss Celia Johnson, Mr Peter Hannen, and Mr Frank Vosper all keep emotion in hand; their acting is easy and life-like. But it has no attack. The elders in this play do attack, not, of course, by shouting, or ranting, or gesturing, but because their technique is far more assertive. They point their sentences; they understand emphasis; they are not afraid to be actors. The younger people, on the other hand, perform as though they were in a deadly fear lest anyone should suppose them to be actors on a stage, and in a theatre.

There you have it.

Perhaps Celia's mistake at this point was not to hold out for more challenging parts to widen her range. Some say that she, in the same way as Sir Gerald du Maurier, knew her limitations and knowingly kept within her range. It is probable, however, that later she regretted not having taken greater risks in her career. She was seriously inhibited by a lack of confidence and this often manifested itself in a somewhat nega-tive attitude. In the early thirties she was enjoying herself and was merely glad of opportunities to act and was hardly reflective about it. In any case, those desirable parts that might have stretched her range were not there in any abundance.

There followed a brief stint in a ridiculous and macabre play set in a castle in Italy called *Death Takes a Holiday*, in which Ernest Milton, swooping around in a cloak, and making full use of 'his excellent powers of bizarre characterisation and sense of the theatre', played Death who takes a holiday on earth disguised as a Russian prince. Then, after having taken over from Madeleine Carroll in a well-established run of a low-key play – 'a straightforward presentation of life in Kensington' – by John van Druten called *After All* (whose cast included the excellent and sharp Lilian Braithwaite and also, in a minor role, Cyril Raymond, later to play Celia's husband in *Brief Encounter*), she did accept a challenge. It was to go to New York to play Ophelia. Raymond Massey, who was to play Hamlet, went to Richmond to ask her father's permission for her to go. It was a thrilling opportunity: 'To say that I am excited would be putting it mildly,' she said to the *Daily Mail*. Unfortunately the production by Norman Bel Geddes was misconceived to a degree, ('This play *Hamlet* has everything. It's an action show. Think of that duel scene – four characters dead at the end of it,' he is reputed to have said) and the designs ludicrous (it was going to be 'a hell of a thing to see'). When Raymond Massey arrived off the ship in New York in November 1931, he was met by Bel Geddes who said ominously: 'I've altered the script a bit.'

They opened at the Walnut Street Theatre in Philadelphia, where the ghost was soon sacked, and from then on Hamlet had to speak the ghost's lines. As the audience went quiet before the play began, Raymond Massey heard Leon Quartermaine, who played Horatio, whisper, 'Forgive us, Master Will, for what we are about to perpetrate.' They then went to New York, to the Broadhurst Theatre. The *New York Times* critic was sarcastic:

Mr Bel Geddes and Shakespeare disagree most violently about the theme of the play. To Mr Bel Geddes it is a play of action, to be interpreted with the nervous agility of contemporary life. Since the drama is heavily encumbered with thoughts, dreams and verses,

Mr Bel Geddes has hacked and transposed until no idle philosophy is left to trip up his scenery. What he has left is, to this department, an incoherent, flat and unprofitable narrative that would hardly be intelligible to anyone unschooled in the play.

He was lukewarm about the acting, admitting that the cast were not well served by the production. But, he added, 'Celia Johnson's Ophelia is one of the loveliest and most poignant descriptions of the part; it proceeds from an interior under-standing and manages somehow to introduce a touch of poetry in the midst of a jabbering production.' Again, she managed to shine through a travesty. The cast meanwhile, bored by the pretentiousness of the production and by directorial notes on their scripts such as 'she razzes him', began to amuse them-selves by looking for animals and hidden characters in the text. One to emerge, for instance, was Marshal Storck, a Scan-dinavian military man:

> MARCELLUS: Thus twice before, and jump at this dead hour,
> With martial stalk hath he gone by our watch.
> [Act I, Sc. 1, 66]

and an Irish Wolfhound called Pat:

> HAMLET: Now might I do it pat, now he is praying.
> [Act III, Sc. 3, 72]

and, finally, Horatio's girlfriend Felicity:

> HAMLET [to Horatio]: Absent thee from felicity awhile.
> [Act V, Sc. 2, 351]

No doubt Celia, who, apart from her visit to Paris when at RADA, had never been abroad, relished New York. After the relative failure of the play, the English members of the cast were sent home on a very slow boat. Celia never acted on Broadway again.

The year 1932 was to bring her back to more typical West End productions. To list them briefly – first came *Punchinello*, a highly elaborate fable about the origins of the legend of Punch and Judy; with a cast of thirty, excluding peasants, soldiers etc., thirteen scenes, and magnificent costumes designed by Laurence Irving, it lasted for four performances, sending tremors through theatrical backers. Then came *The Man I Killed* by Maurice Rostand at the Apollo. This was an emotional piece about a Frenchman (played by Emlyn Williams) who had killed a German in the trenches and, to salve his conscience, seeks out the dead man's parents to confess; in the event he only manages to tell the German's fiancée (Celia). Although soulful, it lacked dramatic tension and came off after only thirteen performances.

Next, *The Vinegar Tree* by Paul Osborn at the St James's was a typical brisk modern comedy. In this Celia came up against an old tyrant, an uncrowned queen of the West End, Marie Tempest, and her husband and producer, William Graham Browne. As star and producer they had been a successful partnership for a quarter of a century. She was an exacting perfectionist, a porcelain prima donna, with a voice described as an 'icy purr'. In her heyday she had had untold glamour (once, when she had opened in Australia she had received ninety cables from the great and the good in England). By 1932 the glamour had faded, but her touch had not left her – her timing was superb and the little gestures with her tiny fat well-kept hands were perfect, even if she did hog the stage slightly. You mocked her at your peril. Rehearsals were very formal, suits for the men, a hat for Marie Tempest. She could be cruel to younger actresses. Celia probably took any autocratic behaviour in good heart and no doubt enjoyed observing her well-honed technique. This play showed Marie Tempest as a vacuous character and her fans did not care for that. It ran for only a month, far less then expected, for usually Marie Tempest was a guarantee of success.

Not only did she rule in any play that she was in, she also reigned at the Ivy, the little restaurant that was the haunt of theatre people between the wars. She would always sit at the same table by the door and Noel Coward, James Agate, others who dared, would pay homage as they left. Lilian Braithwaite, of sharp tongue, would occupy another table, a centre of gossip: 'My dear, I hear that J has been offered a part in New York, but it cannot be a very big one because she is going in a very small boat.'

Later that summer, in August 1932, Celia accepted a part in another play with Marie Tempest, again directed by her husband Graham Browne – *Tomorrow Will Be Friday* by Phillip Leaver, at the Haymarket; it also starred a charming old-fashioned urbane actor, Athole Stewart, as Lord Charles Harley. Celia played the Hon. Cynthia Lynne, Marie Tempest was Charlotte, Lady Immingham, and Leon Quartermaine (Celia's Horatio), Garth Sydney. The action took place in the Music Room at Coaters, Lady Immingham's house in the country. If the *dramatis personae* does not give the flavour of the play, perhaps these lines from it will: 'Enter Butler. "There is a Mr Thomas Cook on the telephone, m'lord; he seems to think you want to travel."' It was almost a parody of the upper-class country-house play of the time. Celia was disgruntled – 'I am sick of old Tempest and Graham Browne too ... There is no more excitement or thrill in one of his rehearsals than in a visit to a house agents – Less ...'; it was clear that the play was not going to do very well, but it trundled on for two months and the management would not release her to take up an offer from John Gielgud to be in *Strange Orchestra* (a play for which he engaged Mrs Patrick Campbell though she was not to last the course). That was a pity as it might well have been a profitable collaboration.

It had been, for Celia, a busy but extremely patchy year in the theatre, although her notices, as had become the norm, were uniformly excellent. She was twenty-four, still living at home at Marshgate House and fussed over by her mother. In the summer she had been a bridesmaid to Pam who had married Nevill Vintcent, a young aviator. John, her brother, was at Trinity College, Cambridge, where he was reading English. However, any dissatisfaction that Celia felt with her parts that year may have been offset by the fact that she was regularly seeing the assistant literary editor of the *Spectator*, Rupert Hart-Davis's friend, Peter Fleming, and that she was unquestionably in love.

6

Flemings

After that initial meeting at lunch with Rupert Hart-Davis, and then the afternoon spent together in Oxford in 1929, it seems likely that Celia and Peter Fleming did not see each other for two years or more. But by early 1932 they had met up again and been attracted to each other, for by March that year love letters were passing between them. It is probable though, as will be shown, that Peter had seen Celia in *Cynara* in 1930. Anyway, however it began, by March 1932, courting was under way – surreptitiously.

Peter was the eldest son of Valentine Fleming, an admired and respected man who had been Conservative MP for Henley-on-Thames and a first-class officer. H₌ had been killed in action in May 1917 while serving in the Oxfordshire Hussars. Winston Churchill, a fellow officer in the regiment, wrote a well-judged obituary of Val, as he was known, in *The Times*, describing in his superb style Val's outstanding qualities. He ended with these resonant words: 'As the war lengthens and intensifies and the extending lists appear, it seems as if one watched at night a well-loved city whose lights, which burn so bright, which burn so true, are extinguished in the distance in the darkness one by one.'

Val's widow, Evelyn Fleming, was left with four small sons: Peter, Ian, Richard and Michael. Peter remembered being recalled from his prep school in Dorset to a sombre household, his mother prostrate with grief, and being told in bleak terms that his father had been killed and that he was now head of the family – words not of comfort but of awe. The family of which he had been informed that he was head was extremely rich and somewhat parvenu. His grandfather, Robert Fleming, had risen from the ranks of one of the big jute firms in Dundee to found a bank in London, Robert Fleming & Co., which continues to flourish today; he invented the investment trust. Once established in London, Robert Fleming bought a house in

Grosvenor Square (on the side where the American Embassy now stands), 2,000 acres of land which had belonged to the Stonor family in South Oxfordshire, and he would rent large sporting estates in Scotland, first Glenborrodale and then Black Mount in Argyll, which the family later bought from the Marquess of Breadalbane. On the land in Oxfordshire, Robert Fleming transformed an elegant house, Joyce Grove, outside Nettlebed into a grotesque palace. The design by C.E. Mallows was ugly, the scale vast (bathrooms the size of tennis courts, elaborate, overpowering marble fireplaces, stained-glass windows), but the workmanship was excellent. Today it is a Sue Ryder home for the terminally ill, but the extravagant and well-crafted details of the interior of the house remain.

Robert was a tall and heavy Scot of few words; his wife, Kate, a handsome woman, liked the tough outdoor life and being fit: she skipped one hundred times every morning, would swim in the sea in all weathers at Glenborrodale with her French maid rowing behind her, and was still stalking at Black Mount well into her eighties. This belief in being physically tough, laughing at discomfort and relishing sporting life was the prevalent ethos in the Fleming family, and is still felt and understood by Robert's great-grandchildren. It was a sort of philistinism well tempered by a sense of humour.

Evelyn, Val's widow, Peter's mother, was not a philistine. She had a daring sense of colour and would wear, say, emerald green and purple, or yellow together with magenta, and it would work. She had an artist's eye, played the violin, and was small and frail and very beautiful. She was not of the Fleming mould and, although she came from a socially respectable family of Buckinghamshire baronets (the Roses), she was not popular with her parents-in-law. They considered her vain and selfish, which in many ways she was. When Val was killed, she was thirty-two; he left her the income from a trust fund, the amount of which would be severely reduced were she ever to marry again. She never did, though in 1925 she disappeared abroad and returned with a baby girl whom she said she had adopted through the good offices of Lord Dawson of Penn, the fashionable doctor of the time. In due course it became clear that Evelyn was the baby's

mother and that Augustus John was her father, though Evelyn
never admitted this to her sons, or indeed to her daughter
Amaryllis. The boys came to love their little sister Amaryllis
who to this day does not know where she was born.

Evelyn, after Val's death, despite being so different from
the Flemings, stuck with them and at weekends occupied a
wing at Joyce Grove, the house in Oxfordshire. (She was in
fact a good fisherwoman and, dressed in a yellow skirt, taught
her sons and their cousins to fish.) Her four sons grew up
partly in the hearty Scottish household, and partly in Evelyn's
bohemian household in Cheyne Walk in Chelsea. They knew
their grandfather was rich (he left over £2 million when he
died in 1933), but Evelyn kept them on a tight allowance;
their share in the bank died with their father. They all went
to Eton, as had their father, Val, where Peter was a brilliant
scholar and became Captain of the Oppidans, Ian a first-class
athlete and Richard and Michael also did well. From Eton,
Peter went to Oxford, where again he excelled academically,
gaining a first in English; he also edited *Isis*, acted in the
OUDS, and was a member of the Bullingdon Club. To those
who know Oxford this shows that he straddled the various
worlds there, an unusual feat, given the cliquey nature of
the university. But it mirrored his life at home where he moved
between the hearty and the artistic, the conventional and the
bohemian. This was the generation of John Betjeman and
Osbert Lancaster, among whom Peter had several friends;
he was, however, too reserved in character and a little too
arrogant to enjoy widespread social success.

On leaving Oxford, at his grandfather's wish he had a go
at banking. He was sent to Wall Street in 1927. He sat in
an office marked 'Research' where even the Wall Street Crash
failed to engage his attention; with no natural interest in
money, no liking for routine and with much of the impatient
undergraduate still in him, he was bored. Only a trip to Guate-
mala to do a report on the railways for his Uncle Phil (Val's
younger brother) for the Fleming office in London cheered
him up. His game-book records for that trip: 1 quail, 1 lardia
('a rather decorative squirrel'), 4 palomas. The following
month on his way back to New York through Mexico, the

bag was 1 tarpon, 2 snakes and 1 coot. An unusual expedition that involved a little shooting was far more to his taste than stocks and shares on Wall Street. Back in London, after a couple of months in the family office in Crosby Square, he decided to give up banking – to his eternal guilt.

His game-book, apart from a gap between 1932 and 1939 ('I did a lot of shooting during those years, both at home and overseas, but was so foolish and casual as to keep no record of it. I regret this very much ...'), he kept scrupulously from his first rabbit in 1918 ('My first day's shooting – Got seven [rabbits] with eight shots – All sitting! Fearfully bucked ...') to his penultimate day's shooting. Shooting was his passion. Best of all he liked to be alone or in the company of one or two in Scotland and trek after the odd snipe or grouse or climb to the high tops in search of ptarmigan. Large, organised shoots in the south, though greatly enjoyed, were less to his taste. Unlike his grandmother, Kate, and all his Fleming cousins, he never cared much for stalking, and he did not fish.

Once he had quit the bank he started writing short stories; none was published. In spite of his millionaire background, he needed to earn money for he had no private income except whatever his capricious mother felt like giving him. Rupert Hart-Davis, who had given up acting and taken a job at Heinemann – the start of his distinguished career in publishing – suggested Peter for the job of assistant literary editor at the *Spectator*. He was taken on in 1931. With, always, a superb mastery of prose, he produced a variety of articles of which some were arch, many facetious, and several brilliant. He had a gift for writing, and the technical construction of elegant sentences gave him immense satisfaction. What he lacked, or what he refused to cultivate, was the creative imagination to inspire his writing.

Although he had found an ideal job, after a few months he was restless and somehow inveigled from the editor four months' leave to travel to China. This he did by way of the Trans-Siberian railway. He gained an insight into and a love for China – and his game-book records a lot of duck and snipe outside Shanghai. He returned by way of Rangoon,

Delhi, Baghdad and Istanbul after an adventurous time that he had much enjoyed. In December 1931 he resumed the de facto work of literary editor of the *Spectator*, and he also wrote some of the film and theatre criticism. It was probably at this time that he met Celia again and that they were drawn to each other.

His first romance, with a childhood friend, Sybil Mayor, had come to an end when he went to work in New York, destroyed, in effect, by his mother who had done her level best to separate them. She, as a straightforward snob, wanted, if not Princess Elizabeth, at least an earl's daughter for her son. Peter, not wanting to risk her interference this time, prudently kept quiet about his new love.

Peter was not very tall, about five foot eleven, extremely good looking with a square, level face, his black hair parted and brushed up at the sides very much in the style of the period. He was intelligent, tough and individualistic; after a dazzling scholastic career and then his clever pieces at the *Spectator*, a great future was predicted. But he was reserved in character and preferred to express himself through jokes or oblique facetiae – or on paper, where his awkwardness in speech would be transmuted into great fluency. Perhaps his exotic, powerful and ambitious mother obliged him to be withdrawn; perhaps it was the Victorian cult of the stiff upper lip very much practised by the Flemings; perhaps the death of his father had arrested him emotionally. Probably it was a combination of all these things. In company he was always a little ham-fisted, and could seem arrogant; with a few close friends he was the best of companions, kind and funny.

Many women found him handsome and romantic (which in a sense he was, though he would never have admitted it) and Celia was no exception. To Peter, Celia must have seemed very different from his mother – more of a chap. She was not at all vain – indeed Mary Pakenham* (an old and close friend of Peter's) remembers Celia pointing at her dressing-table on which lay a brush and comb and a pot of lotion,

---

* Lady Mary Pakenham, writer, daughter of the Earl and Countess of Longford, later married Meysey Clive.

and saying that she thought that she ought to have more things on it but she could not think of anything. She was very natural. There was still a feeling of 'jolly hockey sticks' about her, and she was ready for any adventure. They made each other laugh.

No sooner had the romance taken root than Peter spotted an item in the Agony Column (as the personal column was then known) of *The Times*:

Exploring and sporting expedition, under experienced guidance, leaving England June, to explore rivers Central Brazil, if possible ascertain fate Colonel Fawcett; abundance game, big and small; exceptional fishing; ROOM TWO MORE GUNS; highest references expected and given. – Write Box X.

Lt-Col P.H.Fawcett DSO had last been heard of in April 1925 in the upper reaches of the Amazon where he was in quest of the Lost City. This expedition to ascertain his fate was ambitious, but, with its emphasis on the sporting, irresistible to Peter.

In the event it was ill conceived and poorly led but tremendously exciting, and provided Peter with the material for *Brazilian Adventure*, a brilliant first book, the epitome of the understated style of travel writing in the thirties. It became the most popular travel book of that time. The journey achieved little:

The expedition may claim to have thrown a little (but not much) light, of a confirmatory nature, on the mystery surrounding Colonel Fawcett's disappearance. Otherwise beyond the completion of a 3,000-mile journey, mostly under amusing conditions, through a little-known part of the world, and the discovery of one new tributary to a tributary of the Amazon, nothing of importance was achieved.

Peter never wore a hat; and the last few days of the journey when they were far into uncharted territory and conditions were extremely hard – they were short of food, had to wade bare-legged up a river full of piranha fish, and were surrounded by unseen and probably hostile Indians – he described as 'the best I have ever known'. His descriptions of the virgin terrain, across which they tramped after leaving the river at the farthest point of the expedition, were delicate and inspired.

All Celia knew, after she and Rupert had waved goodbye on 23 May 1932 at Tilbury Docks, and as she returned to face old Marie Tempest at the St James's Theatre, was that he had left for Brazil on a rash quest where there was a distinct chance that he would encounter cannibals.

7

One's Company

Five months later, in October 1932, Celia received a telegram from Peter announcing his return. Not knowing whether he had had any of her letters while he had been in Brazil (he had), she wrote to him, recapping: 'I went to Corsica after *The Vinegar Tree* finished with Glen ... It was lovely but it seems a very long time ago.' (Glenham Bradley, an elderly friend of the Johnsons', a member of a family of furriers, seems to have acted as a benevolent godfather to Celia; he had taken her on a holiday to France and Corsica during which she had thought only of Peter. She had much enjoyed flying for the first time.)

Since then I've been in the world's most stupid play at the Haymarket with old Tempest again – we finish on Saturday the 22nd so, thank God, you won't see it. I haven't got another job yet – though there has been a lot of chat about my doing a film. The first news I had of you was from Ian [Fleming] and Jerry Coke who came to the play about ten days ago. They said that your mother had had a panic about you and so had rung *The Times* who said they had heard Mr R.P.Fleming was on his way home. Darling that was breathlessly exciting. It was queer seeing Ian. The back of his neck is like yours and the way he speaks ... I get more and more grateful for your being safe. It is lovely not to have to stifle an inside terror about you all the time.

Though emphasising that he must not worry about her, she was ecstatic at the prospect of his return.

He came back from Brazil by way of Lisbon and Dover where the customs officials inspected 'two indescribably filthy linen bags full of old clothes: one rucksack containing the small stage properties of aboriginal life (now on view in the British Museum), and a long, lethal bundle, swathed in put-tees, of spears, clubs, and bows and arrows.' He was, as he always would be, glad to be home. In spite of having written to Rupert at the outset of the expedition voicing doubts about his future with Celia, he happily resumed his courtship, and returned to the *Spectator*. In December he went to stay with his grandparents, old Robert and Grannie Katie, at Black Mount to shoot hinds and to finish *Brazilian Adventure*. Black Mount, which Peter visited almost every year from boyhood, was like a sheet-anchor for him; it was a very Edwardian shooting-lodge, resistant to change, where he obviously felt comfortable or self-confident among his nice and funny cousins, the Flemings, the Hannays and the Hermon-Hodges. He sent Celia a little box for Christmas.

She by this time was in a thriller, *Ten Minute Alibi* by Anthony Armstrong, at the Embassy Theatre in Swiss Cottage. She adored his present, but as the romance was still under wraps, was unable to show it off.

It has only one drawback in my eyes. I was so thrilled that I wanted to show it to everybody but I couldn't think of a plausible person to say gave it to me so I couldn't ... Eventually I showed it to Ellen [the Johnsons' old maid]. I should have burst if I hadn't showed it to somebody ... It is very difficult to concentrate. Bobby Douglas is murdering Anthony Ireland only 10 feet away. In a minute I've got to go and discover the body ... (I have now discovered the body and a very moving performance I gave too) ...

In 1933, when Celia was twenty-five, she finally detached herself from her family and left Marshgate House in Richmond and took a flat in Walton Street. She began to meet Peter's friends. Mary Pakenham, one of the closest, remembers that it was generally known that Peter had a secret girlfriend who was an actress, and one day, after counting up to ten, she asked him if she could meet her. When he finally introduced them, Celia, typically, for she was always very clumsy, had had trouble with a gas oven and was a mess. Mary liked her at once. But when she asked Peter what he thought they had in common, he replied, 'Nonsense and passion.'

A great friend of Celia's at that time, and throughout her life, was Terence Nugent, known as Tim. He was a Guards officer, a charming and amusing man of supreme manners, who adored the theatre and had appeared in Celia's life almost as an old-fashioned stage-door Johnny. Tim Nugent took her to plays, and later after he married Rosalie Willoughby, the three of them often enjoyed themselves together. Tim subsequently worked for over twenty years as Comptroller of the Lord Chamberlain's Office, where plays were censored, bringing a breadth of mind to a job that seemed at odds with his upright and courtly appearance. Tom Boase, a historian who became President of Magdalen College, Oxford, was another friend of Celia's, as were Joyce and Reggie Grenfell and Joyce's best friend, Virginia Graham (the daughter of Harry Graham, author of many books of light verse). Celia, especially at this age, was fun to be with; she could enliven any odd outing and, if she found something funny, could spark off hysterical laughter among her companions. Peter, conversely, always found it difficult to give himself to the pleasure of the moment.

Pam and her husband Nevill Vintcent were now living in India, but Celia remained close to her brother John who had just come down from Cambridge and, for a time, shared a flat with him. He was a nice and gentle character, very bookish, and Celia was always very fond of him. Although he and her parents obviously knew about her romance with Peter, as did the servants at Mrs Val's house in Cheyne Walk, Mrs Val remained, or chose to remain, in the dark.

Ten Minute Alibi, the play that she had been in when she had received Peter's Christmas present, was a thriller by Anthony Armstrong. The crux of the plot depended on a large clock in the centre of the stage which was reflected in a mirror. A girl who sat knitting behind the stage turned the hands and, needless to say, forgot one evening, thus spoiling the twist of the play. It was about 'a fiendish white slave trafficker with doped cigarettes, a beautiful girl with the intellect of a hippopotamus, and a hero whose feelings towards the villain are expressed in the pregnant words, "You ..." "I'll ...!"' Although the characterisation was banal and the dialogue uninspired ('My God, Sevilla, you are a swine!'), the plot was ingenious, and it became the most popular thriller of the decade, with over 800 performances.

Celia then took over briefly from Edna Best in *Another Language*, an American play by Rose Franken at the Lyric in Shaftesbury Avenue. And in May 1933 she played Sheila Gray in *Sometimes Even Now* by Warren Chetham Strode, produced by Basil Dean. Sheila Gray had three admirers in 1915. With one she has a brief affair before he returns to the war, in which he is killed. A son is born of this affair whom she 'adopts'. Fifteen years later she meets the other two admirers, both now conventionally married, and reveals that her 'adopted' son is in fact the son of their old friend. The play was described as showing the woman's side of *Journey's End*, and Celia's performance was thought to be one of the best yet of her career: 'indeed it raises her into quite another class of achievement', said the *Daily Mail*. Her dressing-room after the first night was filled with flowers, and also eleven bottles of beer. These, she explained to visitors, were a present from a friend who insisted that she 'must fatten up a bit'. (Peter always thought that Celia was too thin and did not take enough care of herself.)

Before *Sometimes Even Now* came off in July 1933, Peter had gone again. Asking Rupert to take care of Celia, he left for China on a roving commission from *The Times* as a Special Correspondent. He travelled via Berlin and Moscow and then on the Trans-Siberian railway to Manchuria. That long monotonous journey through steppe and birch forest was enlivened at one point by the train going out of control and leaving the rails. No one was hurt and the weather was beautiful; Peter took the accident with his usual sang-froid, managing discreetly to photograph the sprawling carriages. Though ostensibly sizing up the political situation in Manchuria (or Manchukuo as it was called under Japanese occupation) and China, Peter was again looking for adventure. He joined the Japanese army on an expedition after bandits, riding, hatless as usual, under broiling sun through hostile territory. Later on he pursued the communists. Though unrewarded in his search for serious action, he nevertheless had an exciting and interesting time and produced some sound articles for *The Times* on the political developments. Some time afterwards, he wrote a book about the journey, which he called *One's Company*.

Celia, more accustomed now to his temperament with its element of wanderlust, took his departure with greater equanimity than before. After the Chetham Strode play came off she went on a holiday to Mallorca with Comfort Turner, her old friend from St Paul's, now Rupert Hart-Davis's girlfriend, Rupert's sister Deirdre and her husband Ronnie Balfour, and Mary Booker and their children. They stayed in a villa for six weeks; the weather was glorious and Celia flourished in the sun. Her letters show her physical well-being growing day by day. Although stoical in character and seldom ill, Celia had no great physical stamina; she was skinny, ate little, having no particular interest in food, took little care of herself and was therefore prone to get tired and, when tired, depressed. A holiday, such as those weeks in Mallorca, was a genuine tonic.

When she mentioned to an American whom she met there that she had just been working in New York, he said,

'"Oh I saw Massey's *Hamlet* on the first night and couldn't stand the Ophelia – who was that?" In a still small voice I said "Well that was me" – and he spent the rest of lunch apologising and explaining it away, and me by saying how right he was about it over and over again. He has avoided me frantically ever since, smiling nervously when he sees me and immediately starting to talk very hard to someone else.

She was also amused by the local paper, the *Palma Post*, and its notices of the social comings and goings, items such as: 'Captain Baron Boris de Skossyuff finds himself organising a very interesting yachting party.' She also enjoyed observing the Mallorcans talking, 'particularly Margarita, the maid. I can understand her a bit but I could just as much if she were talking Hindustani because she acts everything all the time.'

Celia always preferred watching ordinary people, listening to odd conversations on a bus or children squabbling, snatches of human behaviour, to full-blown social gossip. She was naturally not at all snobbish, and always felt that conversations between smart ladies were more like competitions. Towards the end of the holiday Deirdre was taken ill and a Spanish doctor was called: 'He poked her in the stomach until it made rumbling noises and then said, "Ah, listen to the music of the bowels" – he speaks rather like Mrs Patrick Campbell – "how like Wagner".'

But she missed Peter. 'You would get into a train that goes over sideways,' she wrote to him. 'I wish you'd break this habit of going miles away on curious errands that I can't imagine – I do like to be able to imagine you.' Later, towards the end of the holiday, she wrote:

I thought last night how lovely it would be not to go back to England but to go on to some nasty little boat and sail on and on and on until I got to China. There I would say, 'Where please is Peter Fleming?' They would tell me without hesitation and I should walk rapidly inland avoiding all bandits and fall into your arms.

Peter enjoyed her letters: 'All your letters have an odd sort of gaiety about them which is very like you. They always remind me of you very vividly.'

Aubrey Blackburn, Celia's agent, had been sending telegrams to Mallorca with various offers of work, and she returned in August to find four plays waiting for her response. But what excited her more was to find that *Brazilian Adventure*, which had been published on 24 July 1933 by Jonathan Cape, had been dedicated to her. 'I didn't know you were really going to put "To C" in it,' she wrote to Peter. 'Oh sweet, it gave me the most queer feeling when I saw that. I can't ever thank you enough. My beloved, you don't know how much I loved that.' The book came out to unanimous acclaim, getting reviews from the literary lions of the day (Priestley, Garnett, Waugh, etc.) that young authors normally only dream of. Harold Nicolson picked out five qualities:

In the first place it furnishes vivid information about a tract of territory, a zone of fauna and flora, which is practically unknown. Secondly, it provides the stimulus of all pursuits and treasure-hunts, that delightful sensation of vicarious suffering, that burning question, 'Will they get there in the end?' Thirdly, it illustrates the responses of a highly cultured and intelligent mind to experiences which are physical and dumb. Fourthly, it has passages of keen observation, flood-lit analogies, and sallies of a very virile wit. And fifthly, it conveys a complete, encouraging, and most important portrait of the modern young man.

Three and four, in particular, were spot on.

Peter, in China, was unaware of its success. News had reached him however of the death of his grandfather, Robert Fleming.

I hate these gaps and somebody not being there any more, and he really was a fine old man, and greatly honoured all through his life, which I can't believe is very common in the City if you are as successful as he was. Also it means I suppose that I am now head of the family, technically speaking, and I shall be expected to become more solid and less fitful. It is funny how anxious I am that he has not left me anything to speak of: I really should hate it now, it would make me even more unreal. Poor old man, we never had much contact, and I did badly by not going into the Business. I hope my book had some good reviews, because that sort of thing would please him, he knowing nothing of these matters. You must never die, my darling.

The spurious role of head of the family, first mentioned to him as a small boy after his father had been killed, went very deep. As far as money was concerned, he could relax: he and his brothers were left nothing. It is possible that he never felt quite 'real'.

The serious tone of this letter is not characteristic; on the whole he recounted his exploits, downplaying any danger, puncturing any self-importance and mostly expressing his affection by way of mild teasing insult. 'Well, we are a couple of queer worms crawling about the earth in roughly opposite directions: but I should think much more unkindly of the earth if you weren't crawling about it, my estimable Miss Johnson. Goodnight, my sweetheart, we are a couple of bloody fools.'

As August progressed and he found himself travelling down the Yangtse, he wrote: 'I wish I was with you. I wish I was shooting grouse at Black Mount. But really I am quite happy where I am.' He was pleased to have gained an interview with Chiang Kai-shek, and to have obtained information about the communists, but he was also glad to have been travelling.

We have had a pretty terrific journey, which I think actually has never been done before by a foreigner in the way we did it, though there is no earthly reason why it shouldn't have been. Most of it was in buses, but there was one lovely day coming through some gorges in a sampan where things were more beautiful than you can imagine and some quite amusing rapids . . .

You can be sure that 'quite amusing' meant utterly hair-raising.

It was in Shanghai on this trip that he stayed with two brothers, Tony and John Keswick: 'The latter was at Eton with me, and the former is a director of the local sort of East India Company, which was I think started by an ancestor of theirs. They are both incredibly nice and highly intelligent and I couldn't be in better hands.' They were to remain friends for life.

Celia meanwhile had been receiving what she called 'forceful messages' from Gaumont British about making a film.

So obediently off to Shepherd's Bush I trotted, feeling haughty as usual, and went through the usual formula of being taken from one film magnate (speaking English with a German accent) to another (speaking English with an American accent). They all do the best performance of big business with four telephones ringing and 6 different secretaries answering them – none of which means anything at all. The various interviews took the worst part of an hour at the end of which nothing at all had been said, except they all asked me why I'd refused to do films before. I refrained from replying because they hadn't asked me to, and took a haughty stage star line of not caring or knowing the smallest thing about films.

The following day she had to do a film test:

It was most alarming; they gave me three pages of a closely typed emotional scene and said 'We'll do that' – I said 'What? Read it?' 'No,' they said, 'just say the words' and I had to – I can learn pretty quickly but that beat me. They kept me waiting for ages of course; I sat in a huge armchair in a star-like dressing-room for $\frac{3}{4}$ of an hour. Luckily I'd got 3 of your letters in my bag, so I was quite happy.

Nothing seems to have come of this skirmish with films. Instead, having turned down a part in *Spring 1600* by Emlyn Williams, she went in to *The Key* by R. Gore Browne and J.L. Hardy starring Godfrey Tearle. This was a light drama about a British soldier kidnapped in Dublin in the 1920s. Celia, as the wife of the kidnapped officer, and as the lover of an aide-de-camp, had to express emotional turmoil and sustained terror at the same time. Some thought she succeeded, but one critic felt that 'her voice has not yet the range to express deep emotion'. The play lasted a few weeks. On 4 October, having heard that Peter was on his way home, she wrote:

The Key comes off on Saturday and on Monday I open in *As It Was in the Beginning* (rewritten and now called for no clear reason *The Wind and the Rain*) in Manchester – so I am rehearsing all day, being fitted, trying to learn words, playing *The Key*, dress-rehearsing and being madly excited because of October 20th all day and most of the night. Oh, my dearest love, none of it means a damn thing except October 20th ... Don't remember me as too nice or beautiful or funny because then you'll be disappointed.

8

The Wind and the Rain and the Tsaidam

A good-looking young actor called Robert Harris had been instrumental in getting *The Wind and the Rain* put on. It was a comedy about medical students in lodgings in Edinburgh written by a young doctor from New Zealand, Merton Hodge. Under the title *As It Was in the Beginning* it had been tried out by Bronson Albery at the Arts Theatre Club for four performances; Celia and Robert Douglas had played in it, as had Jack Minster, Cecil Parker and Athene Seyler. Bronson Albery did not want to put it on in the West End without the original cast, in particular Robert Douglas, who was unable to do it. Robert Harris therefore took up an option. He enlisted the support of a young man called Hugh Beaumont who had just gone into a partnership with Harry Tennent under the banner Howard and Wyndham, and together they got the production together. Auriol Lee, an experienced and fashionable director produced it. The play was due to open at the Opera House in Manchester before coming to London. Auriol Lee had taken a lackadaisical attitude to the enterprise and by the time they were due to open in Manchester the play was by no means ready. At the penultimate hour she took a grip, and by rehearsing to 3 a.m. the night before, the play was just able to open as planned. After a tense but successful week there, and then a slow beginning at the St Martin's Theatre in London, it became an enormous popular success. To this day people who saw the play remember the line at the beginning and the end of the play, delivered by the medical students' landlady in a strong Scottish accent: 'It's only hotpot ... but it's awfu' guid.'

Hugh Beaumont, the young producer, known to all as Binkie, and Harry Tennent split from Howard and Wyndham and formed H.M.Tennent productions. Binkie was to become in the forties, throughout the fifties and some way into the sixties, one of the most powerful figures in the theatre. Robert

Harris asked Binkie for £25 a week for his part in *The Wind and the Rain*; Binkie was horrified and offered him less, which Robert Harris accepted. Celia was given £5 more on the strength of having acted with Sir Gerald du Maurier. It was an early example of Binkie's control. The production cost £1,000 to put on.

It was not a particularly distinguished play but, carried largely by Robert Harris and Celia, it had its appeal. 'Celia Johnson,' wrote W.A.Darlington, 'gives Anne the benefit of her greatly increased power of emotional sincerity, and Robert Harris plays Charles impeccably.' Ivor Brown, by now a committed fan, nevertheless said with perception:

This actress either naturally possesses or has brilliantly mastered the art of being adorable on the lines of intelligent sensibility instead of by exploiting glucose charm. It is one of the chief and most commendable differences between the Edwardian theatre and our own that the 'ingénue' parts now demand an aspect of intelligence instead of being vehicles for the Lackwit Lovelies who 'dress' a part rather than acting it.

The play ran for two years, first at the St Martin's, then transferring to the Queen's, and then to the Savoy. Both Celia and Robert Harris kept up their excellent performances. Mackenzie Ward (a late substitute for his brother, Ronald Ward), too, was very good as the comic student. On the strength of his performance he received twelve stage offers and sixteen film offers, all of which he had to turn down because of the length of run; a promising career was therefore still-born.

Before the war, contracts were for the run of a play. Later, during the war, leading actors and actresses could insist on a six-month get-out clause. Binkie refused to let anyone leave the cast of *The Wind and The Rain*. Robert Harris in fact was delighted with the guaranteed income from a long run. Celia was probably grateful for the stability it provided during what turned out to be a difficult period. But Mackenzie Ward suffered, because he was unable to take up any of the offers made to him. And when the husband of Margaret Moffat, who played the Scottish landlady, died suddenly one

lunchtime, she played that evening before telling her colleagues of his death; she had no understudy. In later life, when
people mentioned the play to Celia, as they often did, she
was always rather vague about it. 'Oh, did you see that? Oh,
yes, I was in it . . .'

It opened on 18 October 1933. The first year of the run
was fine. The play was fun, and everybody went to it. Peter
was back from China. He returned to find *Brazilian Adventure*
an enormous success, and himself a celebrated author.
Fashionable hostesses took him up. He enjoyed it all even
though they may have found him a silent and awkward addition
to their parties. An even greater future was predicted for him.

For a while he had a job at the BBC, in the Talks Department,
but after a few months he resigned, explaining: 'I find myself
– by a fluke which could not be foreseen when I applied for
the job – in a position to earn, by writing, at least four times
what the BBC pays me. Economics apart, I should be a fool
not to make the most of the artificial value temporarily attached
to my pen.' But by the spring of 1934, he was planning another
trip, the fourth in as many years. Again he was able to get
a roving commission from the editor of *The Times*, Geoffrey
Dawson. Peter always got on well with Dawson, having shooting as an interest in common. The manager of *The Times*
stipulated:

You are to proceed to Mongolia and to contribute to *The Times*
such articles as the circumstances permit, and if events develop in
or around the area, you will be at the disposal of the editor to deal
with them. As we see it at present, the journey would occupy not
more than 9 months and we are prepared to pay you a sum not
exceeding £650.

Following a rather jolly time staying with the Marquess of
Anglesey, where he directed the guests in some home movies,
and his customary visit to Black Mount in August, he set
off, leaving Celia, after nearly a year in *The Wind and the
Rain*, unwell. He wrote to her from Holland:

I miss you very much. It is horrible being away from you, and horrible
to think that it is probably being horrible for you: if you see what
I mean . . . I do hope you are better. It is miserable for you being

ill on top of everything else; it makes me feel all the worse about going away from you. My poor darling numble, what a rapscallion you have got yourself involved with.

Accompanied by new friends, George and Mogs Gage,* he went first to Moscow and then to the Caucasus, where they had planned a little shooting. His companions then returned, and he took a slow and uncomfortable train from Baku to Vladivostok. From there he wrote:

My food today has been typically unorthodox. Starting with grapes, sardines and brandy at 8, I went on to some chocolate and a dwarf crayfish in the train, and have just lunched at 4 o'clock – off caviar and a jam omelette. You never know what or when you are going to eat in this country.

This was a parting Celia could have done without. She was unhappy. Alice, her devoted dresser at that time, wrote a note to Peter:

You won't be a bit thrilled when you see this from Alice, but I thought if I wrote and told you your loved one Miss Johnson is really better you will at least believe it coming from me – she is really Better I am glad to say. She has got a nice little bottle of Port which seems to be doing her good. I will look after her while you are away as much as I can. Now take grate care of yourself while you are out in China as I dont think China is good for little Boys like you its only good for Big Old Fat Boys. My Very Best Wishes for Speedy Return. Alice. PS. Excuse scrall.

Celia was very low that autumn of 1934. 'Oh I do miss you,' she wrote. 'I get awful fits of black gloom and all the time I have to numb all my real part and live in a superficial casing. I don't think you'll ever know quite how much I miss you.' And, 'September has been beastly.' In October the first anniversary of *The Wind and the Rain* passed:

We had a party at the Ivy which was quite fun – I drank an awful lot mostly because I was at a table with the Masseys and I wanted

---

* The Viscount and Viscountess Gage. Imogen (Mogs) Gage was the daughter of Lady Desborough, a *grande dame* of the Edwardian era.

to keep my end up and appear nonchalant and condescending. I had a new black frock and looked rather like an overdressed pierrot on Brighton pier.

In November she went to another party:

I went to a ghastly party on Wednesday night given by Binkie Beaumont, one of the more effeminate members of the management. The whole of the stars of the West End stage were there, acting their heads off. I stood miserably in a corner clutching a gin and tonic until a woman stepping heavily and suddenly back on me drenched me completely by upsetting the drink all over me – I've never been so wet.

Her father decided she was run down and Binkie allowed her to take a month's holiday at Christmas. Not wanting to go away if Peter was about to return she wired to him to find out if there was any chance. He telegraphed in reply: 'SWEET NUMBLE NO HOPE OF THAT MUST SATISFY TIMES AND WANDERLUST GO SWITZERLAND AND GET BROWN VERY ATTACHED PETER.'

So, after a week with some friends in Devon, she went skiing with Mary Pakenham in St Moritz. This had the required effect. It was the first time she had been skiing and she adored it. Celia often got fits of helpless giggles when she was with friends and something struck her as funny or ridiculous. One such episode happened with Mary on the holiday when they were snooping round one of the grand suites in the hotel, and, 'standing up in the cupboard was a pink thigh-length artificial leg. The shock once over we laughed until tears poured down anyway my face – it conjured up endless possibilities.'

Never very smartly dressed, usually devoid of make-up, and with thick glasses, Celia, throughout her life, was seldom recognised in public. In the hotel in Switzerland, she and Mary overheard some people standing near them say: 'I hear Celia Johnson is staying in the hotel – I'm determined not to miss her.' Much later she would tell a story of being approached by a woman when shopping in Harrods, who said: 'Don't I know you?' Celia prepared herself for a follow-up of, 'Didn't I see you in such and such?' but was amused to hear the woman say: 'I know, you're the person who fainted at the Chelsea Flower Show.' She never courted publicity; she wasn't interested.

She returned refreshed to *The Wind and the Rain*, still a great success, and to waiting for Peter. He had said that he was likely to be away for six months, and four had passed. 'Please, please come home as soon as you possibly can,' she wrote. But he was still roving around. At the beginning of December 1934 he had written from Harbin:

I have got back from the top left hand corner of this puppet state, where I must say it was pretty cold, being indeed more or perhaps I should say less than Thirty Below, whatever that means. I thought my ears were frost bitten but it turned out they weren't. If they had been it would have been like the picture you drew in a letter you wrote from the boat going to America ... Mongolia is a good place. I lived in various Yurts, which are not as you might suppose either a skin disease or a Hungarian composer but rather the rough edifices made of felt which the Mongols throw up with a view to canalising draughts which might otherwise roam the steppe to no purpose. Each yurt is surrounded by a cordon of savage and starving dogs, and when you go out to the lavatory you are accompanied by a woman or child who stands sentry throughout this important process, keeping the dogs at bay with harsh words and frozen dung ... I am sorry to be so coarse in my language; it is the effect of the great open spaces. [By December he was in China.] I have been in the Hsingan mountains which I fear mean nothing to you but which are very nice, and the only major blot on the horizon is that I have missed the last Christmas mail by several long chalks and that therefore the festive season must pass with only a telegraphic salute from your far-flung admirer, who incidentally will not know where to send it. The same very maddeningly applies to your birthday. Oh dear. No moss, no moss as usual. The last letter I had from you was quite a long time ago, the 29th penult. to be exact, but I dare say you have been fondly writing to Peking, which I hope to reach in time for plum pudding via Jehol. When I get there I really shall have to make some plans.

The plans he went on to make, and which he gradually revealed to Celia, were to return – but not by the easiest or quickest route. He was to go to Tokyo, then come back, then do some sort of journey in Mongolia, then set my face for home; but I am bound to warn you that I would like to come home across country if it be possible, so the mere setting of the face may not mean all that much. [After Tokyo, he wrote how he had] stayed with a very nice but clever man called Sansom and his intelligent but talkative wife in the Umbassah, which is how most diplomats pronounce their headquarters. Here I what is known as Broke the back of several articles; my luggage is full of these sadly disabled things, and several others which I have left behind at various places are following me doggedly about Asia. None is finished, but there are going to be several days of mass production in P.King, which I reach the day after tomorrow. I am v. glad to have got Tokyo off my chest, so that I can now concentrate my energies on hacking my way home across country, a project which is most unlikely to come off but which is well worth having a crack at from every point of view.

A few days later he wired: 'GRAND STARTING CROSSCOUNTRY MAY TAKE LONGISH TIME BUT MUST HAVE CRACKATIT KISSIM ALL MY LOVE PETER.' This plan that he so casually mentioned was essentially to walk from China to India, by way of western China, a desolate area of northern Tibet, into Sinkiang, a province by reason of a number of civil wars closed to outsiders (no foreigners had been through it for eight years) and over to Kashmir. There were no roads, only caravan routes – the Old Silk Road through Mongolia for instance – some of which were known not to be operational.

Knowing this news would go down badly with Celia, in the next letter he tried to justify his plan.

I can't remember what I said [in the wire] but what I meant to say was that I was starting home in February across country, that it might take a longish time, but that it was a thing I had to try and do. My sweet, you must forgive me for not being back punctually at the end of 6 months. I feel bloody about it, because I know you'll be disappointed; and it's no good splitting straws and saying that I never actually specified 6 months, a) because I never expected to spend so long in Russia and Manchuria, and b) because I never expected this crosscountry return would prove possible. Now it looks as if – with the help of a White Russian and his wife – it may prove possible; and darling Celia whom I love – I shouldn't be being what you might ponderously call True to Myself if I didn't have a crack at it. I expect I'm being over-gloomy and over-abject on account of the references to 6 months in your letters; because in point of fact this journey will either be a fiasco almost at once, in which case I shall come quickly home, or else at the cost of a few (it's impossible to say how many but not many) extra months it will get me home feeling that I have justified myself and not nearly so vulnerable to wanderlust as heretofore. At least that's how it looks at the moment. But I do feel bloody, I must say. All the same it would be foolish and unreal of me not to try this business, which I may say is entirely free from danger and will take me through the invigorating uplands of Northern Tibet. Once I get started I shall go like a bat out of hell. You must see that it's a good thing for me to do, my sweet. Or at least try and do.

Three weeks later, he wrote:

Tomorrow at midnight if all goes well I board the Flying Chinaman and set off in a B-line Numblewards. How long it will remain a B-line I do not care to prophesy, but anyway I shall be on my way home all the time, even when going backwards. First I go in a train, then in a bus or something, then I vault lightly on to some form of quadruped, possibly a yak. If you look at the map you will see a place called the Kokonor in the north of Tibet and that is where I hope to be. In the meantime I am darting to and fro like a weasel, buying ammunition from lighthouse keepers and Presents for the Natives and Worcester Sauce. I have been inoculated no less than three times against typhus by the Catholic Fathers, who have got a special sort of serum. Each shot comprises the essence of thirty lice, no less. These affectionate little creatures are pastured in the hospital on the legs of three old men who come in for an hour and a half twice a day; each has 6000 clamped to his calves in little boxes and they (the old men of course) get twelve dollars a month ... My sweet Numble, I will make all speed towards you, and will keep you informed of progress and prospects until the time when, and if, I go what we call Out Of Touch.

He set off on 15 February 1935, taking with him: '2lbs of marmalade, 4 tins of cocoa, 6 bottles of brandy, 1 bottle of Worcester Sauce, 1 lb of coffee, 3 small packets of chocolate, some soap and a good deal of tobacco, besides a small store of knives, beads, toys, etc. by way of presents, and a rather scratch assortment of medicines', as well as some old clothes, a few books, two compasses and two portable typewriters.

The following week he wrote to Celia from Lanchow in north-west China having crossed some mountains in great discomfort perched on the back of a lorry.

Sweet numble, I read with great delight the bit about you in the du Maurier book. It looked to me a pretty, indeed a damn, good book, but I thought the Johnson motif was superficially handled ... I wonder where you are now; just finishing lunch with some handsome young man at a Fashionable Rendezvous, I warrant. Celia, my darling love, I do hope you are reasonably happy. I am having a grand though uncertain time, and am making All Speed towards you. Good night darling Numble. This may be the last letter for a bit.

There was one more letter, a month later at the end of March 1935, from Tangar, Chinghai.

This I fear will be your last letter for a bit. The great migration Numble-wards really gets into its stride tomorrow, when I set off with the caravan of a Mongol prince or possibly princeling in the direction of a place called *the tsaidam*. This most maps, if they mark it at all, cover with those little trinities of apostrophes which one imagines to denote a marsh or quagmire; from what I hear however it is no better than a desert, and the snipe shooting very poor. Things have started going rather well, though no doubt all will turn out to be for the worst. I have got a passport of sorts, and have bought a bright red horse, which is most savage. Yesterday morning, in the course of one of my well known Aix-to-Ghent rides it kicked me in the back at 3 a.m., an unpardonable hour, and immediately afterwards destroyed my flask by dancing on my saddlebag. When I think of all the times I have refrained from drinking that brandy my blood boils. Apart from the horse – well apart if they are wise – I have chartered three camels. These are to carry food for the horse as far as I can make out. I have also got a fur sleeping bag and a quantity of what looks like sand. The latter is called Tsamba, and is for me to eat. Altogether it is a very funny expedition. On reaching a place called Teijinor, which is in the middle of the Tsaidam, the object of the game is to slip, or if that proves impossible, to nip, across the frontier into Sinkiang, after which all is plain sailing as far as India, where my Zeppelin awaits me. In the event of no nipping, I shall have to come back, which I shall do in a vile temper and very fast indeed. So either way, my darling numble, you will see me again as soon as I can possibly manage. Perhaps however, you no longer want to see me again. It is such years since I heard from you (I had no mail forwarded from Peking, which I left nearly six weeks ago) and even since I saw a paper with the name of your play in it, that I sometimes think you must certainly by this time have Preferred Another, and that these letters (I say these as if there were a lot of them) are what we of the Upper Shell used to call bombinans in vacuo. I for my part am extremely attached to you, and dream about you literally almost every night. Darling Numble, it really does a chap good to reflect that there is anyone as funny and handsome as you. I miss you much more now that I am definitely going home.

The next three weeks to Teijinor ought to be pretty good fun and I expect to make a good deal of play with my two rather old rifles. There is a kind of wild ass – called, by those who can manage it, Prjevalsky's Horse – which is said to provide good clean sport. Sun and wind are rife, and I am already the colour and consistency of a Gladstone Bag, though perhaps pucer. I will write should it prove possible, but that depends on meeting a caravan coming out and I don't think there are many at this time of year; their Christmas shopping doesn't begin till July. Anyhow goodbye for the nonce, my darling Celia. I am afraid my picture of a Tibetan nonce in the rutting season has been censored by the Dalai Lama. Take care of yourself, my sweet, and I will do the same.

The spring and summer passed before anyone heard from him again. In fact, though he had not mentioned it, he had a companion with him, a Swiss girl, Ella Maillart. She was a tough sporty girl, who had skied and played hockey for Switzerland, and indeed sailed for Switzerland in the Olympic Games. She, like he, had travelled before in Central Asia and had written about it. He had met her briefly in London the year before and had said blithely 'see you in China', and thought no more about it. At the time he had teased Celia about her. Then they had run into each other. Whereas Peter's previous book had been called *One's Company*, hers had been called *Turkestan Solo*. Solitary journeys were what both preferred and though both nursed the same ambition – to walk to India – they had intended to continue travelling alone; they had therefore been relieved to discover that they were planning quite different routes. They parted with mutual expressions of good luck, only to discover that neither of their proposed itineraries was possible and that they must perforce go the same way. 'We got on very well together,' wrote Peter, 'though we both paraded our conviction, which was perhaps not wholly justified, that we should have got on better by ourselves.'

The journey that they completed together was remarkable, covering 3,500 miles and taking seven months, for five of which they were completely out of touch with the rest of the world. It cost them about £150 each. Their means of transport was by train, then lorry, then mule, then caravan-serai, then on sturdy little Tibetan ponies to which they became very attached. Peter named his first pony Greys, after the house his mother had bought near Nettlebed, and Ella called hers Slalom. After a bit Greys became exhausted and had to be left behind to rest. He was exchanged for another horse:

This proved to be a little two-year-old mare. They fetched her in out of the marsh, and at first sight she seemed more amphibian than equine; she suggested, rather than resembled, a water rat suffer-ing from mange and malnutrition. Her hooves had not recently been cut and such patches of her shaggy coat as still remained to her were drably caked with mud. She had abnormally long ears and a general appearance of frailty and apprehension ... I called her Cynara for sentimental reasons.

The title of the play that Celia had done with Gerald du Maurier was *Cynara*: 'I have been faithful to thee Cynara in my fashion.' It was an apposite name.

Ella, who was known as Kini, was very different from Peter. Whereas he liked to get on with the journey, 'walking through' he would call it, she liked to stop and explore and absorb; she was baffled by his references to Eton and grouse shooting, and he underestimated her resourcefulness. At the beginning of the journey he would go out with his rifle into the Tsaidam; she would be obliged to cook and mend the saddles. By the end of the journey their tasks were more evenly divided. They exasperated each other but had great mutual respect. Where he was flippant and ironic, she was serious. The books they later wrote, *Forbidden Journey* (hers) and *News from Tartary* (his) could have been about different journeys, so far apart in attitude were they.

On 25 July 1935, triumphant, they reached Kashgar and Peter wrote to Celia:

Well, my darling beloved Numble, success has crowned the efforts of your devoted admirer, and unless I perish of frostbite or yak-bite in the Himalayas, I should be among you soon after the middle of September. Kashgar I reached the day before yesterday and you cannot imagine how delightful it is to have your first bath, your first whisky and soda, your first toast and marmalade, for 5 months and more. I am permanently in an 'O brave new world' state and in no mood for letter-writing, which luckily doesn't matter much as I should reach England not long after this. What I am v. worried about is you: if only I had had the presumption to foresee success I could have given this place as an address and had a fat mail. There is no daily paper with a list of theatres on the premises, but I have a horrible feeling that your bloody play is still running and you have had a foul summer. Perhaps on the other hand you have Married and Settled Down. Almost anything may have happened. Oh dear I wish I knew.

I for my part am jet black and very well. The journey was uneventful but I am really very pleased with it and hope in future to feel less of a fraud than I did before. I hope that by now you know (if you are still interested) that all is well with Little Rover. The Secy of State, pestered no doubt by my fond mother, has been asking after me here and yesterday they sent a message (by the secret and illicit wireless transmitter) to Simla; so the fears of London should have been allayed today. I wonder if you got any of my letters? It is much to be doubted ... But there is far too much to tell you and I will not try to tell it. Let it suffice that I am still devoted, still bloody and dying to get back. Darling Numble, I do hope you are all right. An honest fellow has now got to carry this letter over the mountains to India so I will, as they say, close. I shall follow it with all speed. It must seem, and indeed is, a long time since I started; but in point of fact I have done the course in little over bogey.

Celia must have suffered dreadfully during this long absence, though few people were aware of it; as usual she revealed little. She was probably glad of the reliable monotony of *The Wind and the Rain*, in which she was still playing night after night. When news at last reached London of Peter's arrival in Kashgar, she wrote him a bewildered letter. 'This desperate long separation has done awful things to me. I am scared of everything.' She also sent him a wire. He replied: 'LOVED WIRE GOT TODAY ANOTHER THREE WEEKS TOUGH STUFF THEN LARGEST FASTEST PLANE JOKES UNFORGOTTEN DARLING NUMBLE.' Later: 'ATTACHED IS STILL THE WORD', and shortly before arrival, 'KEEP YOUR SEATS BELOVED IMBECILE'.

Before setting off on this ambitious expedition Peter had written to Rupert explaining his predicament over Kini, how he had failed to tell Celia about her mainly because, he said, when he had met her in London earlier, he had teased Celia about her, pretending to be very struck with her: 'As far as Affections go she will never mean more to me than a yak. All the same I feel guilty towards the Crackwit and worry a lot about not having told her about the Other Woman, though I am sure it was better not to ... It's a silly situation and would never have arisen if I hadn't cracked jokes about the girl last summer.' Just before arriving back in London, he sent Rupert a wire: 'DUE MONDAY TELL CHEYNE AND DEBAG SWISS CAT IF CELIA'S COMING CROYDON.' Rupert, however, did not have to break the news about Kini to Celia as she did not go to meet him at the airport. Peter, when he did come clean about her, must have done so ineptly, because a few weeks after his return, Celia wrote to him at Black Mount: 'I got very depressed last night on account of Ella who's a new one on me – She's not the Swiss is she? ... I have discovered Ella is the Swiss. I didn't realise you were with her practically from the word go.' He replied: 'Don't worry about the Swiss, my darling little beast. She never poached at all, and maybe, who knows, she did me a lot of good', which was probably true. Peter, inordinately tough and fearless of everything in life, was clearly terrified of female emotion, and shrank before it.

They decided to waste no more time and to marry. Arrangements were made for a secret wedding in December and only close friends were told. Peter wrote from Scotland that he was happy to be getting married and thought it would be a success, 'because after this last fairly non-bogus journey I feel myself to be stronger and because without being able to analyse it I feel you to be stronger too.' Celia replied: 'It's a slightly depressing thought that we've both got to be so strong to carry this off.'

9

Clandestine wedding

And carry it off they did in their fashion. Peter, partly through fear of the press, partly through fear of his mother, and partly because a cloak-and-dagger attitude appealed to him, insisted on keeping the whole thing secret. First he went to Hunstanton in Norfolk to visit Celia's parents, no doubt to ask formally for her hand (he was rigorous in old-fashioned courtesies). 'The news has been well, in fact delightedly, received here,' Celia reported after he left, adding, 'I hope your mother will like me eventually.' The news still had to be broken to his mother – a daunting task and one that Peter felt unable to undertake alone; he called in Mary Pakenham (who had kindly already made many of the technical arrangements for the wedding). They set off for Oxfordshire and went first to call on Grannie Katie at Joyce Grove; she was very nice about the whole thing but not surprisingly foxed by the presence of Mary and began commiserating with her. Mary assured her that Celia was her best friend and she was delighted that Celia and Peter were going to be married. Grannie Katie said that she had seen Celia once in a play but hadn't thought much of her, preferring George Robey.

From Joyce Grove they went to a smart lunch with Nancy Astor at Cliveden – confounding the scent – and then back to Nettlebed, to Greys Court, to face up to Mrs Val. She had recently bought Greys, a handsome mainly seventeenth-century house with some much earlier parts (now in the hands of the National Trust), a couple of miles from her mother-in-law, Grannie Katie, at Joyce Grove, and was doing it up; the Cromwellian stables were for Peter to write in. She showed them round the house, pointing out Ian's room and Peter's room, and when Peter interjected and said, 'Now, Mama. What about this wedding?' she ignored him and carried on talking about the curtains. Peter was floored by this. She was vain and difficult but her four sons adored her; all, especially Peter, were wilfully blind to her faults.

Celia, knowing by now that Peter was unlikely to be an ordinary carpet-slipper husband, wrote:

I do want you to have a grand life. I'm awfully afraid I'll be in the way. It's always seemed to me that our being married won't make much difference to you but I see it's bound to make a bit. Still [she added realistically] being like you are it probably won't make much – anyway you mustn't let it, whatever I say or do, and I don't think you will.

Celia was using the word 'grand' in its northern sense, meaning fine.

She left *The Wind and the Rain* on 2 December 1935 after 900 performances, and the wedding took place on the 10th in Chelsea Old Church, the service conducted by an old Eton chaplain, Ralph Sadleir. It was Amaryllis Fleming's tenth birthday and she was very disappointed not to be a bridesmaid. Celia wore a hat with a feather in it copied from one of Pam's, and a handful of friends and relations attended. Mrs Val rose, just, to the occasion and held a reception of champagne and sandwiches in Cheyne Walk and all went well, Peter having begged Tim and Rosalie Nugent to try and keep her happy. When Peter and Celia left the reception for the station in her Rolls, she did tell her chauffeur not to be too long as Amaryllis had a music lesson to go to.

Mrs Val appeared to disapprove of Celia largely because she lacked blue blood, and also because she was in the theatre. She also resented the fact that with this clandestine marriage she had lost her control over Peter. She had exercised power over her four spirited sons through force of character, control of the purse, and by invoking the memory of her husband Val's exemplary character. Wounded by Peter's behaviour, she made threats about her will, was unwelcoming to Celia, and off-hand to Robert and Ethel Johnson. Celia's parents behaved well and sensibly under trying circumstances and refused to take offence at her high-handed behaviour. Greys Court bought, she said, with Peter in mind, was promptly put on the market.

Celia and Peter went first to Paris and then skiing in Zurs, where they were joined by Mary. They had great fun. Peter was a fearless but poor skier; somehow he never fell down. He must have received some sort of conciliatory wire from his mother, for he wrote to her from there:

My darling Mie. It *was* sweet of you to send that wire. I can't tell you how pleased we were to get it. It makes a tremendous difference. All your worry and doubts were my fault, and I felt awfully bad about it. Perhaps it was wrong not to tell you before, but that would have meant six weeks of misgivings, instead of one and you really were (and no doubt are) working yourself to the bone over Greys, which *must* be a bigger strain than you give yourself time to realise. Anyhow I'm terribly sorry for the pain (or disappointment, if we *must* be polite) I caused you; and you were a darling to send that wire.

I'm about 90 times happier than I ever imagined one could be. Celia is lovely and (believe it or not) a fine person, and the nice thing – as far as I can see – about being married to her is that, funny as everything seemed before, it now seems ten times funnier. At any rate, we spend our whole time being nearly sick with laughter. Darling Mie, I don't think you need have any doubt ...

I thought Am[aryllis] had the other celebrated beauties licked into a cocked hat at the wedding. Give her our love ...

In spite of the placatory wire, Mrs Val must still have been furious about the wedding; she wrote an angry letter to Ian about it, revealing her threat about her will. Ian was better able to stand up to her than Peter and wrote a sharp letter back, showing a shrewd understanding of all concerned:

My very darling Mama, I have just got your letter very late at night and I have even managed to whip my lazy limbs into climbing down to the Cedar room to remonstrate.

Now listen – what ever you may think, I feel that we must all back Peter up in this – and if some testator has cut him out you must go round at once and say you've thought it over and feel after all it's for the best. *You* must not side with the rest of the family and leave Peter all by himself. You *must* put a brave front (once more) on the whole thing and not say things like you wrote to me. It was time Peter got married, I think. He was losing his sense of humour about himself and perhaps not seeing himself objectively enough. Lots of his behaviour has been a little theatrical lately –

even if I do say it and I think some domestic trials and vicissitudes may bring him from the stars a little. He *is* a law unto himself – a genius and an admirable, truthful, good man. We have all benefited by him and his particular personality in some way and I think we must expect – especially you – to put up with the particularities which have made him without question one of the 2 or 3 most brilliant men of his generation. We mustn't get into the way of having a perfection complex about him. The outstanding is always a little inhuman – and always must be, in order to be outstanding, and, darling Mama, we, and ultimately the whole of England, have a lot to be grateful for in Peter's existence. He really *is* setting a standard of sanity and truthfulness for a whole generation – he alone, a lot of people think – and if correction is necessary it should be done gently and in perspective. Don't be carried away on a tide of side issues about Celia's family. I feel disappointed myself and yet glad at the same time that he is married. I should feel annoyed about not being told and not being best man and one thing and another, but I really don't mind him treating me as a minor criminal and as utterly untrustworthy because he does know best in so many other things that one can't expect him to be tolerant and humane in all others.

Try and forgive him for this as you have so often forgiven me for other things and stand with him. He doesn't show it beneath that thick façade, but I know he is longing for you to be on his side if only in appearance (he would be furious if anyone suggested he had such a weakness, but you know it's true and that he is as sensitive as any of us).

I think the great danger is that he should have to turn away from the family for sympathy and support – to Rupert and other satellites when he should be relying on you. He won't get mixed up in the theatre as you suggest if he has another refuge, and I know like all of us, that he looks to you who have made him what he is to see him through things – even if he does appear so self-sufficient . . .

Try and swallow it, darling Mama, and do without the hypocritical sympathy the aunts and uncles will be so ready to give. You must go to this testator and make him change his mind. Admit that you were disappointed at first sight, but that now you are resigned and feel that Celia will do him good. Lie like a trooper if you must but see him through all this and go on helping him when he needs it. He will never say when he wants help, but I know he does now and it is all our duties to do what we can. You must be there in case of anything and so that he can know he will always be able to have ultimate recourse to you.

    I can't write any more,
      Please darling Mama,
        All my love and kisses, Ian.

Powerful forces were at work. Celia, in time, had a reasonable if not close relationship with her mother-in-law, keeping her distance for the most part. For the time being, marriage came first in her life and the theatre second. Having said that, within a couple of months she had one of her greatest theatrical triumphs. In February 1936, a couple of months into her marriage, she played the part of Elizabeth Bennet in *Pride and Prejudice* at the St James's Theatre. The adaptation by Helen Jerome satisfied the Jane Austen purists and the designs by Rex Whistler were beautiful. The whole production was a delight, and the company had many friends in it. In particular Celia liked acting with Hugh Williams who played Darcy. He had a dry wit and was debonair in appearance. Whether she found him attractive or whether she liked talking about cricket (a mutual passion) with him, he became a great friend, probably one of her closest in the theatre. Anthony Quayle played Mr Wickham and Dorothy Hyson and Leueen Macgrath played Jane and Lydia. For once in her life Celia played the romantic heroine rather than the down-trodden or wronged wife. Her unaffectedness was put to full effect. 'There could be no higher test of theatrical tact and Miss Johnson survives it,' wrote *The Times*. The *Observer* talked of 'the best performance of her career. With her wide-eyed innocence she continually adorns the canvas; with her beautiful control of the verbal duel with Darcy, and her discreet intimation of her domestic relations, she gives admirable point to what emerges of the story.' It was a glittering success and ran for nine months. Mary Clive [Pakenham] regards it as one of Celia's greatest triumphs. It was probably one of the happiest times of her life.

Peter was mostly working for *The Times*, and that summer as a Special Correspondent he was sent on the maiden voyage of the *Queen Mary*. Many years later, he wrote:

I find it difficult to recall a comparable event which aroused an interest so worldwide. The ship swarmed with journalists: there were twenty broadcasters of different nationalities. Some idea of the news value placed on everything to do with the voyage can be gained from the fact that *The Times*, in addition to the long otiose dispatches from its Special Correspondent, carried on its main page summaries of any broadcasts transmitted from the *Queen Mary*; 'in the course of the BBC's second News Bulletin the announcer said, "Over to the *Queen Mary*!", and immediately the voice of a speaker in the ship at sea began a report of her progress.' *Immediately*! Just Fancy!

However the ship's transmitters were not up to coping with the traffic of news:

On the second day out *The Times* reported that the wireless transmitters were working at full pressure. By the fourth the operators were dead on their feet, the control-room was knee-deep in undispatched dispatches and the overworked apparatus was in a fair way to being jammed with incoming editorial reprimands. Protest meetings were held, indignant resolutions were passed, but nothing could be done to improve matters. The biggest news-story of the year, and the dullest of the decade, continued to seep out in a belated trickle.

Peter was also involved with Graham Greene, Evelyn Waugh and others in a short-lived magazine called *Night and Day* which aimed at being London's answer to the *New Yorker*. He continued to do theatre criticism. One odd little achievement was to recruit Joyce Maxtone Graham to write a sort of ordinary woman's diary for *The Times*; calling herself Jan Struther she wrote a column about a character, Mrs Miniver, which immediately gained huge popularity. In August *News From Tartary*, his book of the great journey with Kini, was published to fulsome praise. It has lasted well; it is an exciting account of an exacting journey behind which can be found, if you look for them, sharp and jewelled descriptions of the forsaken terrain they crossed together.

Both Peter and Celia were far happier in those few strange years before the war than either had expected, after their long and interrupted courtship. They were both very successful indeed, enjoyed a close group of friends and were settled in a little flat in More's Gardens overlooking the Thames in Chelsea; relations were cordial with Cheyne Walk, Mrs Val's house a few streets away. Celia had no flair for domestic accoutrements; the flats she had lived in before she was married were always on the bleak side. It was not that she did not have good taste; it was more that she did not know how to apply it. She always had a good eye for a picture and she appreciated nice things, but she did not know how to arrange them and was flustered by such decisions. However with the help of some furniture from Mrs Val, More's Gardens became almost homely. Peter had brought back from his travels odd little Chinese ornaments or Tibetan knick-knacks, little toads and dragons. Where she was untidy, he was orderly. Celia was flummoxed by cooking and didn't do it, and in this as in every other aspect of domestic life she never ceased to feel inadequate. Not that this fussed Peter; he would have been as happy in a yurt.

The following Christmas they went skiing again, this time to Kitzbuhel. There were no lifts in those days and skiing was tough outdoor exercise, which no doubt appealed to Peter. Soon after they returned, early in 1937, old Grannie Katie died on the eve of embarking for a cruise to South Africa, for which journey she had packed her golf clubs.

Then, in February 1937, Peter was sent by *The Times* on a lecture tour to various European capitals – Paris, Rome, Prague, Vienna, Berlin and also Moscow, and Celia accompanied him. No record remains of her reactions but to pass through those cities two years before the outbreak of war must have been fascinating and perhaps terrifying, and in later letters she occasionally referred to the horrible atmosphere in a court of law in Germany.

Rex Whistler designed the sets and G.K.Benda the costumes for her next play, *Old Music*. It was by a young playwright called Keith Winter who was much in vogue during the 1930s, his chief success having been *Rats of Norway*. The play was set – for no apparent reason – at the time of the Crimean War and Celia played a Victorian governess who marries disastrously to escape the misery of economic dependence. It was a light modern story in lavish guise. James Agate commented: 'Normally when costume comes in at the door, romantic imbecility flies in at the window. Or, you might put it, that if you have a very good Matisse, you do not hang it in a heavy gold frame above a plush overmantel.' The cast included Hugh Williams again, Greer Garson, Sir Gyles Isham, Bt, and Bryan Coleman. Celia and Tam (Hugh Williams) took against Miss Garson and were beastly to her at curtain calls. In spite of Whistler's sets and the extravagant Victorian clothes, it lasted only ten weeks at the lovely St James's Theatre. Celia had probably been hoping to repeat the success of *Pride and Prejudice*, this play after all having many of the same ingredients. Several times during her career she would try and repeat a success in this way, and usually it was a mistake. This one showed only her old knack of shining in a poor play. Ivor Brown said: 'The noble governess ... is played with such humanity, intelligence, and charm by Miss Celia Johnson that it would be well worth anybody's while to see the piece for her sake alone.'

The 'Quality Street' crinoline that she wore in the play came in useful for a fancy-dress party that Mrs Val held in Cheyne Walk later that summer. Peter, Ian, Richard and Michael, who dressed as Cossacks, invited their disparate friends but in spite of many splendid costumes, and Mrs Val's flair for exotic decoration, the party never quite took off. It was made no smoother by the unsmiling presence of Kini Maillart in full-blown Red Indian costume with vast feathered headdress and smoking a pipe.

The youngest Fleming brother, Michael, had married Letitia Borthwick in 1934; Peter, the eldest, had married next; and then soon after Peter, Richard married his first cousin, Charmian Hermon-Hodge, the daughter of Lady Wyfold (his father's younger sister) and a highly respectable girl. Although it was an excellent match, the marriage caused Mrs Val to remark: 'It only remains for Ian to marry a barmaid'. Old Grannie Katie was found to have left no will, so Robert Fleming's not inconsiderable estate therefore passed to her surviving children, Phil, Dorothy Wyfold and Kathleen Hannay, bypassing once again the four boys, her senior grandchildren. Peter could not have minded less; he never had any interest in or feel for money, nor did he have expensive tastes. Ian, it is said, was rather miffed.

Joyce Grove, Grannie's vast house in South Oxfordshire, continued to run almost autonomously. The four brothers went on using it and inviting their different sets of friends, while Mrs Val and Amaryllis occupied one wing. Their Uncle Phil, now technically the owner of the house and estate, had settled with his family in better hunting country north of Oxford and did not want the house. Nobody did; its scale was so preposterous. Phil therefore gave the house to a London hospital, St Mary's Paddington, as a convalescent home, and, perhaps feeling that his brother Val's children had been hard done by, and also being an extremely kind and generous man, decided to give Peter the bulk of the estate round Joyce Grove, keeping only a small corner himself. The other brothers he saw right in different ways. It was an act of great generosity and Peter, with his sense of family, his love of shooting, particularly there, and his desire now to put down roots, was delighted. The hand-over did not take place for a couple of years and life carried on in its mildly eccentric way until then.

10

The Burma Road

In July 1937, Japan had declared war on China, and Peter saw an opportunity of returning to the Far East. Geoffrey Dawson allowed him to go as a fully accredited war correspondent for *The Times*. His brief was to report on the war which had spread rapidly, the Japanese having captured large parts of eastern China including Peking and Nanking; but before he reached the front he was to survey the Burma Road, now invested with a new importance as one of China's few remaining links with the west.

This time he took Celia with him. They left in February 1938. The Burma Road ran over mountainous country from Lashio in Burma to Yunnanfu in western China. They flew by Imperial Airways in short hops to Rangoon, then took a train to Mandalay and Lashio, and then a lorry to Bhamo. From there they had to go on foot, so they hired some mules and a couple of men to carry what Peter described as 'a gigantic lacrosse bat' in which Celia could ride. She kept a diary:

23 February. After breakfast the mule man appeared. A neat little man. He balanced suitcases, typewriters and pails in 4 symmetrical bundles on to the wooden stands that fix on to the wooden saddles. With one leather thong he managed to get unwieldy objects firmly fixed. Then the chair coolies appeared with my chair. A venerable gentleman who set himself on fire from a cigarette made of Peter's tobacco while helping to load and a younger one with a vague resemblance to Frank Vosper. My chair is made of bamboo and string with a black hood completely blocking out any view so we made them roll it up a bit. Started off in glee ... The road was lovely. Butterflies the size of Puss Moths and much lighter coloured whizz about. Passed several mule caravans carrying according to Robertson mostly cotton and orpiment ... Took to my chair after three miles – v. comfortable in every way except 2, a) VG and FV smell fairly strongly of fish b) I feel tremendously guilty at being carried by humans and guiltier at enjoying what is clearly sweated and / or sweaty labour ... Trying to salve my conscience I determined to

walk a good bit and did 5 miles in the morning and a bit over 2 in the afternoon. Conscience isn't much salved when I realise that's less than half the distance ... Peter shot on ahead most of the time refusing to wear a hat ... So far this is fun and a picnic in perfect surroundings but we leave the British Raj tomorrow and hey for the Sleeping Giant.

24 February. Set off at about 8.30 with slight sadness at leaving the rest house. Walked for a bit and got blisters on my heels from my F[ortnum] and M[ason] shoes. The same sort of country, though it may be my imagination less butterflies. Crossed into China over a bridge but cannot give any first impressions as I was unaware that it was China ...

25 February. Slept pretty well except for shouts from I think the mule man and one horrifying moment when I thought a rat was on my rubber pillow. I woke with a shriek and thrashed about and heard it again when I replaced my head. The monster departed but I slept warily afterwards. Most of the inn inhabitants seem to have hangovers after what appeared to be a thick opium night. We set off again and I walked the first five miles. Quite different country through paddy fields with the bare hills rising fairly near on our right and more distant on our left. A lovely day, hotter than before and we show our first signs of getting sunburnt. Big banyan tree and hedges of cactus. Lots of streams and a variety of methods of crossing them from wading and stepping stones – bamboo poles to nice bamboo bridges curving pleasantly ... Most of the Chinese women have bound feet ...

26 February. Walked 5 or 6 miles through lovely country, for some way along the bank of the river, peaceful and broad with sandy islands ... Sun got very hot and Peter being mad dog and Englishman strode hatless, the back of his legs getting rapidly redder. My chair men had bursts of shouting at each other over the best path to take and even attempted to go different ways whereupon I yelled Ay Ay Ay, hoping it would sound Chinese and angry. Banyan trees got fewer and by lunch time the only shady place was near a farm under some bamboos. Muddy small streams unlike yesterday's clear running ones. Finished *Vanity Fair* in my chair and we amused ourselves by guessing what unlikely people would say finding themselves where we were. Reached Chin Cheng about 3 hot and fliey. Slightly sinister looking landlord and a whimpering baby ... I don't like this place – the wood creaks and clatters and I should guess our last infestation to be as nothing to the one we shall take back

this time. The only nice thing about it apart from the hills which have closed in and remained beautiful all day was a kite flying about the walls of the town humming through little bamboo pipes.

27 February. Took an even more violent dislike to our inn next morning when the spitting was remarkable even for China and not at all sorry to leave. P and I walked slowly for a short time then I took to my chair and was carried I am ashamed to say nearly all the 20 miles. Felt mouldy. Peter angelic and comforting . . .

28 February. Our last stage to Tungyueh and a long one. We set off before the mules and I walked about 7 miles . . . Peter well on ahead when the mules caught me up and on a long climb they too passed me. First sight of Tengyueh as I topped this hill, v. pretty, several villages near it and more bare hills beyond. Was saluted by a policeman and handed a note to invite us to stay with Mr Gardiner the customs man and the escort led us there over graveyards and along the east wall of the town. A very pretty house, 2 courtyards with a white wall round blossom peach and japonica eucalyptus trees. The house is white with high jutting corners to the eaves and the beams are black. From our room we look east and can see our future road to Yunnanfu. Quite cold in the evenings (5600 feet up), a fire was welcoming and honey and scones for tea gave a slightly R. Brooke nostalgia.

1 March. Had porridge for breakfast in the sun with geraniums in pots. Then visited the consulate, an ugly strong stone building cost £20,000. Booked mules, 2 ponies to ride and borrowed a fine large tent. Hoping to do the journey in 11 days. Peter paid a ceremonial visit to the Tupan with whom we are dining. Many bound feet in the town and no wheels except for a rare bicycle. The cook cut my hair with great success and I washed and set it with difficulty, drying it in the sun . . .

3 March. Tremendous cavalcade started off. The mules going ahead and we left about 9.30. We crossed the plain and I rode my pony up the hill. Quite comfortable perched on top of a Chinese wooden saddle and various red cloths on top and round stirrups with a knot in the right leather which is going to rub a hole in my trousers. We climbed steadily. I tried walking a bit but got breath-less pretty quickly owing I suppose to the height. We have a servant (christened Meadows – shades of G[erald] du M[aurier]) and his nephew in very short shorts (John the footman), a mule man and his 2 helpers – and my 2 chair carriers not so attractive as the ven.

gent. and our escort of 2 charming small soldiers with black puttees, grey cotton uniforms, ancient looking rifles and an umbrella each. It's a gay and friendly party.

That night the rain started.

4 March. A huge breakfast of chicken, rice and eggs – folding with some difficulty the wet tent which must have weighed a good deal more in consequence, we started again. P and I slipped and skidded down the stone road to the bridge over the river – I wearing rubber skidded on the mud and he wearing nails skidded on the stones. Then a tremendous climb up the Divide. I rode the pony about half-way and chaired the rest. Peter sailed up; his half of the escort puffing but punctilious behind him. The view was wonderful, the mountains seem softer and less foreboding than most and are extremely colourful ... we are camped in a tiny village above fields of white opium poppies ...

5 March. ... along a flattish road to Fang ma Chang where we camped in a clean yard with a peasant family. Even the youngish women have got their feet bound. The mule man and Meadows are very nice indeed and we pitch the tent in no time. With the exception of the chair men who have no charm and do not enter in, the party is grand. Further hills stretch ahead, not such a towering lot as the last we crossed. So far touch wood it's been great fun.

The next few wet days took them down into the Mekong Valley.

11 March. Slept hoggishly and woke to the now usual downpour. We padded through the mud and went uphill for some considerable way getting very cross with the weather. Lunched at huts with tables and benches around and Peter tried a local sweet, v. sugary, which he had expected to be pea soup. Got to Taipingpu and found the inns full so commandeered the schoolroom, a large room with a fine view, a few dilapidated desks about – Chinese characters on the blackboard telling, so we are told, of an approaching examination. Made a fire on the teacher's dais and were found there by Mr Hall whom we had given up hope of seeing. Went to dinner with him at his inn where Peter had hiccups. Talked of the theatre which he's mad about and of China and news in general. Halifax has succeeded Eden ... Back to our schoolroom where P and I, Meadows and nephew and the 2 ponies slept in amity while 2 thunderstorms crashed over our heads.

12 March. ... We are in an inn recommended by Hall kept by a Chinese woman with a mad husband. It's full of flies and half of it was washed away by the river thus making it airier ... It's still raining.

The following day it poured again, and towards the end Celia's part of the expedition lost its way.

13 March. It was suddenly frightening to have lost the road, to see no signs of houses or life and be getting rapidly wetter and colder. Meadows clambered up a bank and we turned back, crossing the small river and making towards the fort. Suddenly we found the road and on we went. I still thought we'd perhaps missed the town and were now on our way to Tali or Yunnan when John suddenly appeared out of the darkness. P had left him to show us the way in a tricky bit not thinking we should miss it earlier. Nearing the town which we couldn't see until we were right on it Peter called. He realised we were late and was coming to find us. He'd got a clean supper room at the third inn he'd tried and we put on pyjamas and sampled the brandy. It was curiously sweet and we swigged it down, later eating a meal mostly of chilis and bones and rice with the result that we both woke in the night with a raging thirst. John and Meadows shared our room and on the hard bed I dreamt of the most incongruous people like Athole, Leo Hylett, Rupert and an unknown doctor.

For the next three days they were able to travel by bus; however progress was no easier or quicker.

15 March. ... It's a Chevrolet bus ... After we'd been impatient for some time and the body of the bus had some 16 people in it and there was a mass of stuff on top 2 men appeared, evidently of importance, with about 12 enormous packages. Tremendous arguments lasting for hours as to whether or not all this could be taken as well. Several years passed to the accompaniment of yelling and shouting and at last they climbed in with us thus leaving no room for a mouse. Some of their bundles were left behind which pleased us and with a certain amount of feeling rampant we jolted off. The road by most standards would be unmotorable. They are metalling it in patches and we crash up 5 or 6 inches onto a metalled bit and about 12 yards further bash down again. The mud was fairly bad in places and we stuck once or twice entailing the descent of all passengers ... Finally we stuck completely ... Crowds of road workers clustered like ants round the bus enjoying it hugely and

when a bus coming in the opposite direction skidded sideways on the road above us they had their biggest laugh for years.

16 March. Walked about the village planning a pamphlet on See China by Bus.

17 March. [They reached Kunming.] At last arrived. Coolies, rick-shaws and crowds gather and Mr Meyer appears – v. nice, takes us in his car to the American consulate. Lovely compound full of blossom and flowers and luxuriously comfortable. Mrs Meyer has a cold. Have 2 gimlets and get fuzzy as a result of them and being tired. So happily to bed in great comfort after a bath and a huge and delicious dinner. Austria annexed.

After a few days with the very nice Meyers in Kunming, Peter left for Hankow, and Celia was to follow, and then go on to Shanghai and wait while Peter reported on the war. However, the aeroplane that was to take her from Kunming to Hankow turned out to be going only as far as Chengtu; she decided to go all the same.

29 March. Set off waving through the dust with a fairly full plane. All other passengers Chinese men. Fly mostly over the clouds catch-ing glimpses here and there of mountains and steep ravines with winding rivers at the bottom of them. The clouds are annoying as the country is clearly magnificent. About 4 we drop quite low and fly over a plain with arc shaped irrigation like a disjointed river then over Chengtu which seems v. big and grey. Land on the field and I saw the officials waving and then we felt a bump. Less than a train gives when stopping but on climbing out we find that the plane has hit the Eurasia bus fair and square, breaking its glass and the wheels are about a foot embedded in the ground. The plane, far more important, has broken an exhaust and rent some of the right engine cover and seems to have scratched one of the propellers ... I foresee that we may be delayed even with this slight damage.

She was right. The aeroplane was unable to leave and she was stuck on her own in Chengtu for several days. She spent her time knitting, sightseeing and talking to missionaries. Eventually Peter managed to find a plane and come and fetch her.

2 April. Peter arrived and the next day we left for Hankow, a plane suddenly materialising and being entirely empty except for

us and Lutz [the pilot]. Arrived at Hankow in the pouring rain and was surprised to find it huge and tremendously European. Saw a bunch of coolies digging to get at an unexploded bomb which had buried itself 30 feet deep in the airfield. Crossed the Yangtse running thick and fast and fairly choppily in a Jardine's launch. John Keswick came to meet us . . .

A week later they flew on to Chungking, the current capital, where the British ambassador to China, Sir Archibald Clark Kerr, was to present his letters of credence to the President of the Chinese Republic, Mr Lin Sen. Peter and Celia watched the ceremony in the palace (formerly a school) from behind a curtain.

12 April. The President appeared and the ceremony started. The Ambassador appeared bowing low and read his speech; this was translated by Whitamore shaking in every limb. The President replied in a squeaky voice like someone telling a fairy story and his translator boomed out in tones of thunder. Introductions were effected, more bows, a certain amount of back sidling and the party was over. We were amused to see the President after the party had gone, turn and trot out of the back door, no one thinking of opening it for him.

Beginning with the statement: 'Romance has not altogether gone from diplomacy', Peter wrote a highly descriptive piece for *The Times* about the occasion, entitled 'Top Hats in Chungking'.

For the next month or so Celia stayed in Shanghai and Hong Kong with friends while Peter reported on the progress of the war from the front. She always looked back on that wet and muddy trek over the Burma Road as the greatest fun, and certainly, apart from the few days when she was stranded alone at Chengtu, there is no hint of complaint in her diary about the rigours. The expatriate life in which she took part for the next few weeks, although comfortable, was probably less to her liking, and can have been made no easier by the fact that she was now expecting a baby and feeling terrible. Mary Keswick was especially sympathetic, being in the same condition herself.

Peter rejoined her at the beginning of June and they began their return journey by a series of flying-boats. They crossed

India in great heat and some discomfort, reaching London at the end of July. The atmosphere in England had not improved during their absence; war seemed ever more likely. That autumn – the autumn of Munich and Neville Chamberlain's 'peace in our time' – Celia, being now noticeably pregnant, was unable to act on the stage. She did however read a play by J.B.Priestley called *I Have Been Here Before* on the radio. She always read extremely well.

That summer Peter and Celia had spent a long weekend with Joyce and Reggie Grenfell at their house, Parrs, in Buckinghamshire. Parrs, just outside the grounds of Cliveden, the house of Joyce's aunt Nancy Astor, had been designed by Joyce's father, Paul Phipps, an architect who had studied at one time with Lutyens. It may have been then that Peter got the idea of asking him to design a house for him at Nettlebed.

The Fleming estate was about to be handed over to Peter, but there was no obvious house to move into. Peter decided that, with the money that he had made from *Brazilian Adventure*, he would build one. Paul Phipps, Joyce's father, was an architect and a very nice man, and so Peter, with no further ado, thought he would do the job splendidly and engaged him. Peter later wrote:

It must, people sometimes suggest, have been great fun building it. I cannot recall that it was. I had up till then led a mainly nomadic life, devoting small thought to domestic architecture. My wife, equally inexperienced in this field, regarded the whole project with grave misgivings. In her view this house was a Bad Thing; to say that she threw herself with enthusiasm into its planning would not be true.

The site virtually selected itself. 'I always feel', a distinguished soldier said to me the other day as we walked up the long approach to it, 'that I ought to be carrying a white flag.' And I suppose the problems of siting a small country house are analogous to the problems of siting a machine gun. You want a commanding position. For me Dame Nature provided on a plate what my friend would have called the DS solution.

To this agreeable spot we conducted the architect on a very wet day. Rain fell implacably. Under his thundering umbrella the architect squelched meditatively to and fro upon the virgin turf. At length he revealed that the width of the pipe which would bring the main water supply preoccupied him. 'You'll be very isolated here', he said, 'so I think you must over-bid on water.'

We asked why.

'If the house catches fire', he explained, 'you're bound to be on your own for a bit before the Fire Brigade arrives.'

There was then no house, not even a peg in the ground. In the deluged landscape the idea of anything, ever, catching fire seemed remote. My wife, already strongly averse in principle to the construction of her future home, was in no way reassured by this opening gambit.

Celia would have preferred a Georgian rectory with a pretty garden or some such. What she got was a long spacious brick house, a mixture of neo-Georgian and Lutyens in style, with no garden to speak of. She remained hostile to it for many years. Towards the end of her life, when the house in its isolated position was less than ideal for her, nothing would induce her to move from it. They called the house Merrimoles after an old barn of the same name in the adjoining field, which was said to have belonged to a Miss Mary Mole.

11

War and a country house

On 3 January 1939, the baby, a boy, was born in the flat at More's Gardens. Peter recorded:

Outside it was a fine rough winter dawn, with the seagulls dipping in the wind. I read *The Times* until the baby began to lament. Then soon I saw C, who had done it very neatly. She was awfully good in the pain while I was with her and insisted on smiling heroically: no mean feat. Women in real pain have much less self-pity than men. The baby has all the sad attributes of a newly-hatched thrush. C was eating scrambled eggs less than half an hour after he was born.

Celia was thrilled; she had wanted children for some time. Peter, too, was delighted; it was also the first part of the 'bringing him from the stars' that Ian had referred to in his letter to their mother when Peter and Celia had married.

The baby was christened Nicholas Peter Val (known first as the Sausage and later as Nichol) and his godparents were Ian, Tim Nugent, Peter Cazalet (a friend of Peter's since Eton) and Mary Pakenham.

A few months after he was born, Celia took part in a French play called *Sixth Floor* set in a fifth-floor apartment in Montmartre. It had been adapted by Rodney Ackland (the author of *Strange Orchestra*) and was described as 'a long harmless story about a beautiful cripple'. Celia played the crippled girl who, after having been seduced by a songwriter, tries to commit suicide, fails and is carried to the altar by the young workman next door. For her it was the familiar role of the wronged woman, and she carried it off with 'unemphatic tenderness'. One critic found the play so boring that he complained about the angle of the lights which had prevented him falling asleep. Another complained that James Mason, who was also in it, had been filming too much and had forgotten how to speak up. It lasted for eight performances at the St James's.

Sixth Floor was one of the last plays to be put on before the war. It peered over into the vast gulf that was to separate pre-war from post-war theatre. It came off at the end of May 1939, and so in June, in that final summer before the war, Celia and Peter took a short holiday, strenuous as usual, canoeing down the Rhone. It was a last and happy fling. Peter had already joined the Grenadier Reserves. He was still working for *The Times*, though out of tune with its policy of appeasement. He was also trying to write a play; this was an ambition he had cherished for some time.

For 2 September 1939 the Black Mount game-book, written up by Uncle Phil, records: 'Don't feel like any comments. Situation too bad. Richard off and all talking of going.'

And on 3 September: 'After an indescribably black Sunday, war declared, thunder and lightning! Thought best take to the hill and keep going and getting food while anyone here.'

Celia, Nicholas and his nurse left London for safety and went to stay in Wales with old friends, the Barstows (John Barstow was the family lawyer). Celia's sister Pam was still in India where her husband Nevill was working with Jehangir Tata, the founder of Air India; her brother John joined the Buffs. Her father had retired from his practice in Richmond, and he and Ethel were now living in a small house in Brenchley in Kent. Among Peter's family, Richard was to serve with the Lovat Scouts, Ian in due course worked for Naval Intelligence and Michael became captain and adjutant of the fourth battalion of the Oxfordshire and Buckinghamshire Light Infantry. Mrs Val took on yet another house in South Oxfordshire. Peter kicked off at the War Office, from where he wrote to Celia in Wales as war was declared:

Well, my *dear* Mrs Squidge, here we are at War. So far it seems to be much the same as being at peace, only rather more satisfactory. We had a bogus air raid at 11.30. Everyone trooped down to the various basements, which are extremely stuffy but safe and we hung about for three quarters of an hour or so, while what sounded like AA fire could be heard by knowing chaps like Mr Flem. No such fire however seems to have been delivered, and an hour after the raid had taken place nothing was known about it in the War Room.

There are various theories, including one that an RAF plane was flying over a forbidden area but all indicating that it was a false alarm. Nobody in London seems to have turned a hair. The streets are emptyish and very quiet but everyone looks very jolly and glad to have got down to business. Very little news is coming in but it doesn't sound as if the Germans were having a *succès fou*. The Colonel (who looks ravishing in Naval Uniform) claims that we can't fail either to catch or to bottle up the Bremen. So far the chief horror of war is the darkness at night and the fearful expense of having to take taxis everywhere. The Frogs have been tiresome lately and are not yet at war, though they will be some time this afternoon. Not that we know anything here, since there are no evening papers and we are lost without them as far as 'flash' news goes. I am agitating for a ticker to be installed.

And on the 4th:

Just a line to say that I am winning so far. Everything is rather dim here but people are most cheerful. We had another bogus air-raid alarm last night. The censors have been very inept over the torpedoed liner, holding up American dispatches for anything up to 10 hours. During the air-raid alarm the Colonel and his extraordinary Dutch maid trooped solemnly down to the studio and sat side by side in the only corner of it which hasn't got a glass roof, with a night light in a waste-paper basket between them.

On the 5th: 'Nothing to report. The Germans are making fair progress in Poland, nothing has come through from the Western Front, and the feeling in Germany is fairly blue ... London is getting darker and darker.'

The theatres closed on 4 September, but after about two weeks many reopened again, and by December most were in full swing, though performances started at the earlier time of six or six-thirty. In the programme of the Lyric Theatre, Hammersmith, was written: 'This theatre adjoins the Metropolitan station, and the noise of passing trains should not be confused with that of enemy action.' The public did not mind. Indeed the appetite for theatre – of an escapist sort – was enormous throughout the war.

Meanwhile the new house at Nettlebed was taking shape. It was indeed in a commanding position with a glorious south-easterly view over the Chiltern hills. Peter later wrote:

On paper, 1938 was not a good year in which to start building a house in the southern half of England. In practice one could not have chosen a better moment, for one caught the tail-end of pre-war materials, pre-war prices and pre-war workmanship, and the house (which was finished soon after the outbreak of war) provided a firm base for our small son and seven of his cousins throughout the next five years.

It also embodied various pre-war conceptions about the domestic set-up of a country gentleman: there were four tiny bedrooms for housemaids on the top floor (the housekeeping couple was not envisaged), the kitchen was a long way from the dining-room, and there was a so-called servants' hall. The house had ten bedrooms and in style it was a not altogether happy cross of traditional and modern. However with all the rooms, except the bathrooms and the servants' hall, facing south, it was a light and cheerful house. With beech woods behind and flinty fields in front, the garden was non-existent. Peter explained: 'The war, too, prevented us from laying out anything but the most perfunctory type of garden. Since I am indifferent to horticulture and since the environs of the house have a natural beauty of their own, I regard this as a blessing on both aesthetic and economic grounds.' Indeed, in spite of the devoted toil of a saintly gardener, the garden was never a success. Peter never saw the point of flowers.

    Celia and Nicholas returned from the Barstows after Christmas. She wrote a poem to thank Lady Barstow, of whom she was very fond, for her kindness in having them to stay for so long.

> I sing the praise of Lady B
> Who welcomed all my familee
> She never called them utter swine
> But lavished love on me and wine
> For months in 1939
> And even part of 40.
>
> She gave them food and pints of milk
> And toys and coats of Chinese silk
> And things that made a cup of tea
> And Christmas joy and jollitie
> Oh dear, oh wondrous Lady B –

There's no one could be sweeter
So here we state in black and white
We *shout* with all our main and might
That Lady B is our delight.

(Signed) Celia and Peter

And so, along with a nanny, a cook and two housemaids the family moved into the new house. It was raw, the walls bare, rubble lay around. Heavy ostentatious bits of furniture arrived from Joyce Grove. It was soon arranged that Michael Fleming's wife Letitia (Tish) and her four children, Valentine, Christopher, David and Gillian, would move in too. They were expected to arrive early in 1940.

Celia's enormously happy and successful life with Peter in the flat in London, having fun, acting, travelling, was thus brought abruptly to an end. Instead, she found herself in charge of a largish, unfinished house and of what was about to become a substantial household, as well as a sizeable agricultural estate, with farm workers, foresters, tenants and a gamekeeper. Organisation, administration and domestic responsibilities were not where her talents lay. She barely gave a thought to acting. The war completely disrupted her life. The next five years were for her, as they were for everybody in Britain, emotionally and physically hard.

12

Mrs de Winter in the summer of 1940

The year 1940 in fact began rather well. Peggy Ashcroft, who
was playing Cecily Cardew in a glorious and heartening production of *The Importance of Being Earnest*, got measles. She
was compelled to carry on in the play with a rash, partly
because she had no understudy and partly because Edith Evans
(who was playing Lady Bracknell, a legendary performance,
which included the ringing and inimitable utterance: 'A *hand-
bag*!', fortunately immortalised on film) was a Christian Scien-
tist and urged her not to give up. Eventually she had to, and
Celia was asked to stand in for her in Oxford and in Glasgow.
With such short notice, she had to learn her lines in record
time. Margaret Rutherford played Miss Prism, and John Gielgud both directed and played in it. It was comedy of a high
order, and Celia must have relished it. She had had so few
opportunities to stretch her comic powers. A talent for comedy
is not given to all actors, but Celia had it though she did
not use it fully until much later in her career. She got on
well with Gielgud with whom she had a long heart-to-heart
in a cemetery in Glasgow; in later life they would occasionally
remind each other of it. This was just the sort of professional
but light-hearted stuff that audiences during the war enjoyed.
It was put on by Binkie Beaumont who sent many such productions on long tours round the country.

While she was away, Peter uncharacteristically fell ill. As
he was confined to the house, he wrote a short humorous
novel called *The Flying Visit*. It was about Hitler landing
secretly in a small village and getting caught up in a fancy-dress
parade in the village hall, a plot which appeared mildly pro-
phetic the following year when the deputy Führer, Rudolf
Hess, landed in Scotland. The book had engaging illustrations
by Low and was dedicated to Nichol.

Peggy Ashcroft recovered and Celia started rehearsing
Rebecca, a play adapted by Daphne du Maurier from her novel

of that name. Daphne du Maurier was the daughter of Celia's old mentor, Gerald du Maurier; and Binkie Beaumont, thinking that she must know something of the theatre, had persuaded her to make her novel into a play. H.M.Tennent, Binkie's company, put it on, and the set was designed by Roger Furse; the resplendent costumes worn by Celia and by Margaret Rutherford were by Motley.* Margaret Rutherford played the sinister housekeeper, Mrs Danvers ('Prism was banished utterly,' one critic noted, referring to her role in *The Importance*), Celia played Mrs de Winter and Owen Nares, the epitome of a matinée idol, was Mr de Winter; he had to move very gingerly because of a rupture. 'A thumping good plot thrillingly unfolded' again was just what was required during that tense period in the early stages of the war. It opened on 5 April 1940 at the Queen's Theatre.

George Devine, an actor, had tried his hand at directing only once before, when in 1939 he had done *Great Expectations*. His direction of *Rebecca*, wrote J.C.Trewin in the *Illustrated London News*, 'deserves the highest praise. In most productions, when the leading characters hold the centre of the stage they are as isolated as if they were on a desert island. Mr Devine contrives to suggest the movement and bustle of a normal household without diverting the playgoer's attention from the scene.' This was perhaps a sign that the static staging of the old West End was giving way to the more fluid style that was to come after the war. George Devine later ran the English Stage Company at the Royal Court Theatre with great distinction and is remembered as a brilliant and influential director. Celia received her now customary excellent notices for 'providing a show of plucky timidity that was really moving. What a clever actress this is! the child grew into woman before our eyes.' She was well photographed for this production by Angus McBean, the most striking theatrical photographer of this age.

Four days after the opening night of *Rebecca*, on 9 April 1940, the Germans invaded Norway and within three days

---

* Motley was the name used by Elizabeth Montgomery and Margaret and Sophia Harris. They were designers of great taste who were responsible for many theatre productions from 1932 onwards.

had captured all the major ports. On 12 April Peter had orders
to lead a small reconnaissance party (No. 10 Military Mission)
to the small Norwegian port of Namsos to ascertain whether
it was in enemy hands or not and therefore to see if an
expeditionary force could land there. On 13 April, with six
others he flew to Orkney, and the following day crossed the
North Sea in a Sunderland flying-boat.

Suddenly swinging round a bend, we saw Namsos ahead of us: a
little huddle of coloured wooden houses crouched between the mountains and the water. In a few seconds we were circling over it ...
We went on circling over it. There was our objective: so near and
yet so far, like a toy in a shop window. Smoke rose from its chimneys,
trampled snow lay in its streets. A ginger cat walked meditatively
down one of them. But apart from the cat there was no sign of
life at all ... No. 10 Military Mission had been ordered, less than
forty-eight hours ago in Whitehall, to find out who was in occupation
of Namsos. Here it was, hovering over the place like a kestrel over
a rickyard, and for all it knew Namsos might have been occupied
by the Tibetans.

The Germans in fact had not yet arrived; the seaplane landed
and Peter made contact with the villagers. Later that night
three British destroyers slipped into the port and the
expeditionary force under Adrian Carton de Wiart disem-
barked. For the following six nights more troops arrived and
landed covertly. The Germans reconnoitring by day saw
nothing. On the night of the 19th, a French brigade shot at
a German aircraft; the game was up, they were discovered,
and by the following evening Namsos was bombed and burnt
out. The expeditionary force hung on there, in a hopeless
position, for a few days. On the 26th Carton de Wiart sent
Peter back to try and find out from the War Office what intentions it had for the British troops in Norway. That same evening a Swedish radio station broadcast a report that he, Peter,
had been killed in one of the air raids on Namsos. The news
was relayed to *The Times* in London by its correspondent
in Stockholm, who added:

BRITISH LEGATION HERE SAYS LELAND STOWE CHICAGO CORRESPON-
DENT UP NORTH LEARNT FROM NORWEGIAN OFFICER FLEMING WAS
KILLED WHEN BOMB HIT GRAND HOTEL NAMSOS SUNDAY. LEGATION

SO FAR UNABLE GET NEWS CONFIRMED ALSO LIKE STOWE DOES NOT KNOW IF BOMB VICTIM WAS THE PETER FLEMING OR NAMESAKE.

The paper treated the news with circumspection; not so the *Daily Sketch*, which ran a banner headline the following morning: AUTHOR KILLED IN NORWAY, underneath which was a picture of Peter and Celia, and a short obituary. The news in fact was officially denied by the War Office on the night of the 26th, but did not reach Merrimoles soon enough to prevent causing Celia distress. She always harboured a grudge against Ian, who she thought was in a position to check the veracity of the report, for not passing on its denial more quickly.

Peter, on his way from Scotland to London, was unaware of his reported demise, and surprised to find people in London relieved to see him. A letter was written to *The Times* complaining about the irresponsibility of the *Daily Sketch*. Its managing editor defended his paper saying:

The definite statement that Captain Fleming had been killed appeared only in one limited edition of the *Daily Sketch*. Immediately we learned that there was any doubt about the news we gave it the heading 'Captain Fleming reported killed in Norway.' We must give our readers credit for some intelligence. Such a heading would not cause even the most sensitive of Captain Fleming's relatives more than a momentary apprehension.

'We Flemings are a hard-boiled lot', wrote Peter, 'but even so ...'

In May, the British Expeditionary Force was beaten back to the French coast, and at the beginning of June the remarkable evacuation of more than 300,000 troops from Dunkirk took place, blessed by fine weather and good seas. Churchill was now prime minister, and, during May and June, when invasion looked likely, disaster certain, issued his famous rallying calls to the British people. It was a dark time. German aircraft bombed London every night. The government stayed put, the House of Commons continued its business, the King and Queen stayed on at Windsor and at Buckingham Palace, and the theatres remained open (after having closed for a short period).

Performances started early so that people could get home
easily before the black-out. Audiences were told that if an
air-raid warning went off during a performance, they could
either leave or stay put, and if they chose to leave they were
entitled to come back another day. If the air-raid alert had
not been lifted by the end of the play, the audience of the
Queen's Theatre, where *Rebecca* was playing, would join with
that of the Globe next door, and the actors would endeavour
to entertain them until the all clear.

Celia had now been joined at the new house in Nettlebed
by her sister-in-law Tish Fleming and her four small children,
Valentine, Christopher, David and Gillian who was only three
months old, and their nurse. It was an arrangement like many
others during the war where families doubled up in one house.
Michael, Tish's husband and Peter's youngest brother, was
with the Oxfordshire and Buckinghamshire Light Infantry in
France. However, hardly were his family installed at Merrimoles, than news came, soon after Dunkirk, that Michael and
his battalion were missing. 'A whole battalion cannot just van-
ish into thin air,' Peter would reassure Tish. But throughout
the summer nothing was heard until at the end of August
when a POW issue card suddenly arrived from him at the
Henley Post Office saying that he was wounded in the leg.
One more POW card came, written in a shaky hand but not
mentioning the wound. He died on 1 October, the news not
reaching Tish until the end of November. With the threat
of invasion, the blitz and the anxiety about Michael, it had
been a long, tense summer at Merrimoles, throughout which
Tish had found Peter a steady and encouraging support.

It was a summer like no other in British history. Not since
the sailing of the Spanish Armada in 1588 had invasion of
the British Isles seemed more likely. Yet, because danger was
imminent, because the threat was immediate, there was a
strange, almost exhilarated spirit abroad. People lived in the
present, not knowing what the next day would hold.

Evidence that the British, in this crisis, bore themselves well should
not be taken as proof that they had little to bear [Peter wrote later
in his book *Invasion 1940*]. Apart from the fact, of which they were
too preoccupied or too proud to take cognisance, that there was

no light at the end of the tunnel, no discernible pebble in the brook with which Goliath might be suddenly felled, all of them had already suffered loss. The loss might be expressed in terms of bereavement or of separation: of a career interrupted, a house requisitioned, a scholarship forgone: of an oak-tree felled, a flowerbed incorporated in the foundations of a pillbox, a trawler converted into a mine-sweeper: of anything from tragedy to inconvenience. But all had already lost something, and all, as the piles of rubble and the lists of casualties began to mount, knew very well that they were going to lose more: perhaps everything.

Preparations against invasion were made. As it was expected, erroneously, to be airborne, the skies were scanned for Germans landing by parachute. Invasion committees were formed in villages. In their remit were such tasks as earmarking potential sites for mass burial, listing means of conveying instruction and information to the public (the information officer, one village noted, has a megaphone), emergency transport available (this same village listed eleven horses, sixteen wheelbarrows). Signposts everywhere were taken down. It seemed certain that Britain was to become a battlefield, and therefore advisable to get children away from the danger. Many children were evacuated, some from London to remoter parts of the country, some privately to friends or relations in America, and many under the official government scheme to the United States and the Dominions. This scheme came to an end abruptly and tragically in September when the *City of Benares*, a ship carrying evacuee children, was sunk by a U-boat.

Rupert and Comfort Hart-Davis had taken a lease from Peter on a farmhouse on the Nettlebed estate, and had moved there shortly before Peter and Celia had moved into Merrimoles. They decided to send their two children, Duff and Bridget, to America, where Comfort, whose mother was American, had cousins. Peter and Celia thought that they should do the same. It was a dilemma for all parents of small children. No one wanted their child at the mercy of the Germans, or, in the worst eventuality, indoctrinated as Nazis. Celia got in touch with an old American friend of her family, Ruthie Gordon Duff, who lived in New York, and arrangements were made for Nichol to be sent to America. Indeed, she left the cast of *Rebecca* in July to prepare for his evacuation. She, Peter, Nichol and his nanny left by train for Liverpool where Nichol and the nanny were to board the ship for America. Celia, who never had an easy time with decisions of moment, must have been torn.

No one knows how their discussion went on the way to Liverpool, but when Tish welcomed Peter and Celia back at Merrimoles the next day, prepared to commiserate with them on saying goodbye to the eighteen-month-old Nichol, she was amazed to see not only Peter and Celia get out of the car, but Nichol and his nanny as well. They had changed their minds. Celia, who probably knew in her head that it was right to send Nichol away, was ultimately ruled by her heart. It would have been uncharacteristic of Peter to avoid the action; never one to avoid danger on his own account, no doubt he thought that he could risk the danger of staying in England for Nichol as well. Also he was always an optimist. So they brought him home.

The brave and popular run of *Rebecca* (Barbara Mullen took over from Celia) was brought to a halt by a bomb falling on the Queen's Theatre shortly after midnight on Saturday 7 September. Raymond Huntley, who played Frank Crawley, remembers going in on the Monday after to collect his things from his still intact dressing-room. The theatre remained closed until 1959. Many of the cast returned to the play in 1941, when it went on a long tour throughout the country. It seems likely that Celia would have liked to have gone too, but that she felt that her place at this time was at home. Peggy Ashcroft played Mrs de Winter instead, and when she had to leave because she was pregnant, Isolde Denham took over. Described by the critic Michael Billington as an 'imperishable romantic mystery', the play had been an excellent diversion for many.

Meanwhile, the household at Merrimoles was settling down. The house was still unfurnished with bare plaster on many walls. However, with its sunny aspect and rural position, Tish had found it not unwelcoming and her family felt secure there. Nurse Stella Balls, who looked after Tish's children and who was Norland trained, called in her sister, Nora, to help; in the event Nurse looked after the four little Flemings and Nora looked after Nichol. Nurse was rather regimented; Nora was a little more easy-going. The Balls sisters were a huge support throughout the war. Though they were called up to work in a munitions factory, after a short while for some reason they were allowed to return to the families. However the threat of being called up hung over everyone who helped in the house.

Peter, under the command of General Andrew ('Bulgy') Thorne, was based in Kent, where his job was to create subterranean lairs for a resistance force which, in the event of invasion, would be able to harry the enemy from behind as it swept through Kent from the coast. A cellar of a ruined house was one hide-out, a badger's sett another, and a limekiln another. The small units of men who comprised the force he equipped with bows and arrows. It was the sort of unorthodox task which, with its promise of almost schoolboy adventure, most appealed to his Buchanesque nature.

The news of Michael Fleming's death from wounds that autumn was deeply sad. He had been the sort of no-nonsense enthusiastic young man whom it was impossible to imagine dead. As captain and adjutant of the fourth battalion of the Oxfordshire and Buckinghamshire Light Infantry, he had been a brave officer and had been mentioned in despatches three times in May. Tish was glad that when he had been on leave early in 1940 he had at least seen his youngest child, the baby Gillian. Celia wrote a poem for him.

> Where the wild roses took the sun
> Now scattered on the thorn their hearts glow red,
> So on the briars of a conquered earth
> Prodigal lie our English dead.
>
> Gently the petals of that gallant flower
> Do their fierce crimson centres hide,
> And young men, stilled, have gleaming left
> A heritage of pride.

13

Merrimoles garrison

As winter drew on and the threat of invasion receded, life grew no easier in Britain. The household at Merrimoles led a very rural and local life. There was little petrol, so little mobility. Walking and bicycling were the order of the day, and, apart from the times when Celia was working, for the rest of the war, she and Tish went no farther than the village of Nettlebed (a mile away) or the town of Henley-on-Thames (five miles), with the occasional trip to London by train from Henley, or the odd visit to relations elsewhere. Driving at night with only a small slit of headlight uncovered was slow, difficult and dangerous. There were long evenings, listening to the news at nine o'clock, writing letters, reading, knitting, playing bezique. Most nights they would hear aeroplanes going over, and could tell by the noise of the engine whether they were English or German. If the sound of the German bombers was a little way away they knew that they were heading for London; if overhead, then they knew that the Midlands were for it. The night that Slough, twenty miles away, was bombed, Tish and Celia watched the spectacular display of fires from the upstairs windows. Tish woke her eldest child, Val, to see the horizon lit up, but, to his later annoyance, did not tell him the cause of the conflagration.

The village of Nettlebed, an old staging post in the Chiltern hills on the road from London to Oxford, has always been a close community. In those days it had a few little shops – a grocer, a butcher, a baker, a cobbler – all of whom were exceptionally good to their customers during the war, and especially to the Flemings, who were at that time warmly regarded in the village. Tish's and Celia's family benefited from all sorts of kindnesses. Because of that, and because, as they were a sizeable household, they were allowed a joint of meat now and again, they did not fare too badly even though rationing was harsh. Collins, who was part gardener, part gamekeeper, and a general help, kept them supplied with rabbits and vegetables. After the war Celia could never abide rabbit.

They were fortunate too in having some agreeable neighbours. There were the Hart-Davises across the field, Diana Gamble, a friend of Comfort's, nearby, Sandy and Maud Alexander (he was a Scottish sculptor) the other side of the wood, and Donald and Nan McCullough in the village; Donald was a broadcaster who worked in the Ministry of Agriculture during the war and who chaired the Brains Trust, a popular radio programme on which supposed men of wisdom gave their views on issues of the day. He was attentive to the Merrimoles garrison, offering advice on running the estate, entertaining the children, and generally bearing news. Selby Armitage, a son of a former Nettlebed vicar, had grown up with the Fleming brothers; he and his American wife, Bland, were friends; Selby was later awarded the George Medal and the George Cross for his bravery in defusing bombs. Other old friends such as Rosalie Nugent, Mary Clive, Joan Bright who worked for the War Cabinet, sometimes came for the weekend. Walton Butterworth, an American diplomat, was popular not just on his own account, but also because he often brought some little luxury, marmalade perhaps or gin, when he visited.

They were well supported locally by Mr Johnston, who had been head gardener at Joyce Grove and was now the agent on the estate (his son went on to work in Robert Flemings), and by Collins.

The problem with this large household and with people coming and going was the cooking. A cook would be hired; before long she would invariably give notice. For Celia, whose horror of cooking was total, the possible departure of the cook was always a worry. However, the Balls sisters (the two nannies), often stepped into the breach when the latest cook flounced out.

The children, five strong in the early part of the war, had a lovely time. They could roam free round the house and fields and woods. Nichol and David, who were the same age, became partners in many a childish crime, bringing down the grandfather clock, pushing the cat in the pram, enjoying themselves hugely. Parties were held with the McCullough children.

Such was the background of Celia's life for the next four or five years. The life was hard, it was circumscribed, it was anxious, but Merrimoles was where she felt she should be. She could not commit herself to a play with an unknown length of run. Instead, she did broadcasts (nearly fifty in all – plays, novels, stories, poetry), and later made some films which, with their known schedule of work, she felt she could manage, without abandoning home for too long. At the beginning of 1941 she made a short film, directed by Carol Reed, for the Ministry of Information called *A Letter from Home*. She played an English mother, writing to her children who had been evacuated to America; Joyce Grenfell played the American mother with whom they stayed. The film was for export only and was supposed to show America what life was like in Britain: Celia was shown queuing for a bus, exchanging news with a neighbour about the previous night's bombing, shopping for eggs and unexpectedly being given two, going to a fire-bomb practice, and then home to write the letter from the safety of the cellar. It was rather poignant. All concerned gave their services free.

Peter left at the beginning of 1941 for Cairo on another inventive and unorthodox task, known as Yak Mission. Its purpose was to find Italians who had been captured by Wavell in the Libyan desert and who were now in the prisoner-of-war camps in Egypt; the idea was that they could be sent back to Italy and trained to foment revolution. When on the first investigation of the camps, it was apparent that no Italian would volunteer for the task, Yak Mission was obliged to bide its time at Shepheard's Hotel in Cairo, that social mecca of the war.

Peter wrote to Celia on 4 March about the frustrations of his work there, and the friends and acquaintances he had met:

Fleming's Foot are at present in a state of stagnation and it is very difficult to see what our destinies are going to be, except that they are certain to be very safe. We all live very expensively in Shepheard's and I spend my time flapping round and trying to fix things up, which is inordinately difficult whatever the things are. The one incontrovertible fact that Norman [Johnstone] drilled into our heads before we arrived was that it never rained in Cairo, but needless to say it does this time, though not very much and when it doesn't it is very nice. Practically the only thing I have done is to fly up to Bardia where the desert is still black with booty and which was strangely familiar from the news-reels. I have seen a lot of chaps: it is a good place in that way but not a good place to stay in for very much longer. Tom Boase is much the same as ever. Michael Wright's wife was at school with you (she is called Esther), and is very nice. Bill Astor is not in Cairo but is taking two of my boys to see *Rebecca* at the place where he is, all showing smallness of world. Oliver [Barstow] has the smallest topee ever seen ... Peter Sturgis is very well and is here on a course. Freya Stark asked me to send you her love; she is a sort of queen of Cairo and very nice and sensible. Fifi Lampson I have seen once and I fear offended by failing to ring her up. Norman is a tremendous figure, surrounded by pimps and middlemen of all kinds, their horrible faces kindled with the happy and prosperous memories of peacetime Cairo. John Fox-Strangways is installed as usual in a flat full of divans and gin. At any moment I may meet the great Dimbleby in person. All this is very boring and silly but I don't know any news and if I did I couldn't send it. I found a splendid sentence in a thriller the other day: '"My father's bearer was a Pathan", went on Meredith, speaking rather jerkily as he now held Prince Satsui high above his head.' I like 'went on'. Darling Mrs Flem, I miss you and the Sausage [Nichol] very much indeed and would like to hear from you. I do hope you are all right and not being bored or bombed. Ian may occasionally know a way of getting letters out in reasonable time. The ordinary mails are hopeless. Give my love to my mother and Tish and send me a wire to Shepheard's Hotel if you are in doubt or trouble.

Just over a week later, on 13 March:

Here I still am, midst shot and shell, I don't think, trying to obtain *de jure* recognition and a useful job for my small but practically invincible army. This has been weakened (but only numerically) by the loss of Bill Stirling, a tortuous though amiable character who only came for the ride and has been released to seek other employment. I have been up to Palestine for 2 days, also down to the canal where I stayed with Bill Astor. You might perhaps write to his mother and say that I found him in good form and doing invaluable and interesting work, and that I gave him her messages (Actually he isn't in very good form but he is doing good work) ... Give my best love to Tish and say I will write as soon as this rather tiresome phase is over and our destinies are settled. I hope you are not having any troubles or alarms or dread financial difficulties, and especially that you have not sold the house or fallen in love with a colonel. Give my love to Ian and Tim and Rosalie and Mary and all.

The destiny he discovered for his becalmed force was to go to Greece as far as its border with Yugoslavia, and there try and organise little pockets of resistance, much as he had done in Kent, in the face of the advancing German army. It was a somewhat reckless aim. He and his men were too late: the Germans were no distance from the Greek border, and a force many divisions strong was sweeping straight towards them; there was no time. Instead they found themselves part of the general retreat – a headlong rush – to Athens. They used their ammunition as far as they were able, booby-trapping a train or blowing up a bridge. Peter's unit, together with the First Secretary of the British Embassy in Athens, Harold Caccia (an old friend), his wife, Nancy (Oliver Barstow's sister) and his two children and other members of the embassy staff, and some Greek officials, boarded a small boat, the *Kalanthe*, at Piraeus which was to take them to Crete. As the Luftwaffe had control of the skies, it was too dangerous to travel by day, and the boat did not have the power to reach Crete in one night. So the first night it reached the island of Milos and lay up the following day, anchoring off a little beach on Poliaigos, an islet off Milos. A few stayed with the boats and its guns, the rest of the party lazed on the beach. In the early afternoon on 24 April the boat was hit by a German aeroplane; the ammunition in its hold exploded. Oliver Barstow and two others were killed; Peter and Mark Norman, who were also on board, were wounded. It was a horrible and bloody incident. The survivors, with some difficulty, reached Crete and from there made their way home.

Peter cabled Celia:

CELIA DARLING TRANSMIT TO LADY B THROUGH JOHN OR PERSONALLY
FOLLOWING BEGINS OLIVER KILLED INSTANTANEOUSLY IN ACTION
MANNING LEURS [LEWIS] GUN AGAINST LOW FLYING ATTACK ON SMALL
SHIP BY GERMAN BOMBERS APRIL 24 STOP HE HAD SHOWN HIMSELF
A MOST GALLANT AND RESOURCEFUL OFFICER AND WE ARE ALL IN-
TENSELY PROUD OF HIM STOP HE ENJOYED EVERY MINUTE RIGHT
UP TO THE END AND IN EVERYTHING HE HAD TO DO HE DISTINGUISHED
HIMSELF STOP DEAR LADY B MY VERY DEEPEST SYMPATHY STOP HE
WAS A FINE CHAP AND HIS MEMORY WILL BE LOVED AND HONOURED
BY ALL WHO KNEW HIM BUT ESPECIALLY BY THOSE WHO SERVED
WITH HIM OUT HERE STOP NANCY AND HAROLD WHO WERE BOTH
SPLENDID WERE TRAVELLING ON THE SHIP WITH THE CHILDREN BUT
ALL PASSENGERS WERE ASHORE AND COMPLETED JOURNEY SAFELY
ENDS [He continued to Celia:] MARK WOUNDED BUT DOING FINE
MARK'S SERVANT AND SEVEN GREEK CREW KILLED SELF SLIGHTLY
WOUNDED QUITE RECOVERED STOP PLANES PEPPERED BUT WE HADN'T
MUCH CHANCE LOVE YOU VERY MUCH ADDRESS EMBASSY CAIRO.

In the letter that followed, written on 8 May 1941, he revealed
more about his injuries:

I have got three holes in me, head, leg and shoulder, but there
is nothing to any of them and I only limp when entering restaurants
to impress the ladies. I didn't notice them at the time until my
boots began to fill with blood and they didn't hurt in the least.
I do hope John was there to break the news to poor darling Lady
B, and I hope you didn't mind my doing it through you: it seemed
the best and most reliable way ... We lost everything we had in
the ship, which besides blowing up 3 times caught fire, sank, and
generally went through the whole gamut.

Peter was lucky to have escaped death; he always felt very
badly about Oliver. He did not escape criticism for the fact
that there had been men on board and ammunition in the
hold. At the end of May Lady Barstow received a letter from
Nancy describing the tragedy in detail; this she copied and
sent on to Celia.

Almost exactly a year after his reported death at Namsos,
Peter had had another skirmish with danger. Celia's friend
Virginia Thesiger [née Graham] remembers meeting her and
Peter later that summer with the Grenfells at Parrs and Celia
literally trembling with pleasure at having Peter back safe
and well.

Peter remained in England for the rest of 1941, at one stage training street fighters in Battersea. He and Celia saw their friends and in August he took her to Black Mount for the first time. She shot her first (and possibly her last) stag. She had always been rather nervous of the Flemings and their clannish Edwardian shooting-lodge life. But she came to appreciate all Peter's cousins, Flemings, Hermon-Hodges and Hannays. Earlier that year she and Tish had been to the wedding of Peter's cousin Lorna Hermon-Hodge to John Schuster; she described it to Peter:

Today [14 April] we've been to Lorna's wedding. Tish, Amy, Marie and I bundled off in the little Ford (Marie's weight necessitated a periodic blowing up of the tyres) after much difficulty in deciding what I could possibly wear. We arrived about one and found everybody very gay and cheerful eating eggs and raspberry fool and helping Lorna to dress. She looked lovely and decorative and seemed extremely happy. Everything went with a swing except she forgot her bouquet and it had to be fetched by Pet [Hermon-Hodge] half-way through the service. Little Johnnie [Fincastle] who is indeed a wonder child wore a diminutive kilt and held her train up. He behaved perfectly even approving the decorations by saying Nice flowers in a clear little voice while going up the aisle. All aunts, uncles and cousins were there and Hermon scowled at the refreshments which were wonderful, considering, with lots of champagne so that I became dazed and backed into the wedding presents with a fixed smile on my face muttering your messages to Harry H-H which I couldn't properly remember ... We saw Charm's [Fleming] baby which is nice and happy looking and is probably going to be called Jenny; I talked to Phil [Peter's uncle] about the estate ... The happy couple left for Scotland amid a hubbub of hunting yells with three dogs and a still-born foal to feed them on (the dogs I mean and trust). We must give them a present. They had dozens of guns and jewellery and cheques and silver and three hunters (not, I am happy to say, on display) so I think a barometer might fill the bill for us.

Towards the end of the year, General Sir Archibald Wavell, who was Commander-in-Chief of the Allied Forces in the South West Pacific and whom Peter had met in Cairo, sent a signal to the Chief of the Imperial General Staff: 'Should be glad of Peter Fleming as early as possible for appointment my staff.' The historian, Sir Michael Howard, has described Wavell: 'Behind an inarticulate and ruggedly orthodox exterior, Wavell concealed one of the most fertile minds ever possessed by a British senior officer.' He was just the sort of highly impressive military figure to whom Peter looked up, perhaps part of an unconscious search for his exemplary father. He left to join his staff early in 1942, and for the rest of the war he was based in Delhi in charge of deception in the Far East. While he was there he encouraged Wavell, a keen amateur of poetry, to put together an anthology of his favourite poems, and, through Rupert Hart-Davis, helped to get it published. 'Since you were largely responsible for my publishing this, I send you a copy of the result,' Wavell wrote to Peter in a note sent with the book, which he had called *Other Men's Flowers*.

14

The Walrus and the Carpenter

Peter's departure for India at the beginning of 1942 coincided with the start of two new careers for Celia – that of film actress and that of policewoman. So although, as usual, she felt very bereft when Peter left, it was not long before she was busy and happier.

Noel Coward had had some difficulty in finding an appropriate role in the war. He was approached by Anthony Havelock-Allan and Filippo Del Giudice and asked to consider making a film based on his patriotic show, *Cavalcade*; this was not possible, but, after dining with Mountbatten, Coward put an alternative idea to them: he suggested making a morale-boosting film about the navy, which he loved. He produced a rough treatment of the history of the navy from 1922 to 1939 ending with the sinking of HMS *Kelly*, which had happened on 21 May 1941. It took three and a half hours to read and would have made seven to twelve hours on screen. When doubts were cast on this, he said: 'All I know about the cinema is that you can do anything.' 'Yes,' the producers said, 'but you can't get people to sit on their seats for that long.' He told them to do what they liked with it, and in the end it was boiled down to the story of one ship, the *Kelly*. (It was later given the title *In Which We Serve*.)

Noel Coward wanted to play the captain, but when it was put to him that it might not be ideal casting, he said: 'I'm going to play it, but you're perfectly right.' Celia played his wife. She later explained how she got the part. She approached Noel Coward, whom she knew, at a party and, uncharacteristically, asked him for it. It was a bold move; she had done no filming before apart from *A Letter from Home*, the short film for Carol Reed. Camera tests had to be made to see whether she looked right on film, as she explained:

It was a silent test really but Noel wanted me to speak lines so as to get an idea of my expression on the screen. We'd talked for hours about all the ordinary things, plays we'd seen and books we'd read, and actresses we liked and actresses we hated, until we'd exhausted every topic of conversation. Then suddenly Noel began to spout bits of *The Walrus and the Carpenter* at me. What was the sun doing? he said. Shining on the sea, I told him exuberantly, shining with all its might. If seven maids with seven mops swept it for half a year, he said, considering the situation gravely, do you suppose (and he dropped his voice because he wanted a very sad bit for the camera) that they could get it clear? I doubt it, I told him with an absolutely miserable face, and shed a bitter tear ... We recited that poem at each other until we nearly burst, and it looked quite crazy in the rushes. But Noel seemed to like it and I got the part.

In fact, not only was *In Which We Serve* a first for her, it was a first for almost everybody involved with the film. Noel himself had precious little knowledge of films (he had been involved in a small way in a film called *The Scoundrel*), so he had asked around for an experienced cutter, a good technician, to help him direct, and the name of David Lean had come forward. David Lean had not directed a film before – he had held out in the thirties against directing quota quickies – but, realising that a lot of the work was going to fall on his shoulders and that he was in effect going to co-direct, with nervous audacity he asked Noel if his name could be on the credits as such; it was a request of great temerity as Coward was a very big name and Lean completely unknown. It was granted – rightly as it turned out, for David Lean did almost all of the work, Noel just directing the scenes that he was in himself. Coward was interested only in the theatre and David Lean only in films. It was also a beginning for a nineteen-year-old actor, Richard Attenborough, who was cast as the young sailor who leaves his post. Ronald Neame was the camera-man.

Celia's other work, as a policewoman, probably came about because she was a good driver. She joined the Henley branch of the Women's Auxiliary Police Corps, and for the rest of the war served when she could in the police station in Henley.

There were usually two WAPCs on duty there, one in the office and one on car maintenance. The one in the office operated the switchboard and typed out despatches, and the one on car duty would clean the car, sometimes change the wheel (with the duty sergeant doing the nuts) and would then take the despatches round the division. Many of the policemen did not have driving licences. The cars they drove were black Austin saloons, and the uniform they wore was navy blue with a white shirt and black tie. The old superintendent in Henley was horrified at first at having women in the police; in the end he thought that they were very good. Celia enjoyed her work there and was proud of her uniform. She would do *The Times* crossword between calls at the switchboard. Celia had done the crossword in *The Times* from when it began in 1930; she could almost always finish it.

Extracts from her letters to Peter perhaps give the best idea of what her life was like at this time.

[20 February 1942] Well, on the Saturday after you went, the next day in fact, we went to dinner with Donald and Nan [McCullough], he and I having first tried with no success at all to shoot pigeons in Barley Hill. It was bitingly cold and no wind at all so even our wild shooting scared them off. We had the happy fate to run out of petrol on the way back after dinner, just at the edge of the wood, so we walked talking in loud clear voices home so as not to hear the people who always walk with one in the woods at night.

An even more enthralling day on Sunday, a nicish chap called Bowman came to tea. He's a great friend of Nevill's and produced the theory that his plane may have been shot down by fighters protecting Brest. [Pam's husband, Nevill Vintcent, had gone missing when travelling on a plane from London to India; it was never discovered what had happened to him though this theory is the most likely. Pam and her children were still in India.] I do wish to God that we could hear that he is all right. Diana and Jim Bailey came to dinner and we heard Churchill's speech in gloom and sadness. Then the next morning at the attractive hour of 6.30 Shurey [local coach firm] and I wended our way to Denham. It is odd but there is absolutely nix of interest to tell you about it. We did the bit where Noel drives up in his car to the Kinross House and is welcomed by me and the children. That took all day and believe it or not the next sequence, in the hall, I have to do on April 22, when apart from anything else my hair will have grown several feet. I stayed the night with a pleasant and friendly woman called Elizabeth Haffenden, I met her at Shepherd's Bush Studios where she designs clothes and things for films. She is also a friend of Laurence Irving's and I thought it most frightfully kind of her to put me up. She has a tiny house which she shares with another girl and child and her brother, no maids or anything and she was as welcoming as could be. And after all I only knew her very slightly. My second day's filming consisted of being made up at 8.30 and being used at 6.30. It wasn't improved by seeing the rushes in which I looked like a soused herring and didn't register anything at all. I don't look nearly as human as I did in the M[inistry] of I[nformation] film and heavens knows I wasn't Lana Turner in that. I don't think I am going to be the V. Leigh of Nettlebed . . .

I was a policeman yesterday. I took Sergeant George to Wandsworth Police Station and we brought back a prisoner to Henley. He was a chap from the camp here who had found a lovely method of adding to his earnings. He was a clerk and timekeeper and paid out the wages, so he just invented two extra chaps and paid himself for them. You have had several letters but nothing of much interest. An invitation to dinner from Lady Milner, and ditto from Tom Boase. Also a bill from the LCC for £1.2.10d. for damage to boat on lake when shooting . . . what on earth did you do to it?

The Sausage is in fine form. We took them [the children] into Henley this afternoon on top of the bus to have their hair cut and they were thrilled to the core. There's a letter from Kini to you. I'll send it on, but I don't really know how to address it. Just putting HQ South Pacific Command or whatever it is sounds so very trusting, like posting a letter to the moon.

[26 February 1942] Here far from things being in 'bustle and confusion', there is a state of stagnation and continued frost which makes us all fairly cross and awfully uninspired. My parents are still here, they are off tomorrow to Kent.

We are plunging into the turmoil of Warship Week shortly. I have got to do something for the social God knows what. Oh, how I detest village life, it's nothing but doing things with great difficulty that nobody wants done. I think I shall recite them something that they won't understand and that will teach them not to ask me again. A moving passage from the Bard or Hakluyt and I shall be left in peace. I took the sergeant from Woodcote plus two Specials into Henley the other night to see a programme of Min. of In. films.

The Town Hall was packed with police, Home Guard, AFS Red Cross and some other undenoted chaps and the programme was simply awful. About seven films, mostly well out of date and going on much too long. The first was Corvettes and quite good though of no especial value to the audience. Then a sort of map one all about the Far East, explaining the vital importance of Singapore, and how we faced this new threat with confidence ... well that didn't inspire us with much. Next was a Fireguard one about putting out incendiaries, the only one with anything constructive in it, though I should think all the people there have had a fair amount of training in that already. Then a flippant and very old film about the police made long before raids and I should think calculated to irritate the Force if you can irritate those nice chaps; the next was a review of the events of 1941, not encouraging and done in a Daily Mirror Picture Post manner. Then believe it or not one of those Soviet Films of Women cutting corn and singing while they do it. That seemed endless BUT it was followed by an even more eternal one about a chap from Canada, one from Australia, and one from New Zealand, who meet Leslie Howard in Trafalgar Square and talk for Days.

Nichol says that he has just had lovely cauliflower for dinner. He also says he had some trifle at Caroline's.

I have just been sent a play [*Flare Path*] from Binkie by Terence Rattigan. It's about the Air Force and is very good indeed, extremely moving. The only snag is that my part is much the dullest, and might easily be unsympathetic. It's not going to be done until about June, and they want Johnnie Mills to play in it. He would be frightfully good in an excellent part. I think I shall go up to London next week and see Terry who is on leave and discuss it with him. So much might happen between now and then that it's impossible to decide anything.

[1 March 1942] I went to London on Monday and saw Binkie and Terry Rattigan about his play. It really is an awfully good play, Puffin [Asquith] is to produce it in June. I felt very pleased about the whole thing but when I got home I found a dread letter from the Ministry of Labour about Nora, so I suppose they will take her and that knocks the whole thing well and truly on the head. I must say that I am feeling just about as low as I could ... Let us change the subject. I took all my gorgeous jewellery to be valued because I thought it really ought to be insured and the values they have put on things are too odd for words. The man admitted that all values are dotty at the moment but, for instance, you remember that little black bracelet you gave me when you went to Brazil, well they've put that down at £50 and other things just as remarkable. I must be very rich and a lovely jewelled actress, fairly dripping with diamonds, in spite of appearances.

Collins has at last taken his stripes and been made a sort of chief in the district as far as I understand it. He came and told me this and seemed slightly worried because, as he said, if there's any trouble he would have to go to his post at once and leave us alone. Was that all right with me, he said. I said it was splendid and that you would be delighted. He has heard that his brother is a prisoner, in Italy I think. He now has Home Guard every other evening, has decided that he must help with the haymaking and harvest, does everything else as well but is a thought worried as to whether he will find time to keep the keepering up on English [farm].

Tish wrote too about Warship Week:

During the last week all thoughts except of warships have passed from our minds. Celia gave a most soul searing recital last night. She then auctioned some 'mystery' parcels, a shaving brush, some garden seeds etc. In the middle of the sale of the seeds she whispered to me hoarsely to bid for her, and they were rapidly knocked down to the auctioneer, most unorthodox, but the packet contains onion seeds, so was well worth the jiggery pokery. Then we played musical chairs, and together took the floor for a polka and then ate some real fish with Nan, and so to bed. When the bridge tournament at Henley is over, the dread week will be at an end.

[16 March 1942] Here I am in an odd sort of place found for me by my stand-in (fairly classy – having a stand-in, don't you think?). It's quite a nice little hotel full of old family portraits and a mass of rather Joyce Grove furniture, only smaller, and a great deal of wobbly China in cupboards and some ultra Joyce Grove clocks. I seem to be the only inhabitant but dinner is due any minute and then perhaps I shall see the other inmates. Tomorrow I have got to be at the studio at 7.30 to do the Ward Room sequence ...

Did I tell you that Tish and I and Collins went over to Woodcote [Tish's family's old house] to get anything there was to be got out of the garden and came back laden with rhubarb plants, delphiniums and every sort of thing, which have had to be planted in the rocky soil of Moly in the pouring rain ever since. The best moment was when Collins appeared through a pathway with an ecstatic beam on his face bearing most of a beehive which he had found in an incinerator. I've never seen him look so pleased.

Now I will stop because I must learn my lines.

[19 March 1942] Here I am home again, having finished the Ward-room sequence in one long tiring day. I did my long speech and everyone was most complimentary and said it brought tears to the eyes and I saw myself as the greatest emotional film star of all time. So I waited to see the rushes the next day and I've never been so disappointed over anything. I look simply awful, haggard, worn and horrible, my dress which was a very pretty blue thing with sort of sequiny things on it, looks black and minny to the last degree. I swear I needn't look as dreary as that. I'm most awfully disappointed about the whole thing, because I know I did the speech quite well and the effect is just repellent.

We go to what Nichol calls Brightman tomorrow, and I feel v. excited at the idea. Nance [Barstow] is coming too, so it should be rather fun. Alas, Norah has been summoned for her dread interview next Wed. so I expect this is my last fling. I dread the thought of not having her . . .

There was a long letter for you from Lady Desborough enthusing over your book [*A Story to Tell*].

'Dear Peter, what a brilliant book, I have only got to page 148 but cannot wait to write to you – while still looking at my third finger, I wonder if writing could be better?? I have always so minded missing all the fun of the music – but perhaps the ecstasy of words is compensation? How *exquisitely* yours fall – never a click – dead in the right place, and each shade of meaning mathetical, each exact weight of value. You know you have always given me more than anyone that lovely vain-glorious feeling that *no one* could enjoy what you write quite as much . . .

I have an unholy longing to know what Major Hipple's opening chorus was: what a grand slice of life is cut out for the ordinary female – I have tried Rabelais but drew quite blank . . . I do so wish I ever saw you – in this unplumbed salt estranging war – and don't even know if you are in England. If you are, won't you and Celia come here one day when the spring really comes? – This poor house [Panshanger] looks horrible – a Hospital for East End mothers and babies, and Willie and I perching in a wing – but they are so brave and so witty – and it is very comforting work that can be done even in senility – Love to you both, your aff Ettie Desborough.'

Celia and her sister, Pamela.

Celia, her brother John, and Pamela, at the seaside, 1913.

Celia's mother, Ethel Johnson (standing, right) and her sisters, Dora, Amy and Winifred Griffiths (the Ilkley aunts).

Robert Johnson, Celia's father – an early and enthusiastic motorist.

Celia in the St Paul's Girls' School First Lacrosse team, 1925.

Celia in 1929, soon after her first appearance on the stage.

Celia and Sir Gerald du Maurier, a great influence, in *Cynara*, at the Playhouse 1930.

Punch cartoon showing W. Graham Browne, Celia, and Marie Tempest in *The Vinegar Tree* at the St James's Theatre, 1932.

Celia played for over two years in *The Wind and the Rain*. With her here are Robert Harris (seated), Mackenzie Ward and Ivan Brandt.

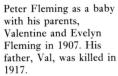

Peter Fleming as a baby with his parents, Valentine and Evelyn Fleming in 1907. His father, Val, was killed in 1917.

Peter at about the age of nineteen on a typical foray.

Peter typing outside his tent on his epic journey with Ella Maillart, from China to India, 1935.

Celia on the
Burma Road,
1938.

Pride and Prejudice, St James's Theatre, 1936. From left to right: Dorothy
Hyson, John Teed, Leueen MacGrath, Celia, Athole Stewart, Barbara
Everest and Hugh (Tam) Williams. The production was designed by Rex
Whistler.

In *Rebecca*, 1940, at the Queen's Theatre. Angus McBean was the most distinctive theatrical photographer of his generation.

Well, that took me a long time to type. All those ——— and ???
which I always leave out, took a lot of looking for ... What was
Major Hipple's opening chorus? You've never told me.

(Celia thought Lady Desborough, with her Edwardian para-
sols and ostrich feathers, ridiculous. She occasionally asked
Peter and Celia to stay; on one occasion, she told them: 'It's
not a party, just a few friends – the Winston Churchills, the
Stanley Baldwins, the Anthony Edens and the Neville
Chamberlains.')

[27 March 1942] First a bit more about Brighton; the thing Nichol
enjoyed most was having tea in a shop in Worthing and drinking
lemonade through a straw. He has given sucking demonstrations
to the other children ever since. I am going to try and get some
straws from the farm to repeat the pleasure but I'm afraid it will
be a disappointment to find that they aren't wrapped in a paper.
David [his cousin] came back today and they had a reunion like
a pair of old cronies, swapping reminiscences and giggling. He is
now v. fond of drawing and at last thinks he can draw lorries, a
thing I am most thankful for as it saves me doing it all the time.

I have spent most of today putting potatoes in sacks, a back and
soul destroying job ... every single potato has to be picked by hand,
put into buckets, after one has decided if it's a big pot. or a small
pot. and they are all fairly medium sized just to make it more difficult,
and then the buckets emptied into sacks and weighed. It is not a
work one can shine at or even put much personality into though
of course there is *something* about the way I do it that one can tell
even if it is only the posture. My fellow workers are Tudor, the
man who looks like a ham Shakespearean comic, and who is fairly
deaf, and Treadwell, a non-speaker who is stone deaf, so there isn't
a lot of happy carefree chat.

Rupert has a week's leave and Eric Linklater is staying at the
farm for the weekend so I am going over there tonight for dinner.
Marjorie Linklater has just had a son [Magnus] and Lady May [Mary
Clive] has cleverly produced a daughter [Alice] in almost record
time.

I wish I had got about six children, all exactly like you.

I have been trying very hard to get a working idea of the estate,
and have spent several days in the office working at pay sheets and
things under Hall's humble but instructive eye. I can't say that I

have yet introduced any startling innovations or that the mystery of the tithe is anything but an unplumbed sort of totem ...

I had rather fun at the farm last night. We ate delicious brawn Comfort had made from the remains of her pig. Their pig slaughtering episode is a tremendous saga, full of horrors, pathos and sordid realism. The really awful part was, I think, that when the pig killer arrived the pig although having been starved for 24 hours and hungry and ramping, immediately recognised his time had come and became a cowed creature with no fight in him at all. Apparently they always *know*.

Brown [the rather prickly game keeper] has killed two badgers to his great delight. I suspect they were not on our ground but on Greys. He doesn't seem to have killed many rabbits, they abound in Merrimoles and Scaffold Wood. His whole attention has been riveted on these badgers ever since he saw their tracks in the snow some weeks ago.

[1 April 1942] I have been learning to drive the tractor, instructed by Harry Smallbones. Much the most interesting thing I have discovered by so doing is that Smallbones is a member of my profession. He shouted at me above the roar of the tractor that he used to be in a concert party, eight of us there were, he said, all men, I used to play the women's parts, a comedian that's me. I was delighted with this bit of information as you can imagine. Do you know *The Merchant of Venice*, he next enquired. I admitted that I did. Shylock I've done and Antonio, I can't remember the names of the other parts. 'Why dost thou whet thy knife so earnestly?' he suddenly yelled and I couldn't hear his answer but he went off into roars of laughter after it, so I don't know if it was the Shakespearean text or a joke they put in. We have long conversations about concert life and he told me of a time when the rest of the party got held up by the breakdown of the charabanc carrying them and how he and another chap had to keep the show going for two hours, first me then him, he said, until they arrived. So if he can plough beautifully straight, I ought to be able to in time. So far harrowing has been my highest achievement ... Don't you think it's surprising about Smallbones? I told him I'd also played in the *Merchant*. What were you, he asked and when I said Portia, said, O yes, the judge and again laughed fit to burst. I don't see that it's as funny as all that. He really is a very nice cheerful man. There is a lot to be said for the theatrical profession.

Today we were invited to lunch by the Alexanders and they fed us eggs and delicious jam pudding until we could hardly walk home, so to work it off I returned to my tractoring and harrowed away in the parks in a wind to take your ears off...

I have had another letter from Lady Desborough, repeating her praise of you (as if I didn't know) and finishing up by saying Moggie's [Gage] children were so 'pointful'. Do you think Nichol is pointful? It seems an odd word to apply to any child, except if they were given to biting people.

[10 April 1942] Well, first of all I as I have said went to stay the day and night of Easter Sunday with Joyce [Grenfell]. Virginia and Tony* were there. Joyce is working at the hospital and has decided against doing the Farjeon revue and is concentrating on doing her turns at hospitals and concerts and places. She is doing quite a lot of broadcasting with great success.

I came back on Monday morning and spent the day chain harrowing the Moley field on the tractor.

On Tuesday I went to London to buy Nicholas some summer clothes, a very difficult job and again full of dread expense. I sabotaged the War Effort slightly and my bank balance considerably by getting him a luscious suit from Debenhams. I can feel you being annoyed and saying why not sacking but I expect it will be sacking by the time you come home so you need never know about it, and I shall enjoy seeing Nicholas looking smart and well dressed for a change. He is in very good form and shows a suitably warlike spirit by being very disappointed when he asked me if there was khaki colour in a rainbow and I was forced to admit there wasn't.

My chief problem – and how I wish you were here to write letters about it – is the calling up of Nora.

[14 April 1942] Amy is leaving us, isn't it awful? She is really miserable about it ... heaven send they leave me Nora or I shall lie down and surrender.

I saw Brown yesterday and was about to tick him off for not killing enough rabbits but he got in first by saying he had heard that you were in India and would you tell Lord Linlithgow that he (Brown) was here as he (Lord L) often used to shoot with him.

* Virginia Graham had married Anthony Thesiger shortly before the war.

This took me aback, I promised to be sure and let you know and rabbits were not brought into the conversation at all. It was on much too high a plane.

Donald has been to see us quite a lot, he is very nice and awfully funny, sometimes intentionally and sometimes not. He is mad keen on making two swedes grow where one grew before and full of enthusiasm ...

Tish has gone with Valentine and Christopher to stay for a week with Edith [Borthwick] and I think next week I am due for the last few days of this nonsense film. It gets more high class every day, they have now had the King and Queen, not to mention your Colonel-in-Chief, Princess Elizabeth, at Denham, to watch the shooting. They can only invite God now and I don't suppose that would make such a good story for the press.

[20 April 1942] Tomorrow I am going to London to go to Denham. I am going to stay with George Thorpe and his wife who live quite near the studio. He was in *Rebecca*, he played Owen's brother-in-law and is now in *Quiet Weekend*. Just to cheer myself up and to curry favour with my favourite Grenadier, Aubrey told me that Clemence Dane had seen the roughcut stuff already shot, and thought I was very good but she is well known as a crank to say the least. It is rather sad that I only appeal to people like her and your chap the ex-c-in-c. You said he was pretty silly too.

[26 April 1942] Here I am home again after nearly a week away at Denham, where I had rather fun and very much enjoyed staying with the Thorpes who couldn't be nicer. I went there last Tuesday, and came back yesterday, and today is Sunday so I feel as if I had been away for months and months. It was nice coming home again and being greeted very sweetly by the sausage who jumped about saying 'My Mummy's comed home' in an endearing fashion ... I found two letters from my love. I also found a telegram from General Wavell saying he had forwarded my cable to you and that you were fit and well, which I think was just about as nice of him as could be. There can't be many busier men at the moment and to take the trouble to send that to me I thought was simply terrific of him. I leave his telegram lying carelessly on the mantelpiece to impress anyone who calls and have already bagged R[osalind] Irving and a girlfriend of hers as well as Nan McCullough and I took it over to the farm to show Rupert and Cuthie.

The film was quite fun, it is the first time I have had more than a day there and I got much more into the swing of the thing and I didn't look quite so awful in the rushes that I saw. I think that, being very hard to photograph, the fact that I was there for several days gave Ronnie Neame more of a chance to get a good line on me so to speak, and I don't look quite so grublike in consequence. I saw some of the rough cut stuff of the film and it is quite good, though it is very difficult to judge. The Carley float stuff is very good, and the film is most heart-rending and everybody weeps buckets all the way through. Whether this is a good thing or not I can't decide. I think it is perhaps too close to people and may upset them too much. Johnnie Mills is as good as can possibly be, and there is a brilliant performance by a young Academy student called Richard Attenborough which should make his name at first go off. Bernard Miles is a bit disappointing, I thought, too slow, and Noel is very good and unNoelish nearly all the time. He has been most nice and complimentary to me and says I am a swell actress and all that but I don't think I am as good on the screen as I am in the studio if you know what I mean. I did the bit where the telegram comes on Friday and apparently made a hit with Lejeune* who was down there watching the shooting and I have been summoned to have lunch with her at the Ivy tomorrow. I had rather secret fun in reducing all the tough film chaps who don't know what the theatre is to tears while doing that bit and thought myself no end of an actress but when I saw the rushes of it the next day I was suitably humbled as you can't hear what I say or see what I do. So though I may have impressed them at the time, the great film public will remain in ignorance of the brilliance in their midst ...

Now I will tell you about yesterday when I went to London to see if I could get anything from Harold [Caccia] re Nevill and Spain. He scoffed in a fairly Foreign Office manner at the idea that there could be any of our chaps there unable to communicate but has promised to send a note to the Embassy just in case. He did put me in touch with a chap in the Air Ministry whom I saw but who could tell me nothing. They simply don't know what happened to

* Caroline A. Lejeune was an early and influential film critic who wrote for the *Observer*.

the plane and that is all there is to it. He thought there really could be no hope and in my heart of hearts I am terribly afraid he is right. That was all most beastly and I met Nance who was in tears at the mention of Ol and I felt an insane fool to have said anything about him at all ...

Today I was summoned to Oxford on Police duties. I set off bright and e, taking Nurse and Nora with me for a day's spree in the dreaming city and leaving poor Tish with 5 children, Brenda and no cook, all on her own for the day. I must say on return she seemed none the worse and the children with the exception of smashing one picture to very small pieces had behaved in model fash. My first job was to drive the Chief Constable to Woodstock. He turned out to be a buddy of my bro. John's, and also equally surprisingly of Merton Hodge's [author of *The Wind and the Rain*]. We went to hear a case re stolen Air Force petrol and he told me all about it on the way there. The case was heard by a bench consisting of three men and two women, all so much what you would expect them to look like that it didn't seem right, and they didn't show a great deal of interest in the case until one of them noticed that the two exhibits of petrol, one clear and one coloured, were in different coloured glass bottles. This made them fearfully excited owing to their smartness and the unfairness to the prisoner. I must say that in spite of my slight scoffing at them, it was a treat to see chaps get excited over a thing like this and I thought of that awful court in Germany where you could feel the hate and venom pervading the whole place. Do you remember? I thought of it sitting on the hard seat in the town hall of Woodstock with the sun pouring down outside and listening to the magistrates saying that they must have the two petrols put in similar coloured bottles ... and this in a case where there can be no doubt that the chap had pinched a considerable quantity of His Majesty's petrol. In the afternoon I drove the despatches round the lanes of Oxfordshire and they looked as pretty as you can imagine. I should have preferred however not to have got a puncture as I did on the Thame road when the steering wheel suddenly lost all control and I heard the air hissing out of my back tyre like a snake. The tyre had an awful slash in it and was as flat as flat in a minute. The usual nice lorry driver stopped at once and changed the wheel for me in a flash, I did practically nothing to help but managed to get covered with oil through just thanking him. It is rather depressing as not only can one not buy a new tyre but even to get it reprocessed entails a great deal of form filling and difficulty. The police station too made me think that there is a lot, oh a great deal, to be thankful for. They are all such nice chaps, very polite and gallant and making small jokes in a human way. I like the English and their ways.

15

'The sprocket-piston'

Celia's letters show clearly what her life was like during the war. As may be inferred, she was often in low spirits; this she hid with a sort of tetchy bravado. She always felt better with herself when she was acting, a fact she would not have recognised; acting was just one part of her life. She enjoyed her work at the police station. Though filled with inconveniences, her life at Merrimoles was comfortable enough, but uncertainty about the future – the next week as well as the next year or years – and anxiety about those (Peter, in particular) overseas, did wear her down. Nichol she adored and was always amused by him, though exasperated when he was naughty. She liked all the little cousins too; when she gathered them together and read *Swallows and Amazons* or some such story to them, the house would become still.

As 1942 continued, so her life changed little – home, the police station, a few more scenes from *In Which We Serve*, a little broadcasting. The neighbourhood was excited by the arrival of American soldiers in the camp which had been erected at the edge of the woods, about a quarter of a mile from Merrimoles. Again, Celia's letters tell the story best.

[5 May 1942] I have just returned from spending the weekend with my parents at Brenchley. I took Nicholas with me and he was as good as gold and very sweet and entertaining. We had an awful journey there as the train stopped at Redhill and we had to change and wait nearly an hour for the connection sitting on the platform, with very little entertainment. But Nichol was fearfully good and apart from saying after about ¾ hour – Mummy I fink we had better go and find vis train – he never made any fuss at all. Mummy had borrowed a most beautiful engine from the little boy opposite who had grown out of it and Nichol pedalled it round the garden happily for hours. It was such a wild success that I asked the parents of the owner if they wanted to sell it and have acquired it for the throwaway price of 10/-. We had a certain amount of difficulty with several jokes from the porters bringing it home as it is what N calls hoooge, but it is the most successful buy and terrifically popular with all. I have just been to say Goodnight to him and said, You have been a very good boy, to which he replied You have been a very good Mummy, so honours are even ...

I have just received a cheque from Capes for £231 odd for your royalties. At the moment we seem to have rather a lot of cash but it changes from hour to hour and tomorrow I shall probably feel poor again. We have been to the Alexanders for a drink and I am slightly drunk. We came home in a giggling state, Tish had her bicycle and we tried to ride it with her on the pedals and me on the seat and I am sorry to say we fell off into a bramble bush and lay there laughing in a sorry state of weakness. We got back so late for dinner that I fear Mrs Phillips will quit especially as we made it too late for her to hear the Brains Trust which is her chief love.

[6 May 1942] I have just come in from harrowing Blackbirds, I swung the tractor about for two hours and am covered in dust and paraffin as a result. It is a dreadfully bumpy field and I nearly lost control several times with the wheel kicking right and left. I sang all the songs I could think of in ringing tones and chanted bits of poetry to myself and the sun beamed down and it was all very nice and pretty, with the lilac coming out in the clumps and pheasants strutting about in a lordly manner.

[11 May 1942] Well now, I posted the last letter in London on Friday when Tish and I were on a slight spree. We did things like dentists in the morning, and in the afternoon we went and watched the Brains Trust recording; an enjoyable and laughable affair. Then we gave ourselves a fearfully expensive tea at the Berkeley and then went to see *One of Our Aircraft is Missing*, quite a good film about an air crew who escape from Holland with absolutely no difficulty of any kind, so pro-British are the Dutch. Then, feeling we were already knee deep in debt so we might as well finish the day in true millionaire style, we went and had dinner at the Ivy. It was wonderful, we had duck and green peas, luscious sticky sweet and washed it down with Pimms. We jolly nearly missed the train as a result of all this eating but just caught it and got home in a fine and cockeyed state. The next day was Christopher's birthday and a party was arranged. The two McCullough children, Anthony Armitage, a school friend named Richard, and our bunch. We had races which were a wild success. I do wish you could have seen David and Nicholas in the sack race. There weren't enough sacks to go round so they were put both in one and as fast as one got up the other fell down and they laughed in helpless peals.

That was last Friday; Saturday I thought I ought to make a semblance of doing some work so in the afternoon I harrowed Hatch Copse. It was quite exciting as the field is so steep that the tractor fairly roared down it and I was mostly hardly in control.

Carol Reed rang me up to ask me to do a little film about ATS officers. It is not for the public but just a training film for ATS officers only. I think it should be rather fun but again it depends on Nora. It is going to be made at Wimbledon of all places, heaven knows how I shall get there, and can you see me as an ATS officer. I think it will be very funny.

We listened to the Prime Minister last night, he sounded in roaring form and completely on his toes.

[13 May 1942] Tish and I are going to see *Macbeth* at Oxford, it is going to be a pretty good expedition as there is no room on the bus so we shall have to go by bus to Reading, train from there, and back the same way and of course nothing connects. I dare say we shall get there some way and I am looking forward to seeing John [Gielgud] as Macbeth enormously.

[14 May 1942] I am bitterly disappointed because after all I can't go to Oxford on Saturday to see *Macbeth* as I have got involved in a ghastly programme on the BBC called Country Magazine which Donald has something to do with. I have simply got myself involved in a most hideous and terrifying mess in which I have got to talk about farming with a Land Girl.

[18 May 1942] Oh dread Ministry of Supply has now swooped down on poor defenceless Mrs Flem and the result seems to be that they are going to raze to the ground the whole of Black Wood, Whitehangings, Barley Hill, and they are trying to get their claws on Bix Larches. Isn't it awful. I tried very hard to vamp a chap called Sir Charles Rose and also to play the pathetic wife who was not allowed to do anything without her husband's permission but he simply said the country needed Pit props and that was that. I think it is adding insult to injury when they take away all our trees for Pit props yet won't allow us coal.

Celia was upset by the felling of various woods and wrote a lament:

A terrible battle is raging,
The losses are all on our side;
Whitehangings and Blackwood have fallen
And Barley Hill's lost its inside.

Bix larches are turned into pit props
And Tylers to telegraph poles,
Scotland no longer stands steady
And where are the once Merry Moles?

[20 May 1942] I went to London yesterday to have the second fitting of my ATS uniform and I can't say I look a glamour girl in it. I am to play a Senior Commander.

Phil and Joan [Fleming] came to tea and were very nice and booming. Phil didn't think there was anything to consider about the trees. He said he didn't see why people minded having their trees cut down so I left the question. I have just been out with the .22 trying my hand at rabbits.

Aubrey rang me up today as Binkie still wants me to do Terry's play [*Flare Path*]. But with nothing settled about Nora and a very dubious prospect in that quarter I can't get involved in a play that may run for ages, and you might come home and I should be in Manchester or some happy Midlands town.

Tish and I took David, Nichol and Gilly to tea with the Alexanders this afternoon and Nicholas I am sorry to say has got the most awful habit of fancying himself as a great wit and thinks it his metier to keep the table in a roar whenever he goes out to tea. The result is that he gets completely above himself and quite out of control. I must admit that he makes me laugh and well he knows it. He spent the morning finding friends for his Alexander Engine [a wood louse] on the manure heap. He collected quite a lot of lice, and caterpillows [sic]. He also got a number of very thick lively worms. I cruelly said that he was to give them to poor Nora as it was her birthday. She was presented with dozens. All the contents of his tin are known as Alexander Engine with the exception of one who is surprisingly known as Mr Cowman ... I have got to go and see Terry Rattigan and Anthony Asquith tomorrow about this play. Binkie says he is sure he can get Nora exempted and I bet he can too, but it does seem monstrous that I can't get her off for useful things like tractor driving and oddments of that kind and that he can just for a commercial play. They sound to have got quite a good cast, including Martin Walker, Kathleen Harrison, Adrienne Allen and a new young man I've never heard of to play the part written for John Mills. He won't do it as he doesn't like the play, I think he is wrong but who can tell? It won't be so good without him, that is quite certain. I don't really know what to do about it. If I do it it means staying in London, which would be terribly expensive, and only getting down here for weekends.

[31 May 1942] Tish and I are rather exhausted as we have had a Czech officer for the weekend. He complained that the fault of our race was that of being too polite to our enemies but the strain of being polite to our Allies was so severe that I have none left for even an Italian ... He was a sad and pathetic chap and I think works with Gubbins [Major-General Sir Colin Gubbins, head of SOE]. His chief attraction was due to the fact that he could mend anything and in no time at all he repaired Valentine's bicycle, Nichol's tricycle, an engine and the children's car. He did all this with a few nails, an old screwdriver and a coal hammer, we rushed round the house looking for things that needed mending, only too easy to find I'm afraid, and set him down to them.

I have stayed all the week with Virginia and Tony in great lux. and comfort and giggling a good deal while making my ATS film. Peggy Ashcroft, Ann Todd, Joyce Carey and I are all in it together and we have laughed without stopping. The real ATS officers who are there to advise and keep us straight though very nice efficient and splendid make us feel quite helplessly weak. It is hopeless to try and describe why we laugh so much as it is all due to little things which won't travel, but the following are oddments. Carol, whom I like more and more, got so rattled one day by them saying that it was wrong to wear a Sam Browne in the mess and that I, being a Major would never lounge over a chair in the presence of my inferior officers etc., was heard asking quite seriously 'Is it all right to leave the door open?' We all become actressier and actressier and catch ourselves saying, 'Darling your tie's divine.' We saw the first rushes one day and were all smitten silent with horror at the ghastly sights we presented, old hideous hags were shown on the screen, acting of course beautifully, but looking like starved gargoyles and as we sat dumb with despair a well-meaning ATS officer came kindly up to us and said, 'You none of you look a bit theatrical.' If she had only known how we longed at that moment to appear like Hedy Lamarr and all the Cochran young ladies rolled into one. Oh, it really has been funny. Our lines are incredible. Peggy has to talk about 'give them all a few fatigues and toughen them up', and I have to say that women's qualities suggest to me courage, endurance and the will to serve. This after Ann has said 'some women's qualities are not to be despised', which unfortunately she would keep saying as 'some women's qualities are not undesirable.'

[6 June 1942] I got to Denham at 7.15 and walked from the station to the studio thinking how odd it was that the first time I went to do a bit in the film I waded through snow and got very cold wet feet. We eventually set out in a car to find the rest of the unit somewhere on Dunstable Downs near Whipsnade. Needless to say there wasn't a sign of them and we wasted petrol, time and our tempers searching for them. I thought they might easily be a bit angry at our non-arrival as there had been so much chat about early starts and in my case not only chat. But, no, when we eventually found the great louts sprawling about with no shirts on and generally basking they only said, 'Oh hello come and sit down there'll be some tea in a minute.' I thought it slightly infuriating. We eventually started shooting about 12 o'clock. There was a great deal of difficulty over sound as there was never a moment without either aeroplanes or tractors. I didn't find it the easiest place to give of my best. We all got hotter and hotter. I can never get over the amount of people needed in the film industry to do nothing of any sort. There must have been quite 50 chaps there and never more than 10 of them doing anything at one time. I think a little doubling could be introduced with benefit. Noel got very angry and I think with sense. He took me and Gladys Calthrop [Noel's friend and designer] back to Denham in his car and we chatted of stage and things with great pleasure. Gladys very kindly asked me to stay the night with her and I rang up Tish when I got there to learn a) to my unutterable horror that Mrs Phillips had given notice and b) to my unspeakable delight that Tish had sent to Virginia's two letters from you. Isn't it awful about Mrs Phillips?

Later. I have just been over to the farm to try and borrow [from Rupert] Fanny Burney's diaries but unfortunately no one knew where it was to be found ... I have got to go to Manchester next weekend for my sins and be in a broadcast by Raymond Mortimer about Fanny B. and I know nothing about her at all, I tried to buy her works in London but the Everyman edition is out of print and a second-hand copy costs quids and quids. So I shall have to bluff my way out of it. Oh, I forgot to tell you that I got in the most fearful schemozzle over the Rattigan play. I had told Aubrey to tell Binkie years ago that I didn't think I would be able to do it on account of Nora and things and the message I got back was for me not to worry as they had plenty of worries of their own. I naturally took this to mean that they couldn't get the cast they wanted and all things of that sort and was amazed when I got a letter from Binkie a short time ago saying that they were starting rehearsing on the 10th June and he was looking forward to my working for them again etc. I rang Aubrey and said what is all this and told him to tell Binkie that I couldn't do the play and then Binkie flew up in the air and said I was the most unreliable actress in London and he would never suggest me for a play again and the whole thing seemed quite frightful. I couldn't make it out as I had previously said it was unlikely that I would be able to do it but at last all was made smooth and amicable again as it appeared that when they had said about worries Binkie was referring to his own domestic troubles and that got us all wrong. I am afraid it is rather hard on Terry as he wrote it for me, but now that Mrs P is leaving it is a very good thing that I am not involved in a play.

[12 June 1942] I had to go to Denham yesterday for a retake. They were doing some stuff in the big outdoor tank, very exciting and good Hollywood atmosphere with dozens of chaps standing about and more tons of water let loose than ever before or so everyone firmly believed. They had two huge tanks hung up in the air, holding 12,000 gallons or 1200 or 12000000 or 12 gallons I can't remember which but a great deal, and they then tipped these into the tank causing one hell of a splash into which several brave sailors leapt from a height of about 20 feet. The whole thing was made quite nice and exciting as the first time they let the water go it carried away the sort of chute thing underneath and everybody got wet. There was always the possibility that this would happen again, and I was looking forward to seeing some of the rarer foreign directors getting soaked. However it didn't bust and we all childishly enjoyed the splash. On Wednesday I went to Reading for yet another panel about Nora.

Walt [Butterworth] is coming down for the weekend to our great delight. Joan [Bright] is supposed to be coming too but so far she hasn't let us know so she may be stuck with work. Unfortunately I have got to go to Manchester on Sunday for a broadcast about Fanny Burney. It is written by Raymond Mortimer who turns out to have a cottage at Culham Court. We have tried to meet to discuss the thing but this petrol business makes it hopeless. We have only got 2½ gallons a month now and it really means one can't move at all. At the end of July they are removing even that amount and we have to apply for it. I have written an impassioned appeal to Harry but have very little hope of getting more than 2½ if that.

I rather expect to be doing a lot more police work as they are calling up a lot of the Police and I hope will use us more.

[18 June 1942] I have been trying to learn to cook but the whole business I find most dreadfully difficult and unreasonable. I can do things like peeling the potatoes and killing the caterpillars in the cabbage with anyone but actually changing them from raw to cooked is a problem that I do not understand. When Mrs Phillips departs we shall live on nuts and berries and a few eggs. The news is pretty depressing from Libya, it is a cold and dull day that looks like rain and the electric light bill has come and is not what you would call small. Otherwise we are all as merry as grigs. But fairly sad grigs on the lugubrious side.

[21 June 1942] It has gone very hot and I decided to sleep on my new and beautiful camp bed last night on the balcony. I couldn't have chosen a noisier night. The Home Guard were having some sort of exercise in the woods at the back firing off crackers like a Chinese festival, this mightily disturbed the sheep in the field and they baaed and maaed at each other without stopping. Motor cycles rushed up and down the lane and it would have been a good deal quieter in Piccadilly ... Just heard the news that Tobruk has fallen, oh Lord, how simply frightful. I suppose they will sweep on to Egypt now and things will get worse and worse. We never seem to be able to win anything at all.

[23 June 1942] Yesterday I had the most fantastic day. For my sins I got myself let in for driving around the countryside calling out through a loudspeaker for people to support the Salvage drive. Never have I done a sillier thing nor one of less use. They gave me a large piece of bumf with slogans and things on it, and long speeches I was supposed to make to the gaping village. I was provided with a car and a driver, a young Irish chap who was so like a stage Irishman that I really expected he would say Begorrah but though he didn't he got very near it. It was a very hot day and we trailed through the county, me occasionally startling chaps with a resounding call to Save Their Waste Paper Their Rubber Their Metal and so on. I got so sick of the sound of my voice repeating all this nonsense over and over again that I varied it as much as I could with the result that I think I said in a clear bell-like voice: 'Are you sure that there are no pieces of waste paper anywhere in the house ... Have you looked out all your old rubber goods ...'

We got a puncture up near Nuffield and the Irishman had characteristically left the thing to open the spare wheel case behind, so he kindly let me walk a good mile to the nearest telephone to find out whether there was anything else that would open it. I had a set-to with a man at Rotherfield Greys who said very reasonably that it was intolerable that a voice should come shouting out of the blue telling him to save metal when he spent the whole morning collecting tins and things from the village and hammering them flat. He calmed down after a bit but is clearly going to hold a grudge from now on. Later at Kidmore End a woman came rushing out of the house not so much to chat about salvage as to tell me that it didn't matter at all about Tobruk as the whole thing was in the book of Daniel and she couldn't wait for Egypt to fall as then we were really all right. I must say that I could have hit her with pleasure but instead led her gently away from Daniel and back to the absorbing question of Salvage.

[26 June 1942] I took Nicholas to tea and a party at Sylvia Thursfield's this afternoon. He refused to be at all social and grabbed an engine which he played with happily all by himself all the time. I think he feels rather like me at parties, slightly dumbfounded and idiotic.

Rosalie [Nugent] and I are sitting in the sun which is hot and delicious on the loggia. Tim had to go back last night to our sorrow. We felt the news was quite bad enough to play bridge and Rosalie and I took on the Colonel and Tish. We won after a very exciting game and it recalled to me us playing at Munich and during invasion scares. Rosalie is staying a week. I hope she won't be too bored and made to do too much washing up. It is lovely having her.

It is really very tiresome the way whenever the weather is nice the news is particularly bloody. It was the same during Dunkirk and last year during Crete and Greece. One really holds one's breath when the sun comes out it is so alarming and ominous.

I am frightfully lucky I have been allowed 4 gallons of petrol a month by Harry. I didn't think I should get more than 2½ at the most. I shall really try to do some broadcasting if I possibly can, I don't think I shall be able to be away for more than an odd night or two so that will knock out any films though I shall try if they ever ask me to do any more, particularly Min. of In. or Training ones. Just heard the news it sounds worse and worse.

[5 July 1942] I have caught a new cook which is so surprising that I can hardly believe it. Poor Mrs Phillips has a bad knee so is leaving on Tuesday and we await with some trepidation a Mrs Musgrove. I have got to do a reading for the BBC next Wednesday and after a great deal of cogitation and complaining, I have decided to read a bit of Katherine Mansfield. I think it might quite good, her writing is so simple and effective that it should read well.

[17 July 1942] I had a merry two days in London since I last wrote. I stayed with Tony and Virginia, and the first night we went to the ballet. I saw the new ballet of *Hamlet* and started rather prejudiced against the whole idea, but as a matter of fact it is very good and most exciting. If you know *Hamlet* well it is interesting and gets practically everything in, but if you had never seen the play it would hardly give one a sound impression of it. The killings come thick and fast with hardly a pirouette between them. The place was packed with wild enthusiasts and a good time was had by all. Tim and I went to see John's *Macbeth* and it is very disappointing. He isn't good at all and looks awfully wrong. It isn't nearly such a good production as when Laughton did it. I think *Macbeth* should be played as a thriller with lots of speed and zip. The poetry can't help coming out however you do it and it really is so exciting that it should be allowed to excite. Gwen [Ffrangcon-Davies] was good in her way but she really isn't right. Curiously enough Francis Lister was remarkably good as Macduff.

I came home this afternoon to find that we are now occupied territory, the camp* being stuffed with Americans. The village is in a great state of excitement and so I may say are we. We have asked some of them in for a drink tomorrow and are pouring out our precious fluid in the hopes partly of cementing Anglo-American relations but more in the hopes that they will turn out to be generous to a fault and we shall never want for anything again. They look terribly funny with German tin hats and German coloured uniforms (except for pyjama trousers) and when they are not wearing tin hats they wear little stitched linen ones like children have in the summer. They drank the village dry the first night they arrived and not only the village but also Highmoor and as far afield as Rotherfield Greys . . . It is all rather funny and a delightful source of gossip and interest.

[19 July 1942] We had our party and it was a great success. Tish mixed the most startling drink, taught her by a stock exchange pal and consisting of Champagne, gin and cointreau. It seemed fairly

* Early in the war, a camp had been built, about a quarter of a mile from Merrimoles at the edge of the woods, for Polish soldiers. After America entered the war, it housed US Engineers, and at the end of the war, it was again occupied by Poles.

... but and hands across the ocean fairly
... very nice old fatherly men. Tish and I
... dsome young college boys but they were far
... ...ple fellows became flowerier and flowerier as
... ...er and I became more and more American.

... ...ded to take the children to the seaside, to Cornwall.

[... July 1942] The children left this morning in a wild state of
hilarity and excitement. They have by now I hope arrived and I
should think are worn out poor little things. I do hope the journey
wasn't too exhausting for them and for the nurses and Tish. Nichol
was so thrilled going down the platform that he had to stop and
clench his fists and utter a great sigh to gather himself together.
They were looking as sweet as possible, all holding hands and beam-
ing. I wished I had been going too and felt almost tearful as the
train with these gleeful small faces peering out went out of Henley
station. Fortunately I had to go at once to the police station to
drive my CID chaps on further enquiries. They got the stuff they
wanted and then we had the wild thrill of getting a search warrant
and a warrant for arrest and going after a chap who had been stealing
Air Ministry aeroplane wheels.

She had three offers of films, one about Yugoslav guerrillas,
one about fetching a flag from Belgium, and *On Approval*,
based on Lonsdale's play of that name. 'I feel pretty undecided.
I think they have had more than enough films about occupied
territory but I don't feel any urge whatever to go so far to
the other extreme as to be in a very old Lonsdale film.' She
was more taken with an offer from Binkie – who must have
got over his rage with her – to take over from Vivien Leigh,
who needed a rest, in *The Doctor's Dilemma* at the Haymarket.
('It would be fun to be in the theatre again for a second or
two.')

[6 August 1942] I have turned down the Jugoslav film and *On
Approval*, and that at least is a relief as they would have entailed
an awful lot of arranging to do and again dread conscience would
have socked me all the time. All the same I hope they ask me to
do some others that a) I like and b) fit in with things a bit better.
I enjoyed my day as a policeman quite a lot. We had to take
the police car into Oxford to have its speedometer tested. You have

no idea how pleasurable it is to drive somewhere that isn't just as far as Henley and back. One feels wicked and adventurous and really seeing life ... I think I shall like being a police lady, though I dare say it will pall more than a bit when I have as my companion Jeanne Stonor, who I hear alas is the other on duty with me ordinarily.

[13 August 1942] Yesterday I spent the day in the Henley Police Station answering the telephone and trying to fathom the mysterious way in which switchboards as well as God move. I think I have got the thing taped now and can say Henley Police and Hold the Line with exactly the right air of boredom and slight malice that all telephone girls affect ... Jeanne Stonor was there and snitched all the driving owing to having a uniform which I as yet do not own. Nothing very funny happened except, believe it or not, a harassed looking woman came in to say that she had lost some very important papers all about Nursing in Newfoundland and on being asked her name said, quite unaware of the fact that she was dropping (to me at any rate) a bombshell, Miss Florence Nightingale. People do lose the oddest things. I found in the Found book, 1 cwt of coal, one set of false teeth (upper), one pair ladies' stays (found in a field I am sorry to say), one part of an aeroplane (unspecified), a whole set of garments belonging to the Victorian era discovered under a tombstone in Henley churchyard (setting the entire Police Station in an uproar as they all tried them on) and five horses.

[16 August 1942] Well, the little monsters are home again and very nice it is to see them too. They all look most bronzed and fit and appear to have had a splendid time. Nichol greeted me with loud laughs which is his way of showing pleasure and endearingly flung his arms round my neck, a thing he hardly ever does. They went scampering round the house exclaiming as if they had been away for months, and were delighted to find some flowers had grown in their gardens.

Tomorrow I have to go to Denham to make a soundtrack of 6 words. It seems a long way to go for that. I am wondering if they will pay me £50 for it. I can hardly believe they will be so foolish but am quite prepared to accept it should they press it into my grasping fingers. I should think they must have nearly finished the great opus by now.

[22 August 1942] I have been to London to have my clothes fitted for *The Doctor's Dilemma* and they seem all right if nothing startling. I stayed up to see the play that night and thought it very good and well acted which is a change as I have seen very few plays, but what I have seen have been third or fifth rate in both acting and production. I think I shall rather enjoy playing it if I can ever learn it, which I doubt. It isn't a very good part, in fact it is a very dull one but it will be fun to be back in the theatre. Austin Trevor is in it and Frank Allenby and Peter Glenville and they are all good.

Did I tell you about the most enjoyable day I had at the Police Station last Wednesday? I have seldom had more fun, we had a Red Warning while I was on duty at the telephone and so I sounded the siren. I have seldom enjoyed anything so much. Instead of getting a sinking wobble inside at the sound of the thing, the fact that I was responsible for the noise made me feel as if I were God or Hitler and running the entire raid. Anyway I felt intensely important and passed the message on to the various places one has to in a suitably nonchalant but efficient voice, I think, copied it all into the telephone book and settled myself to await the next vital news. This consisted of two messages coming through at once, a thing I find very difficult to deal with, one to say that One Light Pump and crew had taken up action stations at Clark's Garage in Bell Street and the other, which I enjoyed very much, was from Stoke Row Police Station to ask if the cricket match was cancelled as it was raining with them ... That was a week ago and I don't seem to have had a calm moment to sit and write to you since. Rosalie came down for two or three nights and I have been making her hear me my words and there seems to be a great deal of washing of nameless veg to do and I have had to go to London to fit my clothes and what with one thing and another I have been dizzy with bits and pieces.

I had lunch with Ian and David Eccles in London yesterday. Ian was in very good form indeed and most nice and friendly. He disclosed half-way through lunch that he had been at Dieppe and told me lots of queer and frightening things about it. He said that when all hell broke lose and everything was whizzing round everywhere he began to think Is my journey really necessary? (I forget if that depressing slogan was stuck up on all booking offices when you left but it is now.) Don't mention to Mama that he was there as he doesn't want her to know and there is no point in her knowing after all. He told me a good bit about one of the Oerlikon crews. Most of them were shouting madly at dive bombers and things but one who I suppose had done his job for the time being was sitting just behind utterly engrossed in a paper cover called *A Fortnight's Folly*. It must have been hair-raising and awful and wonderful and as fearful as anything could be. Even Ian who in Fleming fashion understates nicely seemed not exactly staggered but as if he had had his breath taken away once or twice. To me it sounded like blank stupefying chaos. I don't really see how chaps do the things they do and then appear quite sane and ordinary afterwards.

Peter, in Delhi, found Celia's letters vivid and often moving. He tried to send her encouragement, and to give advice when needed, but it took letters so long to travel from India to England that, by the time they arrived, events had generally moved on. He described to her her life as he saw it:

Running a creche, drinking port out of her slipper, wrestling a living from the soil, averting mutiny in the ATS, unravelling nameless crimes in high-powered cars, winning the King's Cup at Bisley, rallying the nation with a well-timed broadcast from *Clarissa Harlowe*, keeping down the weasels, and altogether being the very sprocket-piston of Old England at War!

16

This Happy Breed

Peter, although unable to say exactly what he was up to, wrote frequently and often amusingly; his letters were eagerly awaited in the house. When he had reached Delhi early in 1942, he had written, 'I feel I am doing more good this time, though most of it is rather (to coin a phrase) a Bow at a Venture.' He set up an office: 'I have just got a very efficient secretary called Miss Noad or Noade or Node or possibly Knowed. She is said to have a Temper but seems mild enough.' After a while the office grew:

Having been single-handed and not had a day off since I got here, my pathetic little branch is now what they call being put on a proper basis, with a full Colonel on top and a Naval officer and an RAF officer and all sorts of trimmings. This is a very good thing because poor Miss Noad and I, splendid though we are, are hardly a match for the combined Intelligence staffs of the Axis powers.

But gradually he became more and more frustrated by the sedentary nature of the job, the idleness and obtuseness of some of his superiors and the irritations of the bureaucracy. In a letter on 16 August 1942, he wrote about his office being moved:

We moved in this morning, by bullock cart, in pouring rain. We are now twice as far from the main building as we were before and that was far enough. This greatly increases the difficulty of getting anything done at all and involves endless sweating round corridors and waiting for people who want to see us but have always become immersed in something else by the time we get over there. The premises themselves you have often seen before in films of Devil's Island. Most of the windows are high up in the walls so that people cannot look in and see what we are doing. Some are at normal level and protected by flaccid-looking bars. You can't see anything out of them except another row of barred windows. The floor is uneven. There are no electric light bulbs. It is physically impossible for anyone to find out our telephone number and indeed it is only by the veriest fluke that we have been able to do so ourselves. In the course of the move many of the contents of our former office went astray and the only department which is really up to strength is the happy band of grigs (or whatever they are) that live in the drawers of our desks and come leaping merrily out whenever the drawers are opened and go and lay eggs behind the maps on the wall. Beyond providing a Link with the Past, however they are of little use to us. These hutments have been built in a most ingenious way so as to minimise the effects of blast, the verandahs being not so much verandahs as tunnels and light and air being very largely excluded. Something tells me that Miss Noad is going to resign and that, as the Bard would say, presently. Ah well.

Alongside the grigs in one of the drawers was a hand-grenade: 'It became attached to me in Burma and has followed me about ever since. I keep on meaning to get rid of it, as Miss Noad tends to use it to hammer nails into the wall and to the best of my knowledge it is primed ...' Peter would never be happy in an office.

However, the work in which he was involved – deception – in theory suited him well; it was to devise all sorts of inventive and cunning schemes to foil, deceive and confuse the enemy in the Far East. 'The whole point of the job is to be creative and destructive at the same time, both of which suit me.' He could not elaborate on it in his letters, but instead would refer to it as playing at Red Indians ('I'm afraid it was Red Indians again, but on an amusingly rarefied and cosmic scale'), or 'hide and seek in the shrubbery', or, if it involved something to do with a river, as 'put it in the Swimming Bath', in the style of Edwardian thrillers. He always enjoyed the trips out of Delhi to, say, Chungking or the Irawaddy to see to the various ruses: 'The only night I have felt really natural and contented was in Burma, sleeping in the dust of a bombed-out temple,' he wrote in August, and later, after a skirmish with the Japanese: 'It's extraordinary how I do enjoy myself when I get anywhere near the war.' Probably what he would have liked best would have been to have been a straightforward regimental officer involved in some action, but, as Duff Hart-Davis says in his biography, Peter was too individual, too clever. He longed to fit in, but he never would entirely.

In the autumn of 1942 he came home unexpectedly for a
month. He was in England not only for part of the pheasant
season but also for the first screening of *In Which We Serve*.
It was well received and immediately a success. Fifty years
on, owing probably to the combination of David Lean's direction and Noel Coward's script, and despite its dated jargon,
its well-intentioned jingoism and full-blown sentimentality,
it still works in its way, though Noel Coward himself looks
out of place. At the time, it cleverly hit just the right note;
the contrast between the ordinary home lives of the sailors'
wives hiding a constant anxiety and that of their husbands
overseas in some respects mirrored Celia's own. Anyone
involved in the film remembers how she did the ward-room
scene – in which she had to address other officers' wives about
the difficulty and the pride of having a ship as one's rival
in marriage – in one take. It was one of the two technical
feats of which she occasionally boasted (the other was that
of doing her own stunts at the age of seventy-one on the
Eiffel Tower in an indifferent American television film called
The Hostage Tower).

'We did have a lovely month,' Peter wrote to her when
he returned to Delhi at the end of October:

Try and find out when your film is coming out here; everyone wants
to know. Also tell me how it goes in USA. It's hard to know which
to be proudest of – the policewoman's truncheon, the chatelaine's
seccaturs, or the film star's ... well, whatever corresponds to a truncheon. I bet you didn't realise I knew the word seccaturs. Is that
how you spell it?

His work in Delhi however continued to be hamstrung by
bureaucracy and office administration.

We are having a very bad spell in GSI(d). The Colonel and the
Wing Commander sit around like a couple of effigies doing absolutely
nothing at all, I mean really literally nothing. This does not fail
to make the section look pretty silly from outside and thus further
queers our chances of getting the sensible chaps, let alone the oafs
and demi-oafs who abound, to take an interest in our abstruse and
unfamiliar racket. It isn't so hot inside our section either. The two
girls, who are loyal and hard-working and invaluable little creatures
[Miss Noad had left for Calcutta] resent the Colonel's idleness and

futility and will sooner or later drift off into some other section where the atmosphere is less Chekhovian ... Short of learning ventriloquism one has to do all the talking [at meetings] oneself (with frequent pseudo-obsequious asides, like 'As I think you decided the other day, Colonel') and thus gets the reputation of flat-catching, bumping and boring, talking out of turn and generally confirming the Indian Army's worst suspicions.

He welcomed the odd wild-fowling expedition to the jheels outside Delhi.

I had a splendid time, sleeping in the frost by a fire and swigging rum and reading Henry Wade ... and finishing up with a cracking meal of six tinned sausages and a whisky and soda at 10.30 on Sunday morning after being up since four and in the very cold water since half past five. I took an inordinate amount of exercise, sucking first one foot and then the other out of the rich but gelid mud and got 27 snipe, 5 duck and a curlew.

On another occasion: 'We shot duck last night and this morning and slept happily on the ground by a camp fire, full of rum and bully beef and coated with mud.' Wavell invited him to go shooting:

This involved getting up at 3.30 ... a 50 mile drive and wading about half a mile through deep mud in darkness. It was a failure as a flight but I shall always find that sort of thing tremendously exciting, the noise of so many and such various wings, the moment when you first see things like cannon balls against the pale colours in the East, very close to you but only visible at a certain angle, then the moment when they have suddenly grown wings and necks, then the first shot and the great roar like a huge breaker on a long bank of shingle as almost everything gets up, the different calls dominated by the throaty confidence of the geese, and later when the front is stabilised, the warmth of the sun, which has suddenly jerked up above the horizon as it does in a theatre, and in its light things identifying themselves – mountains turn out to be trees and trees mountains, from the village you now see the smoke but not the fires. By God we have run into some Fine Writing ...

As usual he punctured any show of feeling – this would always be the case.

The Chief enjoyed himself I think and killed 8 duck which was more than anyone else. He was awfully nice to me, at least I thought he was; but as neither of us ever speak more than about 6 embarrassed words to the other it is hard to tell for certain.

He went on a tiger-shooting expedition which he found interesting but not so much to his taste. He sent Celia a little bone from the tiger that they shot:

I have got the clavicles, which are spare bits of bone somewhere inside the shoulder about the size of two halves of a wishbone, and these I have been told I must have mounted into a brooch for you, so I will do so, only I'm not sure it's quite your style to go about with your *fichu* gathered at the throat with whole segments of a carnivore's skeleton. Still, it's what one must do, it seems, and they may by that time come in handy for the soup.

Celia and Tish meanwhile prepared for a wartime Christmas 1942:

Christmas Day started with Nichol waking at 0400 hours and wanting to look at his stocking. This was thwarted but he was pretty wakeful until allowed to open it at 0700. He then came dashing along to me and he was very sweet and thrilled at his presents. He sat on my bed pulling things out by one by one as he calls it. A paint box was almost the greatest success with a pencil sharpener a close second. Breakfast was enlivened by a delightful paper fairy made by Nora and Nurse with a lot of skill. She was most beautiful but had clearly got mumps ... Next in this breathtaking day was the Christmas tree with presents under it. Nichol did very well and had a most lovely aerodrome from Lady May which was I think the high spot ... Lunch went off well, with a turkey and the most sumptuous pudding made by Nora and a positive dream. We had threepenny bits in it and wonderful brandy butter made with whisky and maple sugar ...

After a long and absorbing day we got the children to bed at last and then we remembered that in a moment's unwonted expansiveness we had asked the Alexanders in for a drink and then felt sorry for the Nares and asked them too. [Owen Nares and his wife lived in a cottage nearby.] So in they all trooped and our hearts sank slightly at the thought of fairly boring chat for an hour at least. However so imbued were we all with the Christmas spirit that we all started telling stories about children and the mad cook who is an unfailing source of humour that we eventually rolled about helpless with giggles ... The mad cook was very funny on Christmas Day. Tish and I had given her a quid each and wrapped it up in a dingy bit of tissue paper and given it to her in a fairly shamefaced way. I went into the kitchen in the middle of the morning and asked brightly the way one does, How's the turkey? Well, Mrs Michael, I mean Mrs Peter, she said (she always calls me that and Tish the other way round), If the dinner's spoilt you've only yourself to blame. I was horrified and thought the worm had at last turned, and she had had enough. Why? I asked in a timorous tone. Oh, she said, Giving presents like that on Christmas Day, you've quite done for me. There's no work in me. With a good deal of relief I said, Oh, I'm afraid it was very dull. Dull, she said, I thought it was most interesting ... All she says is Isn't it funny Mrs Michael, I mean Mrs Peter.

Peter replied: 'I think you and Tish must have done wonders over Christmas and it is – quite truly – stirring and *émouvant* to read about so much cheerful and really not at all easy improvisation in this atmosphere of bloated, overstaffed but joyless ease.'

Celia's spirits dropped rapidly as 1943 began, mainly because she was not feeling well and had an outbreak of impetigo on her face. The petrol ration was now four and a half gallons every three months. Nichol's fourth birthday in January went well. 'The McCulloughs came in their pony trap and looked very sweet trotting away in the dark with candles winking in the lamps at the side and all the children wrapped to the ears singing "Oh dear, what can the matter be", whenever one of them went out.' Nichol was given a toy lorry which he was thrilled with.

'Isn't it lucky the war's over,' he had said ... it was because I had told him to take care of his cars and things as there weren't any more until after the war was over, as the stuff they were made of was needed to make tanks and guns and things. Having been given another lorry after I'd said there weren't any, he naturally assumed that the war must be over.

Tish paid Celia 3s. 2d. in winnings for a year's bezique. 'We have started again and am about 4d. up on this year but intend to improve.'

Imagine therefore her surprise when her agent, Aubrey Blackburn, rang up to say that the people making a film of *Dear Octopus* (a successful pre-war play by Dodie Smith) wanted Celia to play Cynthia and would offer her £2,000. She wrote to Peter on 5 January 1943:

Isn't it simply frightful and shaming and appalling? I don't know how they have the face to suggest such sums but it makes it very difficult to refuse. In fact to my shame be it said I have accepted and am consequently in a good deal of confusion what with the police and Nora's day out and *War and Peace* and *everything*. Aubrey rang me last night to tell me about this dreadful offer and I have been cogitating and racking old brains since. It seems pretty good madness to refuse all that mon. which even when halved, if put into War Loan and left severely alone will pay for a good whack of Nichol's education. On the other hand it seems so disgraceful to get so much money for doing practically nothing when chaps are fighting for 2s. a day that I can hardly bear the idea ... I wish you could have seen the sought after film star talking to her agent on the telephone. No one would have thought that that was what she was. A serious blemish on her face, chilblains on her fingers, a pair of very dilapidated shoes and darned stockings on her shapely legs, and her hair tied up in an old scarf as I was in the middle of dusting the drawing-room when Aubrey telephoned. Tish and I got the giggles at the idea of glamorous film star after this.

She had already agreed to read *War and Peace* on the wireless; she was to be Natasha in a radio dramatisation of the novel. It was thought to be an apposite moment to attempt this ambitious task, as parallels were drawn between the campaign of 1812, and the German invasion of Russia in 1942. 'Apart from all other reasons,' wrote Val Gielgud, director of drama at the BBC in a letter to *The Times*, 'we feel that listeners will welcome the production as in some sort a gesture of appreciation to our ally's magnificent military achievement.'

Noel Coward was also pressing her to act in his next film, *This Happy Breed*, the saga of an ordinary working-class family in Clapham from 1918 to 1939, from one war to the next. Peter had sent his advice:

I am most awfully impressed by the spate of film offers. I never saw *Dear Octopus* ... and the nearest I got to the Coward play was hearing a very good description of the first-night broadcast in the Empire service while marooned in the Ikoyi resthouse at Lagos – I thought it was just the sort of thing they ought to put in those broadcasts because it gave chaps the feeling of being in the swim at home, which is what they like. I should do it if you possibly can. Old Crusty's view is that you are a very good and highly skilled actress and can play anything within reason, which this is. I believe in a way it's a help not being an actress (or an actor) all the time because the ones that are – and this applies very much to proper theatricals appearing in British films – tend to label themselves the moment they open their mouths. They may be jolly good but there's no question about what they are up to. When I say 'very good' (above) it is the old habit of understatement bursting out because I know and always have known that you are easily the best actress there is, whether reading Poe – like an eager stoat with earrings – in Rotherfield Greys village hall or prancing about dolled up to the eyes in any of the West End pieces I have without too much difficulty sat through. There may be a better one somewhere but I haven't caught her at it.

It was an opinion, expressed most typically, that he never had reason to change.

Celia did them all. She read *War and Peace*, during the broadcast of which they had an air raid,

but it finished about half way through the broadcast and I went back to the hotel thinking all was peaceful. But no. At about 5 in the morning the sirens went again and the most almighty din started. The guns in Hyde Park were booming and barking and there were a lot of new noises that I have never heard before. It was most frightening and I am ashamed to report that my knees actually shook ... I decided to keep very quiet about having been frightened to people who had been in the Blitz, as I hadn't heard any bombs fall, and thought it very chicken-livered to be frightened of what some old lady called 'our dear good guns'.

She did eleven days' work for *Dear Octopus*, complaining the while ('Never again will I do a film unless I am absolutely *mad* about the part'); and after much cajoling by Noel Coward she took on the part of the Cockney Ethel Gibbons in *This Happy Breed*. She had to do a test for it first, which she wrote to Peter about on 14 February 1942:

Did I tell you that it is all in Glorious Technicolor? They give one the most peculiar makeup. All very pale so that one looks like a ghost all wan and rather blue. I felt it only needed a touch of

phosphorescence and I could haunt with any old ghoul. It all takes
ages too. Goodness knows that filming is slow enough at the best
of times but this is far worse. All the lights have to be arc lamps
as ordinary ones give a yellow light and the camera picks up the
colour. It is the most gigantic camera and takes twenty minutes
to reload. So you can see that things go anything but rapidly.

Let me tell you [she wrote to Peter a week later] that Mr Noel
Coward thinks I am the greatest actress ever, or jolly near it. I
had a session with him the other night. I will tell you all about
it. On Sunday afternoon when I was walking over to the farm to
invite Rupert and Comfort and Diana to tea, Noel rang up and
asked to speak to me. Tish said I was out and he said he would
ring later. Which he did and started raving to me about the tests
which he had just seen. The upshot was that I said I would come
up that night and see him as it was impossible to talk properly
on the telephone. So I went up with Rupert on the late train from
Henley which was bitingly cold and entailed a long wait on Twyford
platform and then standing all the way to London in a very crowded
train, and I couldn't find a taxi at Paddington so I had to carry
my by this time extremely heavy suitcase in the packed tube to
Trafalgar Square and then walk along the Strand as far as the Savoy.
There I found Noel and Gladys Calthrop who proceeded to tell
me that they had seen the tests that afternoon and thought they
were staggering, stupendous, colossal and that I am the only actress
in the world with the possible exception of Helen Hayes. Noel is
mad for me to do the film. I don't know what to do. He had talked
to David [Lean] and Ronnie Neame who said that I didn't particularly
want to do the film and so he had said there was no point in pressing
me if that was how I felt and then he'd seen the tests and according
to him had been knocked all of a heap by my brilliance. All this
sounds a thought conceited but I am just repeating what he said
and this is only the half of it, but I have no one really here to
tell about it and it was very pleasant to be so fulsomely praised.
So please forgive this back-slapping ... I said in the intervals of
blushing hotly ... that my home life unlike that of our dear Queen
was complicated and that I didn't really see how I could leave Moley
for about 10 weeks to stew in its own juice having already been
away for some time doing this present silly film. All of which he
schwep aside and said that my great gift (Oh Yeah) should come
first and so on and so forth. I am now in a torment of indecision.
I can't really straighten it out with my conscience and convince
myself that there is any sort of contribution to the war effort by

my knocking the world sideways as a Cockney mother of three (always providing that I did, which I doubt) ...

While trying to make up her mind, she had set off with Nichol for a weekend with her parents: 'I am taking so many things over to Mummy, what with a rabbit and camelias and our lunch for the train and rations for the days we are there and books to keep Nichol amused and the film script to make up my mind over, and some *New Yorker*s for Daddy that I shall need a cabin trunk at least.'

Peter wrote back:

31 January 1943 Don't worry about anything. I know how bloody difficult things are, but if it is anything to do with the theatre or films I should make a snap decision on womanly intuish. and stick to it and if it is anything to do with the Estate or the house I should either do that or make an interim arrangement and refer it to me or to Richard [Fleming]. Don't worry about making wrong decisions. There is nothing you can make a wrong decision about (except Nicholas – e.g. putting him down for Harrow) which really matters to anyone or if it does can't be remedied if wrong. You've got excellent judgement, at least I think you have, in all what you might call human matters; all you want to do is to have a bit of confidence in it and stop *saying* to yourself and other people 'I'm no good at this sort of thing'; because it isn't true ... We're very alike in some ways and I know how it is ... The great thing is for us all to be alive and to have enough to eat and a chance of doing some mischief to the other side.

In Which We Serve, meanwhile, had reached India and Peter went to see it again:

I took an enormous party, consisting of the entire Wavell family, less Archie John and the daughter in Cairo, the GOC in C Eastern Army, the GOC in C West Africa, Freya Stark, Ralph Edwardes, and a Major Mumblemumble-mumble who was staying at the Chief's house. The Chief said he thought you were very clever; he doesn't use many epithets and he can have had few previous occasions to use that one in India ... The ADCs appeared to be bowled over. I have heard of one or two people who thought it was all rather too sad and it is indeed all rather too near the war to give undiluted pleasure in Delhi; but I think it has done as much good here as anything short of a series of sustained attacks from the air (or, far

more unthinkable, half a dozen dismissals) could do ... I think that
you can take it that the first phase of your Conquest of Asia is
complete.

A few days later he wrote: 'More and more people keep telling
me with tears in their eyes how good you were in the film
and how it has made them think differently about the war.'

With trepidation, Celia had started working on *This Happy
Breed*. Accents were not her strong point and she never felt
very comfortable in the part, and, according to David Lean,
would tear up her script when she had finished a scene. On
22 April 1943, she wrote:

You asked me to tell you about the other people in the film. Well,
Robert Newton is playing my husband, he is nice and very good
and has the best part in the picture, the part Noel plays in the
play. Then our children are played by Kay Walsh (in *In Which
We Serve*), Eileen Erskine, whom I don't know and haven't so far
met and a rather spotty young man called John Blythe is my son.
Alison Leggatt plays the sister-in-law who is maddening anaemic
to start with and Christian Science to finish up with, the part I
mean, actually she is charming and an excellent actress. Johnnie
Mills is in it as the son of the man next door, who is played by
Stanley Holloway, a cheerful and full of stories man whom I've
always admired, then my mother is played brilliantly by Amy Veness
and that is about the lot. It's a nice cast and I like David Lean
more and more. He is not only extremely efficient but very nice
and thinks I am good which is always endearing. It will be most
well acted by everyone and I am not fishing when I say that I think
I am the weak spot. It is such a totally different part from anything
I have ever tried before and I cannot think that I *look* right. To
me I don't look like a real person and that is so important on the
movies. Still Noel saw the first stuff we had done and seemed pleased
with it all.

Celia was struck again by the unreal life at Denham Studios.
On 8 April 1943 she wrote:

This really is the most extraordinary place. No one appears to take
the *faintest* interest in the war. Literally not the faintest, though
now and again they are annoyed because they can't get 500 horses
without going to Ireland for them. So they are going to Ireland.
They are going to do *Henry V* with Larry as the King and to get

enough men and horses for the battle scenes they are all going to Ireland.

Her film took about ten months to make and cost about £200,000. It had not in fact had an entirely easy passage. The play had ended with the character played by Robert Newton addressing a patriotic sermon to a baby ('Life isn't all jam for anybody ... We know what we belong to, where we come from and where we are going. We may not know it with our brains, but we know it with our roots'), and David Lean had some difficulty persuading Noel Coward that a jingoistic monologue to a baby simply would not work on the screen. Robert Newton, though excellent, was inclined to drink. One incident was reported by Celia, on 5 July 1943:

On Sat. night Noel gave a party at the Haymarket to which everyone was invited. I didn't go, wanting to go home and see Nichol and let Nora out and I think on the whole it's as well I didn't. Getting to the studio today I asked how they'd all enjoyed it and everyone said 'Oh v. much' rather vaguely, and then Bob Newton appeared at lunch with a terrific gash on his cheek (this necessitating shooting him from only one side and then in the dark) and I, still the little innocent, thought vaguely – oh, he's been on the booze and fallen over – and said lightly How did you enjoy the party – did you go? He said unblushingly Oh I just looked in – which turned out to be the understatement of all time – it seems he went and got stinking and while Noel was singing one of his songs he stood up – took off his coat and shirt and fairly let fly. Ronnie Neame and Tony and William got him out and he was last seen almost naked being hustled down the Haymarket by the police and spent Sunday day and night in the cells. He had only just got out after being charged and fined and had come hotfoot from there to the studio just in time to shoot this afternoon. They managed to get the charge of nakedness shelved and he only got fined for being drunk and disorderly, and we trust and pray it will not get into the papers. Ronnie and David hadn't told me to show him they were not telling tales so I of course jumped in with both feet. Tomorrow I am lunching with Joyce Grenfell who was at the party and shall hear the rest. He is an idiot.

They had had some trouble doing the last shots in July, as the sun refused to shine, and the final scenes were delayed.

Celia had hoped to accompany Tish and the children to Cornwall for a seaside holiday in August, but instead saw them off from Paddington on the Cornish Riviera.

By the saddest of mischance everybody else in the world had decided to travel on that train. It was an indescribable scene. No porter would carry anything – if they knew that was the train one was making for they simply gave hollow laughs, pocketed kindly 2 or 3 half crowns, said they would be back in a minute and were never seen again ... the final result was that we were some of the thousands one keeps seeing pictures of who were left behind. We fought our way out of the mob, went into the GW Hotel and reviewed the situation. There was another train at 1.30 so we planned a sort of commando attack on that and after standing on the platform for one hour, we did, by biting, kicking and shoving, get into the carriage where we got 3 seats for 3 grown-ups and 5 children, and so I left them.

Yesterday I was also engulfed in crowds [she wrote]. We did the scene in Hyde Park and the entire population of London tried their best to get in front of the camera. Bobby Newton and I had to stroll along together he saying 'This is the first time you and I have been out alone together for years' – every time he said 'alone' the crowd bellowed and whistled and by the time we reached the camera we had a mob several thousand strong pushing and giggling and peering out from behind us to try and get their silly faces in the picture. I can't think the shot will be any good but it's done and that's all I really care about ... I am longing to get down to the sea and wallow.

However, the last day of filming was a little tricky, 'as R. Newton had slipped a bit and we were all a little nervous particularly as the shot was at a church door in Clapham. It would hardly have been the place for a strip tease performance. He started rather aggressive but finished giggly.' The filming came to an end and with a sigh of relief she, too, left for Cornwall.

17

Thanksgiving at the Albert Hall

Celia then joined Tish and all the children at the Atlantic House Hotel in New Polzeath on the north coast of Cornwall. The Atlantic House, a modest hotel in the middle of a short row of Victorian terraced houses, stood on the cliff above a huge surfing beach. Celia, on arrival, found it cold and rugged with a strong north wind blowing. It continued cold and wild for the rest of August, but Celia, within days, was enjoying herself. She got the hang of surfing in the icy Atlantic rollers ('You have no idea what fearful fun surfing is'), – she walked along the cliffs; she visited Padstow on the other side of the Camel estuary, and was entranced by the little seaside church of St Enodoc, which had once been buried in sand dunes and had earned the name of Sinkininny. Her spirits, which had not been high that year, recovered, and she conceived for that little bit of North Cornwall a passion that never faded.

Although they were not entirely safe from danger there – Tish remembers running with the children from the beach when an aeroplane with a swastika on its side flew low over them – it was a tonic for them all.

We go off the day after tomorrow [Celia wrote on 31 August 1943] and already the first sandy remnants have been squidged into trunks and sent off luggage in advance. Already the children unmournfully and unsentimentally say 'the last but one bathe', or 'the last but two elevenses'. We hear dread reports from them who are gone before that the journey back is little if anything better than it was down . . . Oh, dear, back to dread grindstone. Not that I can possibly begin to complain and am really not. There can be very few people who in this year of grace can have had the luck to spend 4 carefree weeks at the sea. I am a lucky pig and well I know it. Pause for listening to Winston's speech from Quebec which unfortunately was not spoken by himself on account of atmospheric conditions but read instead by Mr Snagge (wonder if you were listening too) and missed a lot by this. I like to hear the old boy roll out his words smacking his lips over words like mighty combat and such like. The

Russians seem to be doing wonders. Old steamroller is fairly hurtling over the barren steppes. I suppose their losses must be fearsome but so must the enemy's ... I sent you a few cuttings about *Dear Octopus*. I seem to have come out of it rather well, God knows why. Aubrey sent me a letter saying he had been to the trade show and was sorry to say we had been rooked as my perf. was worth far more than a paltry 2000 quids. I shall try and go and see it some time though I know it's not at all my c. of t. as a piksh.

The grindstone was as before; policing, shooting rabbits, dealing with squabbling estate tenants or the cantankerous gamekeeper Brown, trying to protect the woodlands, to hang on to Nora and to keep all the children happy.

Did I tell you about Nichol and David playing Ludo. They are mad on the game and very funny playing it. They get wildly excited and their counters are always tanks or lorries or jeeps and when Tish and I play, there is great and rather sweet partisanship. Nichol yells, 'Quick, Mummy, run', if there is danger of my getting sent home ... They never think of cheating (they doubtless will soon) and they get so thrilled they go pink with pleasure if they throw a six.

The mad cook was away so cooking had to be done and Celia continued to be anxious about it.

[1 October 1942] Cookery still rages, in fact I now dream about it. This is beyond a joke. It is bad enough pondering all day and weaving about the kitchen in a haze of indecision with countless cookery books on the table, but when I start dreaming I am taking the lids off pots and wondering what to do with the contents, it begins to get me down ... We had such a nasty pudding that we had to grate it and even then it wouldn't crumble up to be cooked so then we put it through the mincing machine and it stuck that up so then we gave it to Monty [the dog] and had rice pud instead. I also made some spaghetti which tasted of absolutely nothing at all and that took me the entire morning. Monty is most frightfully useful, if one has a failure he eats it up in a flash and no one is any the wiser ... Next day. This letter goes on and on and nothing happens in it, like one of those dreary novels silly women are always writing. I had a lovely letter from you today, it made me laugh 'ha ha' about the rats in Kunming. Of course I remember you winging off from the airfield there and wish I could now stand on some nearer airfield and see you winging your way towards me ... Today, except for your delicious letter, has been a fairly boring one. I cooked like mad this morning and produced a well-nigh uneatable meal. If the children were not so exceedingly well trained they would have struck. As it was they asked for second helpings and had to be prevented from having them as it was so indigestible and nasty. It had taken me all the morning and really even Tish who tried to be polite could not do anything but agree that it was the nastiest meal she had ever had.

Cookery she felt was rather like her bank account: you did things to it, you tossed things in but fundamentally it had a life of its own.

You have no idea how terrifying cooking can be. I made a white sauce to put on the wodge [of tinned salmon] and it turned into sticky dumplings before my astonished and horrified eyes. A very surprising thing is porridge which obeys no laws at all. I have made it three times now and each time, though I have done exactly the same thing, the result has been totally different. No one can say that luck or God or totemism or something doesn't come into it because it just must.

While she was making a name for herself on the screen as the epitome of the English housewife, it was in reality not her natural metier. Her inadequacy, as she saw it, in that role always made her feel guilty. 'I am not much catch as a helpmeet,' she would write to Peter.

As the year wore on, she went to London to look for a few Christmas presents:

There wasn't a thing in the way of toys but I managed to spend a lot of money on books for the children, and was maddened to hear on the wireless the next morning that after all they are going to release some proper toys in December ... then I went to a film show arranged by Donald [McCullough] for the Duke and Duchess of Norfolk at the Ministry of Information. There were two films, one called something like *The Rise of Nazi Power* ... and the other *The Battle of Britain*, made from cuttings of our and captured German films of that time ... They were both excellent and should be shown everywhere at once. Even if they had not been good films, everyone would have enjoyed the party no end as we had tea and lots of delicious chocolate biscuits. No one made the slightest pretence of doing anything but lamming into them; it was quite funny to see well-dressed ladies in fur coats and Air Vice-Marshals and Cabinet Ministers tucking into the goodies in a less well-behaved way than our children.

Just before Christmas she received a fan letter from a tank driver:

He says he is going to call his new tank after me when he gets one, as he says it is unlucky to change the name of his old one and is looking forward to fighting his way forward in a tank called Celia. I have seldom been more delighted with any letter. It was most awfully funny. I suspect though that he writes similar ones to all film stars and that his tank at the moment is called Greer.

The next year, 1944, was generally a very local one for the household at Merrimoles. Celia continued to enjoy being a policewoman; she adored driving – and occasionally had to meet people, such as Churchill's scientific adviser, Professor Lindemann, off the train at Henley and drive them to the secret headquarters of RAF Reconnaissance at Medmenham. There were one or two drawbacks to the work, as she wrote in January 1944:

Yesterday, I policed and fear that there is a nasty affair blowing up in the shape of a request from the Superintendent for me to entertain the specials and the regulars at their dinner which they are having shortly. I can't think of any way of getting out of this without looking snooty; they will never understand that it is the sort of thing I am utterly hopeless at, and I am awfully afraid I shall have to promise to do something and then I shall go quite mad trying to think of what to do. Oh dear, dread notoriety can get one into a terrible predicament. Talking of this I am going to read Gray's Elegy on the radio on the 30th Jan. before the 9 o'clock news.

There were also advantages:

Pause for – what do you think [she wrote in a letter to Peter] – eating an *orange*. I was given one the other day by one of the police and Tish and I have just shared it ... We had such an argument as to the best way of eating it, that we had to toss up and I won so we ate it in pigs and now the drawing-room has a lovely old-fashioned smell like the gallery of a theatre.

In February she wrote:

We had a funny time last Friday when I was on duty at the police station. There had been a raid the night before and a message came in from one of the specials that there was a canister of some size in a field and would we send for it and see what it was. So I drove Sgt Bott over to the field and he peered at it and finally hoisted it on his shoulder and brought it back to the car, saying that it was a flare. In the afternoon I was told to take it in to HGs at Oxford and duly did so with it bouncing in the back of the car. I was not in the least perturbed by having it there as I have (or had) complete faith in Sgt Bott and felt he knew his stuff. I took it in to HQS where they received it quite calmly and that was that. The point of the story is that, in the evening at the lecture, Sgt George said at the end that as the enemy had started what is known as Activity again, it would be just as well to brush up on our instructions in case of bombings and not to forget that one of the latest orders was that in all cases of unexploded flares they were to be treated as unexploded bombs and roped off and so on ... I intend to make a much better story of it in the future and shall end up by saying I drove a 500 pounder that ticked all the time from Ghent to Aix.

Tish and Celia made camouflage nets in the village:

It is a beastly job. You have to wind bits of scrim through in an exact and complicated pattern, and it's far more difficult than one would think. Typically I worked most hard, achieved very little and at the end Yvette and I, feeling we'd done a bit to win the war, goodly struggled with the black-out shutters, tidied all up, and I, saying scathingly of the other woman who had been working there too, she is the most half-witted woman I have ever met, slammed the door and shut the keys inside. So no more netting can be made for several days. Wasn't it awful? I had to go and confess to Nancy Jackson and have most successfully sabotaged all village projects for some time. I am a fool and so very well intentioned.

Celia and Tish were delighted to be asked to an Air Force party. 'We feel as thrilled as if we were débutantes going to the Queen Charlotte's Ball.' When they got there

We could hardly believe our eyes at the sight of so many lovely MEN. There is something very touching about them, they all look a mixture of very young and yet most old. There was a young Wing Commander who was in our party; he was 26 but in the dark looked about 16 and in the light about 46. He writes music, we asked him what sort and he said either a symphony or else songs simply dripping with love. We drank beer and danced and stared with open mouths at the chaps covered with DFCs and DSOs, and were mightily impressed.

A sweepstake was organised among everybody in the house as to when the invasion, which was expected, would take place. 'I can't help feeling,' she wrote in March, 'that this invasion thing must be blowing up quite soon. Our bombing is getting undoubtedly fierce and there is an air of stern endeavour about, also a great many troops.' But time wore on, and the children lost interest in the sweepstake. However, with the increased activity and in spite of the buzz bombs that were hitting England, the end of the war could be envisaged. Celia and Peter occasionally mused on what they would do after it was over. In a letter on 29 August 1943, Peter wondered whether he would write:

I have been reading some Maugham short stories, including the splendid one about the man who reads his *Times* every day in the right order in the heart of Borneo, and for a moment I was smitten with the desire to write again. I expect it will go on recurring but I don't think I shall ever write anything good and I rather doubt I shall try to. I haven't got the right sort of self-discipline and I can't take m'work sufficiently seriously and after 15 years of dodging about from one thing to another – plus, now, a lot of other interests and not enough economic incentive – I can't see us working up from *Love's Labour's Lost* to *King Lear*, or even from *Psmith* to *Jeeves*. Never mind. I shall always rather enjoy using unexpected words and inventing preposterous situations, in however second-rate or catchpenny a cause ... The only other thing is that in my poor fumbling way, and with unaccustomed fingers, I am getting rather good at *The Times* crosser and quite often finish it, half at breakfast and half in the lunch hour, and thus Britain marches on to victory.

Celia had replied:

Darling, I am delighted that you should have a hankering to write again. Do bear it in mind and jot down a little morceau now and again or ponder on a few plots ... and don't go thinking that economic necessity won't arise, you should see the bills for the new chair covers and then there's always the billiard-room, to say nothing of the marble swimming-pool, squash court and tennis lawn ... It will take several of your bellest lettres to cover the few little improvements I have in mind. But joking apart, do write if you possibly can ...

This referred to Peter's growing fantasy, as usual rooted in Edwardiana, of his future as a reclusive landowner at Merrimoles, now to his mind clad in creeper and boasting a billiard-room and a swimming-pool. He joked, he mocked, but in due course the billiard-table arrived, a swimming-pool was dug.

Celia herself expressed doubt about her own profession. 'After the war, I am never going to act any more but just be at your beck and call and be a gorgeous chatelaine with gracious mien and clanking keys and a .22.' Her declaration was less convincing, and stated in a moment of exasperation. But, strangely, both were now in their late thirties, and each had an exceptional gift, which in each case had been recognised and acclaimed, yet Peter, though enjoying the use of words, did not believe in himself as a writer and Celia, though confident when actually acting, still did not see herself completely as an actress. That is why Peter wrote after he had received some rather depressed letters:

What you must allow for is being by profession and circumstance an individualist with high standards, which always tend to create gloom and despondency from time to time. All good actors are individualists, and on top of that you have fallen in with old Crusty, a Lone-Hand-cum-Spoilt-Child if ever there was one. The net result is that in idle or unsatisfactory moments you get a strong wish to be other than you are, to be doing an 'honest' routine job under somebody else's orders, to be quit of uncertainty and the need to take decisions to which you can't find a guide in the Answers at the back of the book ... You really do get, as you said in your letter, white mice waltzing round in your head and you feel completely lost and desperate. Being more fatalistic and animal-like, I've probably never had it as badly as you, but I know the form. [11 April 1944]

Uncertainty about the future was not peculiar to them; the war had changed people and their circumstances, and in some cases had revealed new aspects or talents; few people knew quite what the future would hold. Peter wrote:

I've learnt a lot in the last 5 years (it's *astonishing* how little I knew before: the life of an individualist is very unenlightening in some ways) and it's been most interesting and I suppose that on the whole I've thoroughly enjoyed it all. Not that I shan't be simply *delighted* when it's all over.

For the time being he had acquired a horse, Red Queen, 'a great success so far', and a young dog, Blondie, both of whom gave him great pleasure. He described Blondie's effect on his office:

There are now twelve men and two girls working in our two very small rooms and if there is another dog there the sort of non-stop *haute-école* boxing match which is Blondie's idea of how to behave indoors doesn't increase efficiency ... Blondie's attitude to life on the staff is very much the same as his master's and I don't think I shall take him again until he is a bit older. It isn't so much that he eats Most Secret papers when no one is looking – not a mere telegram here and there – but the best part of a file – but he has got, not alas from his master, the idea that whenever you see a lady you should leap on her, and the shrill screams of the Anglo-Indian beauties in khaki who perambulate, dusky, languorous, and always going to the lavatory in pairs, the corridors of GHQ, pursued me wherever I went. A little friend of all the world, he is particularly keen on bouncing through any open door he sees and first licking, and then gently but firmly biting the nerveless hands of Indian Army Brigadiers ... During this phase I am whistling like mad in the corridor, which passers-by find odd, and Blondie is doing a sort of fan-dance with the plans of the Fortifications of the Khyber Pass.

Celia did little professionally in 1944, apart from radio. She read Gray's 'Elegy' on the wireless – 'It was odd I was so nervous that I shook all over when waiting for it to begin, and yet I'm never in the least nervous when broadcasting.' Although friends had said they were moved by it, it attracted one of her rare bad reviews – 'insensitive reading of a beautiful poem ... I could hardly have been more damned'. She also read *Sense and Sensibility*; at the police station, one of the policemen said 'that he was sorry to have missed my broadcast, and asked what it was. When told *Sense and Sensibility* he said, "Oh, a propaganda thing." They all listen like mad which is really rather endearing of them.' She did the first of several

'How to ...' programmes devised and produced by Stephen Potter.

In March 1944, she was one of the judges at the RADA public show, with Lord Cromer, Binkie Beaumont, and the Lunts. 'It was quite fun to do and very impossible to judge. There was a generally fairly high level but no one was outstanding and that made the awarding of a Gold Medal most difficult.' (They gave it to Patricia Lawrence.) She had lunch with Binkie and John Gielgud.

They want me to play Ophelia when John does *Hamlet*, which he is hoping to do fairly soon. They are hoping to do it for half the week with *Love for Love* the rest of the week so as to make it possible for people like me who can't do a full week's work to play in some of them. They are also possibly going to revive *The Importance* and certainly going to do the *Dream* at Christmas. John suggested that I should play Helena in that but I would rather play Titania only I suppose I am too old really. I think it might be possible to do one of these things but you never know.

It wasn't – for the household at Merrimoles was about to swell to fifteen. Pam and her three children, Charles, Henrietta and John, were on one of the first boats to come back from India through the Mediterranean. They arrived at the beginning of April with measles, much luggage and no home. Celia had searched Nettlebed and around for a house for them, to no avail. So they squeezed into Merrimoles – Celia, her widowed sister Pam, her widowed sister-in-law Tish, seven children under eight, two nannies, a housemaid and, luckily, a cook. (The mad cook had given way to another cook who had squandered all the rations, who in turn gave way to an efficient Mrs Burns who saw them through the influx.) The little Vintcents soon settled in, and, being the same age as the little Flemings, had a wonderful time.

Well, my darling, here we are, thousands of us, all different ages and sizes all over the house. So far, thank goodness, it all seems to have worked out very well. I don't know how long it will last in this amiable atmosphere or how soon we shall all start back-biting and snapping and the children biting and hitting. They, the children, have paired off wonderfully well. Charles and Valentine rush about together setting rabbit traps to catch rabbits in and planning books they are going to write about their adventures called 'We met our cousins' cousins.' Henrietta has been rather the odd man out, but that is because Christopher has been away for the weekend, I think he and she will be the pair now that he is back. John and Nichol are buddies and discuss their books a good deal as they like the same sort of literature. A great mass of cooking has taken place without stopping. I know there will come a moment when there is nothing at all for lunch and then I shall burst into tears and sob and sob.

A few days later she wrote:

There are so many people about all the time that one never gets anything done on account of answering questions, preventing rows, and going to see something funny that has happened. So far, all is very well and I for one am enjoying the maze of children that like an infestation or infiltration swarm over the house.

(The McCullough children and others, seeing that Merrimoles was where all the fun was going on, would come and join in too.) Pam, who had arrived in England nervous and dejected, began to recover her spirits. It was still hard for them all with heavy rationing and little mobility.

But it was a beautiful spring – 'even the old clubman Ian was moved to tears (almost) by the prettiness of it all' (he had come to visit). Peter came home on leave briefly in June. With much talk of invasion, for reasons of conscience Tish cancelled their rooms in Polzeath that summer. Peter's brother Richard was slightly wounded with some shrapnel in his leg. Relations with Peter's mother were good and she would occasionally take Nichol to the pantomine or have him to stay. 'She is frightfully good with children,' Celia observed.

In May *This Happy Breed* was released, and was on the whole very well received. In the *Observer*, C.A.Lejeune compared it with the taste and art and honesty of French films. She also compared it with Coward's first film, *In Which We Serve*:

It hasn't the common, emotional surge of the naval picture; it hasn't the glow of service pride; it hasn't the high moments the watcher himself half-created from the hints of emergency still fresh in his own memory. It is a deliberate study of the lives of an ordinary suburban family in the flat years between the two wars, and the trouble with any honest study of ordinary people is that ordinarily it tends to seem a little ordinary. The special talent of *This Happy Breed* is so quiet that it hardly becomes manifest. It appears to record drab, physical facts from the outside, while actually indicating a mute spiritual experience from within.

Another critic punned, with apologies to Mr Coward: 'This bitter sweet family album of the private lives of people with no design for living is too much a conversation piece to make a perfectly satisfactory film, amusing and moving though it is.' 'Historically superficial, it is emotionally superb,' wrote another.

Celia did not care for her performance, or, more accurately, her appearance. 'I look so awful that even Ginny [Thesiger] who came with me to hold my hand, couldn't say anything but that I was meant to look very drab and certainly succeeded. Most of the time I don't appear to have any teeth ...' She may not have 'knocked the world sideways as a Cockney mother of three', as she had written before the film, but she certainly extracted glowing notices from the critics; all singled her performance out. C.A.Lejeune wrote:

The acting is good to serviceable apart from some rather fugitive Cockney accents but there is one magnificent performance. Celia Johnson plays the wife, the drably named Ethel Gibbons. She plays her in drab silk blouses, drab skirts, drab hair, and sometimes a positively fierce Technicolor makeup. Often she looks awful, but by thunder! as an actress she's superb. The wife with diplomatic relations to preserve between husband and family; the mother of a son, lost in thoughts of her lost son; the mother of a daughter, harshly tender with the daughter; the grandmother, ardent but a little tired, heavily applying herself to the cares of a younger woman; there are not many actresses of Miss Johnson's age who could even begin to rough out this manifold personality. And yet she does, in a quiet sketch that will touch many people in a large, loose way, and move not a few personally and poignantly. This is beautiful acting; the sort of acting that the French have been taught to understand; confessional acting from the inside outwards.

These effusive words drove Celia, unusually, to write to Caroline Lejeune to thank her and also to remonstrate. 'As Ethel Gibbons would say: "Don't talk so soft."' She got this reply:

Dear Miss Johnson

I've been trying to find time to write this line for a fortnight. I nearly sat straight down and wrote to you after the press show of *This Happy Breed*. Then I thought you'd think it 'soft'. But your letter fixes it. Don't fool yourself. You are that good. You'd have found you were even better if the sub-editor hadn't been so heavy on my copy. Maybe I'm extra sensitive just now, because my own boy is rising sixteen and I'm getting into a funk about him, about actresses who can act what it really means to be the mother of a son. But you do get under one's skin, you know. 'Oh, do listen to Sylvia, she's off on to Bird of Love Divine now. That always makes Reg laugh.' Just one of the little moments – but there were so many of them – when you seem to touch off something so much bigger than any silly old picture. Anyway – don't dare to say you're not that good when I say you *are* that good!
    Yours,
        Caroline A. Lejeune

The film, although patronising and dated, is still watchable.

At the end of August the liberation of Paris lifted everybody's spirits.

The news is really too thrilling for words and the BBC is really doing a tremendous job, their recording vans in Paris have produced the most vivid and stirring accounts of de Gaulle going from the Place de la Concorde to Notre Dame with snipers shooting at him and the tanks raking the Crillon with fire, all of which came through on the air with staggering exactitude. I have had tears in the eyes every news time for ages, I cannot take people being rescued or cheering crowds, it always makes me cry. [But a week later:] The victory feeling we all had a week ago seems to have worn off and everything seems dim dreary and endless.

However some offers of work began to come in. Among other things she was asked to give a talk to her old school on the Art of Acting ('I've got to talk for 3/4 hour and all I know of the art of acting you could say in 3/4 minute and then speaking slowly'). She was also asked to read a poem at the Albert Hall for Thanksgiving in November.

I have these maddening commitments of the Albert Hall and other stupidities. I wanted to cancel them but Pam says don't. But really it's not easy to look after a great many children (Nora is still away) and write a long dissertation on the Art of Acting (I *ask* you) to shatter my little schoolmates with on Tuesday. I have scribbled things down in between answering the telephone at the Police Station, while playing cards with the children and in between trying on everybody's dresses to try and discover something that I can wear for this Albert Hall schemozzle. Oh dear – we all got quite distraught, unstrung and hysterical on Friday night, all of us having a thousand ridiculous things that *had* to be done – like the village jumble sale and the trains not fitting and came to the decision that the planners of D Day had nothing on us.

However, her father, Dr Johnson, was taken ill and rapidly became worse; it was thought that he might not live. Pam rushed over to Kent to see him and Celia cancelled St Paul's and attempted to get out of her engagement at the Albert Hall; she was unable to do so. She and Tish knelt in front of the fire at Merrimoles trying to decide what she could possibly wear for the occasion. Bits and pieces of their meagre wardrobes were produced, and Celia stood on the stool trying them on and asking advice. In her own words, writing later from her parents' home at Brenchley:

Last Monday my father got much iller and they thought he wouldn't live through the night. So abandoning all the children and poor Tish I rushed over here and cancelled my St Paul's thing and tried to cancel the Albert Hall thing as well. They wouldn't let me do this so I had some complicated and pretty insane packing to do – late on Monday night Tish and I were to be seen feverishly packing things I should need here and also a white evening dress and jewellery for this Albert Hall thing. I don't suppose it has often happened that it has been essential to pack a white evening dress to go and see one's poor possibly dying father. I left at crack of dawn on Tuesday and arrived at the nursing home very frightened lest I should find he had died. On the contrary he was a little better and has gone on like that, rather up and downish, till now.

I went up to London on Wed. afternoon and rehearsed at the Albert Hall feeling rather dazed and wretched for my mother. As it turned out it was a very good thing that they wouldn't let me off from the performance as Daddy was well enough to listen to it and loved it and it gave him something to think about and talk about and he loved the whole broadcast. From my point of view the whole thing was terrifying – we had a whole day and a half's rehearsal but most of the time was spent (naturally) in rehearsing the orchestra so that we poor speakers felt a bit uncertain and worried. I had really not given very much thought to it and suddenly found it upon me with a packed house, and the Albert Hall is no mean edifice – a worldwide hook-up or network or bit of knitting or whatever they call it – the horror of realising that with bright pink spots focused on me – in spite of the fact that I had the script on a lectern in case – I wouldn't have been able to read it if I did dry up. It was nerve-racking, I came very near the end of the show and had two solid hours in which to work myself into a frenzy of fright and panic. Winston was there and made a speech at the end and it was all very exciting and tremendous and I got a lot of compliments, so that once my bit was over all was fine.

We were given a supper by the *Daily Telegraph* at the Savoy afterwards which was an odd affair with drinks flowing and turkey and cranberry sauce and speeches and general hilarity and Thanksgiving that it was over. I had no idea I should be so nervous but come to think of it with the exception of *The Doctor's Dilemma* it is about 5 years since I have faced an audience and then nothing like this – it was an ordeal. The Albert Hall has the effect of making one feel the size of a small worm but an ultra-conspicuous one, and when empty it echoes so that you have to wait between each syllable to let the boom die away but when full does nothing of the sort thus disconcerting one to start with.

The poem she read was by Jan Struther, whose real name was Joyce Maxtone Graham (the creator of Mrs Miniver). The poem, a nostalgic celebration of London in wartime, written from America where she was living, verges on, but just avoids, the trite, and, beautifully and movingly read by Celia, it struck a chord. Tim Nugent kept a copy in his wallet for the rest of his life. Tish and Pam, listening at home, to their surprise, found tears welling up.

'To You America' was what the celebration was entitled, and the programme, a long one, consisted of a mixture of English and American music and narration and poetry; there were trumpeters, there were American soldiers carrying the flags of each American state, there was the London Symphony

Orchestra conducted by Sir John Barbirolli; above the orchestra hung a thirty-foot portrait of Abraham Lincoln; five hundred performers took part. It was a veritable pageant which drew on Anglo-American history and culture. The Albert Hall, bedecked with banners, was packed, and when Churchill entered the Royal box, 'the audience gave one tremendous roar of applause'. His speech, following that of the American Ambassador, was eagerly awaited.

We have come here tonight to add our celebration to those which are going forward all over the world wherever Allied troops are fighting, in bivouacs and dugouts, on battlefields, on the high seas, and the highest air. Always this annual festival has been dear to the hearts of the American people. Always there has been that desire for thanksgiving, and never, I think, has there been more justification, more compulsive need than now ... We are moving forward in this struggle which spreads over all the lands and all the oceans; we are moving forward surely, steadily, irresistibly, and, perhaps with God's aid, swiftly towards victorious peace.

It was a fine and emotional occasion, but even in such illustrious company and in such awesome surroundings, Celia managed to catch the attention and to convey feeling. The *Daily Telegraph* reported:

When Celia Johnson recited very beautifully Jan Struther's moving poem of the London blitz, there was complete silence. Four red spotlights focused on the platform lent effect to this item. When she cried, 'How can London fall?' the orchestra swept into the final bars of Elgar's 'Cockaigne' Overture.

W. A. Darlington, writing of the spoken performances, said:

All spoke well. Indeed, if I were asked to suggest how that team could be improved I should find it difficult to leave anybody out; but there must be a special word of praise for Miss Johnson. Whether her entry on the scene goes to the credit of Mr [Stephen] Potter or of Ralph Reader the producer, I do not know. This I can say, however; that a woman's voice coming at the end, when we had been listening for some time only to men, gained greatly in effect by sheer force of contrast. Partly owing to this, but still more by reason of that indefinable emotional power which is the secret of her success on the stage, she was able both to lift and to lighten

the atmosphere, and to create a sense of intimacy – the word is
not too strong – even with so vast an audience.

Celia ended her letter to Peter: 'I would like you to have
been at the Albert Hall. I think I had rather a success.'

18

Brief Encounter

Shortly before the Albert Hall performance, Celia had had other offers of work, as she wrote in a letter to Peter at the end of September 1944:

I have been much in demand today. Starting with a request to go to Coventry to make a personal appearance at the opening of the film there next Sunday, with any luck I shall get out of this as it is my policing day; the next offer which might be interesting is to be in a new film of Noel's, founded on one of the plays in 'Tonight at 8.30' called *Still Life*. It must have been one of the ones I didn't see as I have no recollection of it at all, but it sounds rather fun and a very good part. I am going to have lunch with Noel tomorrow to hear more about it. It wouldn't be until after Christmas so the whole thing is a bit vague and seems to me Other Things Being Equal to depend on whether or not we have any form of cook by then ... and who on earth can say that?

Aubrey Blackburn also rang with an offer of a part in a new play by Daphne du Maurier.

A few days later: 'I read the new play by Daphne du Maurier that Binkie wanted me to be in [*The Years Between*] but I didn't like it very much, in fact not at all, so that makes one decision a lot easier.' However she was intrigued right from the start by *Still Life*, Noel's sketch that he wanted to make into a film.

[2 October 1944] Since I wrote I have been to London and had lunch with Mr Coward who read me his new film that he wants me to be in. There is no getting away from the fact that it is a very good part and one I should love to play. In spite of the appalling-ness of Denham, the cold corridors, the getting up at crack of dawn, the revoltingness of all the people who have anything to do with films, the not knowing where to stay, the vain struggle with trains, buses and Shureys, the abandoning of all (or nearly all) that I hold dear, the fact that a film always takes weeks longer than they say it will, etc., etc., etc. I have found myself already planning how

I should play bits and how I should say lines that I can remember from Noel having read it to me, in fact it has been whizzing round in my mind ever since last Friday. That is the trouble with being an actress, you do want to act even when in such an unsatisfactory medium as the films, and a good part sets one itching. And it is a good part. It's about a woman, married and with two children who meets by chance a man in a railway waiting-room and they fall in love. And It's All No Good ... It will be pretty unadulterated Johnson and when I am not being sad or anguished or renouncing, I am narrating about it. So if they don't have my beautiful face to look at, they will always have my mellifluous voice to listen to. Lucky people. I sent you a cable about it but I don't suppose it made much sense. It was rather fun, my day in London. For one thing I went up by car.

Still Life was to become *Brief Encounter*. Noel had found, during *In Which We Serve*, that he didn't particularly like making films; however he was well pleased with the team – David Lean, Anthony Havelock-Allan and Ronnie Neame – that had come together originally to make *In Which We Serve*, and had gone on to make *This Happy Breed*. He was more than happy to let them go on making his works into films; he wrote the dialogue, and they got on with the rest. They called themselves Cineguild; he called them 'my little darlings'.

After *This Happy Breed* in 1943 Cineguild had gone on to film *Blithe Spirit* in 1944 with Rex Harrison, Kay Hammond and Constance Cummings. It was inappropriately cast and remained too rigidly in its play form. David Lean was on less sure ground with comedy. It didn't quite come off and has yet to make its money back.

Still Life was not an obvious candidate for the screen, being small in scale and not particularly visual. David Lean and Anthony Havelock-Allan were certain that Celia would be right as the suburban housewife who falls in love with the doctor she meets by chance in a railway station. For *In Which We Serve*, after Celia had put herself forward for the part of the captain's wife, Noel had very much wanted her, thinking she would be perfect. For *This Happy Breed*, the question was 'Would she do it?', but for *Brief Encounter*, it was 'How can we get her?' Not only did Noel Coward and David Lean have a high opinion of her acting, they also thought that her looks were right for the part of Laura Jesson. Celia was not exactly pretty and so when the doctor (Trevor Howard) goes to help her get the speck out of her eye at the beginning of the film, it is clear he is doing so out of a pure desire to help, not to pick her up. No doubt in their initial meetings about the film Noel cajoled and flattered as he could. However, as is clear, she was hooked from the start.

But who was to play the doctor? Casting such a part in wartime was not easy. In Celia's next letter she reports: 'Roger Livesey is going to play the doctor.' This was not to be. In the end, after a search, David Lean spotted an actor in a small part in a film made by Anthony Asquith called *The Way to the Stars*, and thought he would be ideal. His name was Trevor Howard. 'Who is Trevor Howard?' asked Peter, 'and what has he done before? New one on me.' 'Trevor Howard is a new one on everyone,' she replied, 'he has been invalided out of the army and did I tell you the really terrible thing about him is that he is *8* years younger than I am. Isn't it dreadful? When I first realised it I nearly fainted with shock and horror but now I am getting acclimatised and treat him like a mother.' In the film the difference in age does not show up; Trevor Howard's face with its slightly rough complexion is rather grave and not at all boyish.

As another Christmas approached, and before work on the film started, Celia's spirits failed.

I hate the Japs, the Germans, moths and sweeping floors to which may be added all sales of work, all travelling and most children on wet days. [Their ninth wedding anniversary passed] I must say I don't seem to have been married very *much* as you might say. Certainly not 9 years' worth, still maybe that has prevented you from feeling constrained as it might have done if we'd had peace, prosperity and the 9.15.... I feel rather gloomy at the thought of this film. I shall be in almost every shot so that there won't be much chance of getting a day off now and then. Please send me a cable if there is the slightest chance of your getting home between now and May as if there is I shan't do it and I must know before I sign the contract ... I have got gloom tonight. It is partly Christmas and partly the news which makes everyone feel that the war is never going to end even this end and as for the Far East ... oh dear.

As before, Christmas was a huge success, and again Celia wrote a touching account of it, starting with the children opening their stockings,

crammed chiefly with pencils and apples and an odd sweet or two. We'd filled the drawing-room with all their parcels in different piles, decorated the Christmas tree and stuck some rather pathetic bits of holly along the curtains – we got the giggles as well as a lot of scratches in the face while doing this and when it was done it looked like spinach and there was no jollity about it at all .... I acquired a turkey at the eleventh hour – this was due to my friends the police. There are many unexpected advantages of being friends with detectives – no one else could have found a turkey on Christmas Eve and it was a fine, stalwart, if rather small, bird.

Apart from a lavatory overflowing and the refrigerator 'giving out noxious gases on Xmas Eve so that we had to put on our gas masks to clear it out, all went swimmingly'.

Peter cabled from Delhi: SIMPLY LOVED YOUR LETTER ABOUT CHRISTMAS WHICH WAS MOST VIVID AND SWEET THINK BRIEF ENCOUNTER IS FINE JOB AND MOST MOVING AND SUPERB PART FOR YOU NOEL SHOULD CHANGE CATCHPENNY UNDER-GRADUATE TITLE YOU WILL BE TERRIFIC. PF.

He reassured her by letter:

Don't worry about the film clashing with my leave a) because everything this end is so imponderable (this is one of my favourite words: I never write about a situation without saying that it is 'full of imponderables' and sometimes even that it is 'governed by so many imponderables that' it's not really worth writing about. I have a clear vision of these imponderables. They are small people, rather round and malicious and extraordinarily numerous. They giggle a good deal, often pretend to be asleep or dead, and live mostly rather high up in rooms and offices, for instance on the tops of cupboards. Their favourite things for hiding behind are Brigadiers and works of reference. They all have little crowns and wands of office, to govern with, but they are only allowed to put these on when I say they can. The exception is a rather fat one called Earthquake; he is allowed to wear his all the time and is the object of much jealousy – well, as we were saying, there are so many of these little creatures about that it's no good my attempting to make a plan and therefore it's no good worrying, and b) in any case I can almost certainly make my leave conform to your programme.

Early in the bitterly cold winter of 1945, work started on the film. On 9 January she wrote:

I can't tell you what agony it is getting my clothes for the film. It is like a sort of Tantalus thing or whoever it was who could see the things but not have them. Here am I down to one of everything and pining for some splendid clobber and having made and designed delicious garments which are just the sort of thing that I would like to have for myself and not allowed to have one of them. I long to have even the mackintosh, but no.

[The following week, she reported:] We have got to go up North for 4 weeks' location on some horrible railway station. I don't yet know where. Please write as often as you possibly can as I shall feel low and lonely and shall pine more than usual for letters. All the police force have been to see my film in Henley this week. All approved but for a variety of reasons.

The station which the Ministry of War Transport allowed them to use was Carnforth in Lancashire. In the north west of England, it was sufficiently removed from London to be safe from attack, even with all the film lighting, and also had very little traffic passing through at night – only the Royal Scot – so that filming could continue throughout the night without interruption.

Contrary to her expectations, she had a wonderful time at Carnforth; they all did. It was a very happy unit. She wrote from there on 11 February:

Well, here we are on the film and for the first time enjoying it ... The reason that I am enjoying it is that away on location and all of a unit one gets a good compact atmosphere, much more like a theatre and away from all that awful factory dreariness of Denham ... and I dread getting back there after the fun of this. You'd think there could be nothing more dreary than spending 10 hours on a station platform every night but we do the whole thing in the acme of luxury and sit drinking occasional brandies and rushing out now and again to see the expresses roaring through. [She and David Lean in particular loved standing at the edge of the platform in the middle of the night as the Royal Scot whooshed through.] The unit is mostly mad or pleasant with a sprinkling of bores among it and a great many gamblers. I have played a little poker with a certain amount of trepidation but have stayed even so far. We are living out at Windermere in a frightfully comfortable hotel where we have fires in our bedroom and breakfast (or rather lunch) in bed, in fact every mod. con. We go from here to the station every night in a Rolls-Royce – one night we were forced to travel in a Packard and there was a good deal of mutterings and complaints and the next night I am happy to say we got the Rolls back. We could hardly be expected to put up with anything less. I had no idea I should enjoy it so much, in fact I never thought I should enjoy it at all.

In spite of her Lancashire antecedents, she had never been to the Lake District before and found it quite beautiful.

I am scared stiff of the film and get first night indijaggers before every shot but perhaps I'll get over that. It is going to be most awfully difficult – you need to be a star of the silent screen really because there's such a lot of stuff with commentary over it – it's terribly difficult to do. I hope to goodness it will be all right. At one in the morning we have a great meal in a restaurant car in a siding – The food is uneatable (and I'm not fussy) but the whole set-up being ridiculous is fun – we manage to giggle a good deal. The food at the hotel on the other hand is stupendous and beats anything in London hollow. We are really very lucky. I must go now and do a beastly difficult shot on a frightfully cold platform.

At the end of their week there, she wrote

I have got awfully fond of Carnforth station. It seems most unlikely, but all the guards and porters and people are most awfully nice and even the station master, a large man in stern bowler hat who is renowned for his grumpiness, raises his stern hat unceasingly to me and I am continually being besought to sit by the fire in his office. We had a very long night two days ago and didn't finish in the station until 7.30, by which time the fish train from Aberdeen had pervaded the place – not really awfully encouraging to Art(!) at that hour of the morning. I was playing a sad little scene with the scent of herrings in the air and milk cans rattling ... The whole affair has been very funny and odd. I wish I could be funnier about it but it's all so fantastic and ridiculous I don't know where to start.

One of the more absurd scenes is at one in the morning when we all troop into a restaurant car in a siding and have a huge meal. We, the Snobs, have the first-class part and all the electricians and hoi polloi have to pig it in the 3rd. Would you believe it – there are at least 80 people up here to do this stuff. We could easily fight a small war on our own.

She returned to Merrimoles to find that her father was ill again and

obviously in a poor state and very hard to deal with, and my mother is worn out and pining for some sort of help and we can't even get a nurse, let alone a body who would monger around and be useful. My aunt [the saintly Amy from Ilkley] is still there but she is naturally getting a bit restive as well as exhausted and everyone seems at the end of their tether. I can't think what on earth to do about it, and alternate between worrying myself sick and dismissing it entirely from my mind. Neither at all helpful attitudes. Oh dear. We finished up north with a wonderful day when we got three shots on a bridge in record time and so had the afternoon free to do a major walk (my standards, not yours) over the hills and far away. It was really lovely and the whole day was made pretty ridiculous by the fact that one of the assistants discovered that the cellar of the little pub was stocked with the most wonderful wines, brandies, liqueurs and things that no one has seen for years. We all lost our heads and bought great armfuls of bottles and general hilarity prevailed ... Now I have to go and have a drink with the Alexanders and exchange views on the Lake District, which is apparently Maud's home. She was worried to hear that I was living at the wrong end of the lake but on investigation it turned out that it was a mistake and I was after all at the right end. A narrow escape.

The part of Laura Jesson's daughter had been given to Pam's daughter, Henrietta Vintcent, who was eight. Nichol and the other cousins at Merrimoles were wildly jealous when she set off, grandly, for the studio, and returned later with film make-up still on her face.

Celia settled down to two months' work in the studio which, again, she enjoyed more than she had expected – 'in fact I am almost enjoying it quite a lot'. Not only did she find the part of Laura Jesson satisfying, not only did she like David Lean and the others, but also the end of the war really did

seem at hand at last. 'The war here looks very good and fine.
But I do wish it would stop. Oh, I do wish it would. Will
we ever live happily here at Merrimoles, you and me and
Nichol?'

We have been doing all the dream sequences the last few days [she
wrote in the middle of March 1945] and the whole of the hairdressing
wardrobe and makeup departments have been on their toes in a
wild attempt to make me look glamorous. On the whole, they succeeded fairly well but I saw some of the rushes today and the whole
thing is perfectly pitch dark so all their sweat and toil has been
completely unnecessary. We did today the dream shot of us driving
in a car with wind blowing etc. and we had the most gloriously
ridiculous car you ever saw with a bonnet stretching from here to
Delhi and great shiny snakes sticking out of its bonnet and every
horn, light and gadget imaginable. It was a Mercedes and had to
be pushed as it was perfectly immobile and had to be brought to
the studio on a trailer behind a lorry ... There is no doubt about
it – I do like acting – even film acting if I can't have any other
– it's better than no acting at all. Cyril Raymond – did I tell you
– plays Fred and is and will be excellent ... There is a roar of
bombers at this moment going out to wreak havoc.

[A week later] Today we've been doing some of the stuff in the
station refreshment room. Joyce Barbour plays Dolly Messiter and
she is a dear and very funny and nice but she's been very ill and
can't remember her lines easily and gets sort of scared of the camera
so it means things go terribly slowly and lots of takes on each shot.
It would be maddening if she wasn't so nice and I didn't feel so
sorry for her. Perhaps she'll get better about it.

She did not, and her performance as the loquacious friend
who ruins the lovers' parting was played too much for laughs;
although she was a friend of Noel's, he agreed that she had
to go, and she was subsequently replaced by Everley Gregg,
who played the bore perfectly. 'Trevor Howard is going to
be good I think and has the mentality of a born film star.
Rather pleasant but pretty stupid (shhh).' And he was, of
course, very good indeed, but it was hard work. Whereas Celia
was quick and malleable, and if she didn't get something right
first time, with a little suggestion, would almost always get
it right second time, Trevor Howard was slower and took

longer. He had particular trouble with the scene in the station refreshment room where he is listing diseases while she listens and gazes at him. Gradually – although they are still talking about medicine – it becomes evident that they are both thinking something quite else (a hallmark of Noel's); he took ages to get this right. But, then, with every repetition of the scene he improved, while Celia, losing the freshness of her performance, got worse. His attitude on the whole was a little cruder; he could not understand why, when he and Laura, alone in his friend's flat, simply don't get on with their affair. David Lean particularly admired in Celia her professionalism and her no-nonsense approach to her work: she was talented; she made no fuss, she got on with it. Lean, in his work, always had a very exact visual image in his head of each shot; Celia was able, intuitively, to pick up that image and translate it to his satisfaction.

She wrote to Peter at the end of March:

Victory and Easter are upon us. The news tonight sounds stupendous although as there is a security black-out on where Monty is getting to it has to be rather nebulously stupendous. Everybody is in a varied state of excitement. Some refuse to think the end is in sight – others expect it hourly ... I do hope I'm good in the film – I really do want to be – most dreadfully badly but am very dubious about it.

'Something tells me,' wrote Peter, 'you are going to have a major triumph.'

On 15 April she was writing: 'Victory is at hand so they have been saying for some days. Poor old FDR. I am sad about him.' But Victory dragged her feet. 'What do you suppose you will do after the war?' she wrote a few days later.

Are you going to be a stick-pointing Squire or literary gent? or Press lord? or simply wealthy recluse? or will you as I suspect spend the week in London with your pals and bring them down here for weekends, a dozen or so at a time to your distracted chatelaine with no cook? Not that I mind, you understand, and I should like you to have everything heart can desire but I rather hope you won't desire this too much or I shall hardly ever see you. I also think I shall not want altogether to stop being an actress though how I'm going to fit that in I don't quite see.

Meanwhile she got rather bored having to redo the scenes with Everley Gregg instead of Joyce Barbour. ('She is certainly very much better.')

May 4th and victory was imminent.

You ask me to tell you about it but as a matter of fact I can't tell you much, being in the studio all the time and not seeing or hearing much. It's so obviously coming any day and the announcements as to how we are to behave and whether the grocers will stay open, come thick and fast so that it's all getting rather like a municipal festivity and won't be at all spontaneous or unexpected. The studio is mainly concerned with whether, if the news comes this weekend, Sunday will count as one of the days off on full pay or not. They are having their usual labour troubles there and we have an overtime ban on at the moment which may delay us a bit but not much as we are getting on for finishing – we've only got another 10 days in the studio (VE days excepted) and then about 10 days night exteriors which will of course depend on the weather as to how long they take to get that.

Later After Dinner. The 9 o'clock news has just given us the news of the German surrender in Northern France. To my everlasting shame we missed the beginning announcement so that I'm now waiting for 10 o'clock to hear exactly what's happened on the Forces wavelength. Oh Gee. I can't take it in. We seem to be getting Victory in instalments so that one gets more and more accustomed to these gigantic bits of news – just as in the old days one got more and more prepared for what Churchill called Hard and Heavy news.

Our first real excitement (apart from the return of prisoners of war which was a major delight and omen) was the surrender to Alexander of Northern Italy 2 days ago. I was out to dinner at Ronnie Neame's with John Mills and his wife when we heard this. We got v. excited and we played poker with them in a gay and abandoned way.

[5 May 1945] Victory gets nearer and nearer until the very sound of it begins to get a bit boring and tiresome and no one can plan anything for fear of getting stuck by the celebrations, and no one knows whether the children are to go back to school or not ... We have a bonfire in the garden for the children and one up on the common for the village but already there are rows about it and Mr J. has annoyed 10 people separately before the thing starts. Just heard the news that Winston is to speak on Thursday night, the 5th anniversary of his taking office as PM, and that it is expected that he will have announced VE day before then ... The Brenchley ménage is all very difficult. My poor Papa now can't get out of bed at all and the doctor says that he may go on like this for a year or more, my mother is as good as dotty, at least judging by her telephone conversations and I really feel terribly sorry for Pam having to go there for a month to let my aunt off for a rest.

At last, on 8 May, VE Day came.

My darling, we have really won the war and I can't believe it ... To start with we all got in a state of rising excitement culminating on Monday (V-1) when rumours were rife and all expected the news of victory from moment to moment. At the studio excitement became intense at lunch-time by the report that all Technicolor cameras had gone up to the Palace and bets were laid and work haphazard on account of having to rush out to listen to the radio between every shot. A sign of the tremendous upheaval was stressed by the unprecedented buying of a bottle of rather nasty white wine by Tony Havelock-Allan at lunch-time on our table. Well, it went on and on and no news came and I didn't know whether to go home or not. Eventually I decided I would and risk the next day not being VE day and tremendous alternative plans were made for any eventuality. But we'd guessed right and by the time I got home the news had come through that Churchill would give the official announcement the next day at 3. So I got back to Moly to find they'd hoisted the flag over the front door and Pam and I had a couple of drinks and Margot and Nan appeared and we all felt rather overwhelmed and peculiar; however in a moment of quixotic insanity we decided to suggest to Nora and Nurse that they could go to London for the next day if they wanted to. It never really occurred to me that they would but to our horror they said they'd like to – so we had a pretty devastating VE day coping with all 8 children (Tish incidentally had gone to London to meet Jamie [Thomson, her fiancé] who arrived in Edinburgh on Sunday and she rushed up there to meet him and she is being married on Saturday).

I took Nichol, Gilly and Detta down to Henley to buy some bread and they got very excited by the flags and bunting which appeared pretty rapidly on all sides – when we got back they rang up from the farm in a fury to say that the boys (Charles, Val, Chris and John) had been over there behaving very wildly and the culminating crime was that they'd let the bull out. I *was* furious and waited like a witch for their return and ordered them to their rooms and made them go and apologise to Copeland after lunch. In a way, apart from the fact that it must have ruined Copeland's VE day by forcing them to spend a good bit chasing the bull, it was not altogether a bad thing as it gave us a slight respite and bit of peace while they were confined to their rooms. It did them a lot of good and they all became good and sweet from then on.

We had a bonfire in Polly's field beautifully made by Collins in which we let off thunderflashes and things, remnants of the Home Guard. (Nichol I am sorry to tell you took cover.) All the McCulloughs came and Rupert and Comfort and their bunch, and Margot and her 2 girls and Nancy Jackson and Jill and all got very hot and delighted. We had previously gathered in the drawing-room, Pam, me and the 8 children, to hear Winston announce it. They all sat goodly on the floor waving their flags and trying not to talk but I doubt if many of them really followed what he was saying. After the bonfire (which Nichol always calls a bombfire) we put the horde to bed and then rushed down to church where I'm sorry to say we arrived rather late and had to stand. Then back to hear the King and after that up to Windmill Hill for the village bonfire which was a beauty, with beer flowing (provided by us – *hope you agree*) and 4 returned P of ws and I lit it (I don't quite know why me but still –). It blazed up wonderfully and was a fine and satisfactory sight. It was a beautiful night and the whole village and a few others were there dancing and singing and thoroughly cheerful. Pam and I stayed for quite a time – it was a lovely sight flickering away against a navy-blue sky with a few stars about. At last we got home and sat on the loggia with the light on and took in the fact that there was not an aeroplane in the sky and all that you could hear was a nightingale singing and an occasional cracker or firework in the remotest distance. That was lovely and I wondered if you were having a nice time and a snipe or two in celebraggers. At last, worn out with Victory, we fell into bed.

The next day I cleaned like mad and dusted and swept in a frenzy and then in the evening I went to London having rung up Gin [Virginia Thesiger] and asked if I could stay the night. I arrived to find Gin and Tony had been out the night before and walked and walked and cheered and sung and were speechless and incapable of more but Joyce [Grenfell] had just arrived from Wales so she and I sallied forth. We were asked for a preliminary drink at Clemence Dane's so we battled our way down there – she has a flat in Covent Garden – where we found Gladys Calthrop, Dick Addinsell and Victor Stiebel. So the six of us set out, C.Dane sailing like a ship in full sail and along the Strand we went, gazing in wonder at the floodlit Tivoli and arrived at Trafalgar Square which was lovely. The National Gallery floated away above a mass of cheerful people, and Nelson on his column was lit by several arcs which were just on him leaving the column in darkness, and Admiralty Arch was lighted with the White Ensign flying above in a proud and lonely fash. We walked up to the Palace with thousands of others meeting crowds coming back and it was fine. The crowd was never too thick and as nice a crowd as you could wish to find, cheerful, weary, and extremely good-humoured and not a bit drunken – mostly I imagine as beer is pretty short. We sat on the Victoria Memorial and sang and shouted, We want the King, and talked to one and all and cheered the King and Queen when they came out and having seen them once, stayed for the second house as it were and saw them come out again which wasn't until about 12.20. There were searchlights doing a sort of ballet and fireworks coming from Wellington Barracks and the usual chap who climbs to the very top of the Victoria Memorial and gets told to come down by the police (who were I may say wonderful) and it was all fine and dandy and occasionally funny and always a bit emotional too. We started back home fortified by the sight of 3 most charming sailors who were paddling in the fountains – one walking about, waist-deep, reading a paper, one fishing solemnly with a long stick and the third was being the fish. They were very sweet, rather serious and perfectly silent, encouraged by the crowd and managing to remain remarkably dignified. We trudged home, Victor, Joyce and I past a brilliant Dorchester and an almost as brilliant Grosvenor House and also past a very small serious bonfire watched by a few intense soldiers – from their faces you would have thought the liberty of these islands depended on their never taking their eyes off it – and so home with our feet several sizes larger than when we started and our shoes a great deal smaller – I'm glad I went up. It was a satisfactory evening and I wanted to cheer someone – I really would have given a lot to have been in Whitehall the day before and seen Winston conducting 'Land of Hope and Glory' from the balcony of the Min. of Health and heard him speak. His announcement on the wireless was less exuberant and characteristic than I expected but his speech in Whitehall was both. I should have liked to hear that.

Well, that baldly is that – odd items are a rather nice v sign outside a house full of billeted American troops consisting of a pair of long underpants hung upside down. Flags and bunting everywhere – the biggest flag in Henley is that of Brazil rather surprisingly. Everyone pulling a long face over the Poles, or rather over the Russians being tiresome over the Poles, when they stop being relieved and ecstatic that we've won. And cheers for Rangoon so you're not altogether forgotten. I must go to bed because I must be up at 6.30.

The Merrimoles cousins during the war: (from left to right) Charles Vintcent, Valentine Fleming, Henrietta Vintcent, Christopher Fleming, John Vintcent, David Fleming, Nichol Fleming, Gillian Fleming.

Ann Todd, Joyce Carey, Peggy Ashcroft and Celia as ATS officers in a training film, *We Serve*, 1942.

During the making of *Brief Encounter*
1945: Celia and Trevor Howard.

As *St Joan*, 1947.

Kate and Lucy, aged four and three, at Merrimoles.

Celia and Nichol at Eton.

Peter with owl.

Paula Long at Merrimoles with one of Peter's dogs.

Celia, travelling.

Opposite above *Hay Fever* on BBC Television, 1968. Charles Gray, Celia, Ian McKellen, Vickery Turner, and Lucy.

Opposite below Celia won a BAFTA award for best actress for her BBC television performance in *Mrs Palfrey at the Claremont*, 1973.

Merrimoles c. 1979; Kate and Celia dabbling.

Celia and her first grandchild, Flora
Laycock, at Merrimoles.

Opposite above
The making of
Staying On, by
Paul Scott, in
Simla, for
Granada
Television: Trevor
Howard and Celia.

Opposite below
Celia as the Nurse
and Rebecca Saire
as Juliet in *Romeo
and Juliet*, 1978,
part of the BBC
Shakespeare series.

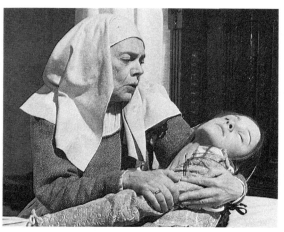

Sir Ralph Richardson and Celia rehearsing *The Understanding*, 1982; she died a few weeks later.

Celia, at rehearsal, March 1982.

19

Peace

To begin with, peace made little difference. Petrol remained in short supply and rationing was still in force. The main things that Celia remarked on were that you knew that no one was being killed any more and the return of the prisoners of war.

On 18 May 1945, she wrote:

The chiefly thrilling thing is the return of the POWs and the various stories they have to tell. I met a very nice chap who was just back at the studio the other day. He was shot down while being a photographer in a Lancaster and had been a prisoner for about 18 months. He'd escaped and had some extraordinary experiences. I still feel rather censored and will wait to tell you until I see you. I'm sure it's silly even now to relate all the things they did too freely. But one tears-to-the-eyes thing happened to Kay Walsh who was in a train with 5 returned Scotch POWs who were so excited they couldn't sit still and kept gazing out of the window. They said that from the stuff they'd heard about the flying-bombs, they didn't expect to see any of Southern England still standing and told about the accounts the Germans had given them of the success of V1. But, and this is the touching bit, they said to her, We knew you wouldn't give in. I haven't perhaps made this sound moving but it was and particularly with a Scotch accent ... We have now only about 10 days of exteriors to do. These start on Tuesday night at the Metropole Cinema, Victoria.

But before the filming was finished, old Dr Johnson, who had been ailing all year, died on 31 May.

I am really v. glad that it didn't go on any longer because he obviously wasn't going to get better. He just went on and on getting worse and worse. Poor Pam's had an awful time and so has my mother. She needs a complete rest and change and we are trying to persuade her to go back with my aunt to Ilkley for a week or two anyway but she's in the mood that whatever one suggests is useless.

Peter wrote back with sympathy, saying of her father: 'He was a most sweet and endearing character.'

Celia's work in *Brief Encounter* came to an end in June.

I've had another session at the studio doing all the commentary as well as some post sinking [sic], it took ages and was not helped by the fact that I am at the moment riddled with catarrh so that a lot of the time I sounded like an adenoidal child. However, after four solid days' very hard work it is at last finished. I saw the rough cut of the film and can't decide if it is good or not. Some bits come off very well and some bits are not so good. But what I can't decide is whether the story itself is strong enough. I'm not bad in some bits, in some I'm rotten. I'm longing for you to see it, and see what you think. David has promised that you can see it when you get back but it won't then be in a finished state, I don't suppose, so it may be a bit unfair on it. All the music and stuff will make a tremendous difference, especially of course to you who will be miserable without Rachmaninoff's Piano Concerto swishing through it. Perhaps you can hum it to yourself while watching it. That might help.

Peter had no sense of music whatsoever.

Noel attended the showing too and wrote in his diary: 'Saw rough cut of *Brief Encounter*. Delighted with it. Celia quite wonderful; Trevor Howard fine and obviously a new star. Whole thing beautifully played and directed – and, let's face it, most beautifully written.'

C.A.Lejeune, a wholehearted fan of Celia's, went to Merrimoles in August to interview her for *Picturegoer*.

There is a school of thought, including Noel Coward, that holds that Celia Johnson is just about the most talented actress on the British screen today.

This is not an opinion shared by Miss Johnson, who insists that any merit she may have shown in pictures is due, in the first place, to a run of good parts, and in the second to short-sightedness.

'You can do anything with her,' says her cameraman. 'Stick lamps under her nose, she's got such technique, nothing bothers her.'

'It's just my eyes,' says the actress. 'It's a great advantage when everything is a blur beyond a certain distance. I take off my glasses to do a scene, and I don't see all those terrifying tough men in sweaters standing about with their hands in their pockets. It's like the theatre, when nothing is very distinct beyond the footlights.'

This is not a pose; it is the genuine Celia Johnson.

She went on to say that Celia was

something quite unique in film stars. She is an extremely personable
young woman who has never found the time nor the zeal to settle
down in front of a mirror and deliberately acquire glamour. Sometimes she thinks about it in an academic sort of way.

'Perhaps I ought to try to be glamorous, in the evenings anyhow,'
she says spreading out her practical hands with the short unvarnished
nails, and looking ruefully at the marks left by potato peelings. 'But
it's awfully difficult to find time with eight children.'

Lejeune then described the house –

a pleasant place; a place possessed by children.

Bookshelves line the walls; the books are mainly travellers' tales,
records of journeys in China and South America and the East, reflect-
ing Peter Fleming's taste; but the children have occupied the floors.

There is a doll's pram in the hall, spilling over with dolls; there
are bits of toy trains; a windmill on a stick; a child's painting; a
tin can on a string; a pair of small stout shoes.

At one end of the terrace is a miniature chute; at the other a
caravan, used once to house food for the pheasants, now the children's
playroom.

A large black Labrador dog, a fox-terrier bitch, and a very small
black kitten run under your feet. On the grass are odd erections
made of deck chairs draped with black-out material, children's tents
– 'so deplorably squalid,' says Celia Johnson shaking her head.

A small boy comes into the room on all fours, rises with reluctant
courtesy to shake your hand. He is Nicholas Fleming, aged six.

He has an imp's face, and a naughty, infectious laugh. His bare
arms are scratched, and there are stains on his brown legs.

'Red currants, Nichol?' asks his mother, suspiciously. 'Paint,' says
Nichol, 'just purple paint.'

He strikes a match for no apparent reason; throws it nonchalantly
into the big fireplace; hurriedly unscrews a screw-up pencil to see
how it works; and goes out again on all fours.

From the next room comes the sound of cups and saucers and
children's chatter, where the eight cousins are eating their tea.

The household was, in fact, about to disperse; the Merrimoles
garrison was breaking up. The children, so tiny at the beginning of the war, had grown. The eldest two, Charles Vintcent

and Valentine Fleming, were already away at prep school, and Celia was starting to look at prep schools for Nichol. That May Tish had married James Thomson who was serving with the Cameron Highlanders, while he was on leave. When his leave was up, she returned to Merrimoles, but began house-hunting, and later that year she and Jamie and the four little Flemings moved to Sussex. Pam and her three children remained at Merrimoles until early 1947, when they moved into a house in Nettlebed. A few years later she married Ralph Dennis, a widower with two sons, and in 1952 they had a child, William.

Peter, too, had some leave that summer and returned home in July. The war was over in Europe, the filming of *Brief Encounter* was finished, Peter's work in India was coming to an end, but the privations were still there and, in spite of the euphoria and the relief, there was a sort of cumulative exhaustion. The anticipation of peace had been so great, the reality was always going to be harder.

When Peter left for India for the last time to finish his work there and clear his desk, Celia took the children to Cornwall. To her delight she found she was expecting a baby. Peter responded:

I can't tell you how thrilled and delighted I was to hear that you are once more in trouble. I do hope the Precious Burden has a smooth passage. It would be splendid if we could get two for the price of one but I suppose that's a bit much to hope for. *Do* take care of yourself and behave in a very gingerly way if that is required and lay off the gin ... *Oh*, I am pleased about your dread predicament. I think it is a splendid thing. Nonchalant old flint heart that I am, I had really forgotten that one could be so pleased about anything.

For the time being he was sifting through old files in Delhi.

Honestly you know, when I glance through the rubbish I've been wrestling with for the last 3½ years I'm amazed how much sense of proportion (not much, I admit) I've managed to retain; after read-ing through the old controversies, complaints, attempts-to-get-a-move-on, insincerities, eyewash, long analyses of things which eventually turned out to be of no importance at all, complaints about pay, about the telephone, about correspondence going astray, nonsense about security precautions, requests for an electric fan, raspberries, reconciliations, 'Following personal for Fleming', 'To be opened only by addressee', more complaints about pay, about aeroplanes, about the lavatory, about the American General Staff, about topees and travel allowance and time-saving – you never *saw* so much bumf. After reading about all the muddles and squabbles and changes of plan and hurried flights hither and thither I feel as if I'd just woken up from a particularly horrible and arbitrary nightmare. I am glad it is all over. I don't think I ever allowed myself to realise how badly I wanted the war to end.

He made a bonfire of most of the files and finally left in October: 'I am glad to have left Delhi, though it was sad parting from Hassan [his servant] and Red Queen and Blondie and the lovely dawns and dusks on the jheels.' He returned to London in time for the premiere of *Brief Encounter*.

No one knew how the film was going to be received, least of all David Lean. First he showed the completed version to Noel Coward and Noel's friend and associate, Jack Wilson. There was a silence afterwards; then Jack Wilson said he liked it, and Noel Coward said: 'I don't know how you could have done it better.' But they still didn't know whether it would appeal to the public. They thought that it was unlikely that it would be popular in America, but after a private showing for *Time* magazine, a man rushed after David Lean exclaiming: 'It's brilliant.' They did, however, think that it would appeal to the French; it was not unlike a French film *L'Orage*, made in 1937 with Michelle Morgan and Charles Boyer. To their surprise the French distributors, Gaumont, turned it down; the French saw no interest in a love affair that never happened, and considered it typical British hypocrisy. However, after it won the Critics' Prize at the Cannes Film Festival the following year they took it and showed it with success. In 1946 Celia was nominated for best actress in the American Academy awards and David Lean for best director; neither won. (Laurence Olivier won a special award that year for his outstanding achievement as actor, producer and director in bringing *Henry V* to the screen). The British were the last to appreciate *Brief*

Encounter, but over the years they have come to love it and it has become one of the classics of British cinema.

David Lean has always given Celia credit for the success of the film. Her acting throughout has great truth and subtlety. Her thin old-fashioned upper-class voice speaking Coward's clipped dialogue, so easy to imitate, is outweighed by her acting; the feeling she conveys transcends those now ridiculous very English tones. There is a moment when she has to begin to tell lies about what she has been doing, when deception comes in to her life; she looks at herself in the mirror, and it is clear from that look that she has never told a lie before in her life – a simple point but so difficult to express. On another occasion she decides, just as the train that she is on is pulling out of the station, to keep an assignation with Dr Harvey (Trevor Howard) after all, in a flat that he has borrowed, an assignation bound to consummate their affair; she distractedly jumps from the train, runs down the platform, stops, collects herself, starts walking and then can't stop herself from breaking into a run. She did this sequence of movements on her own initiative and David Lean thought it was marvellous; by rushing, trying to walk and starting to run again, she so clearly showed all her fears, hopes, excitement and worries. He congratulated her and asked, 'Why did you do that?' 'What?' she said. He explained and she just said, 'Well, she would, wouldn't she?'

Almost the only feature of the film that jars today are Celia's hats. Gladys Calthrop, Noel's friend and the designer of the film, had insisted on them at the time to pinpoint Laura Jesson's class. In other respects it has proved remarkably timeless. David Lean never liked the comic banter between Joyce Carey and Stanley Holloway in the station refreshment room which interrupts and contrasts the main romance, but no one has ever criticised it.

Noel Coward, delighted again with his team, said they could do any of his works that they wanted. But David Lean wanted to move on to new things and in particular to make a costume film; he abandoned Coward for Dickens and went on to make *Great Expectations* and then *Oliver Twist*. He thought that Noel Coward was rather put out to be deserted by his 'little darlings'.

Hollywood made a tentative offer or two to Celia but she remained at home, delighted to have Peter back at last and to wait for her baby.

20

Daughters and *St Joan*

I was a bulge baby; that is, I was one of the children whose numbers swelled the birthrate immediately after the war. So was my sister. I was born on 24 May 1946, and Lucy was born, less than a year later, on 15 May 1947. So although Celia did not get two for the price of one, it was not far off. Celia was in her fortieth year when she gave birth to Lucy in the spare room at Merrimoles.

So much had changed in the six years of war. At the outbreak, Nichol had been a baby, and Peter and Celia a glamorous young couple. Now they were both rising forty, Nichol was about to go to prep school and two baby girls had appeared. Nichol thought the babies a poor swap for his jolly cousins. Celia had made the David Lean films and done a lot of broadcasting but had not been seen in the theatre, with the exception of *Rebecca* at the beginning of the war, and two short spells in first *The Importance*, and second *The Doctor's Dilemma*. With Tish's support she had coped with the house and estate. Now Peter was back, unconsciously imperious, such was the force of his character, taking charge, asking friends to shoot. Nichol he scarcely knew, and now had to get to know. He was delighted with his little daughters, one fair, one dark. Celia was relieved that he was back, but the readjustment must have been harder than either expected. Peter always said that those shattered years after the war were a nadir for the country.

Celia continued to feel inadequate as a housewife, and the problem of the cook was to recur at intervals. However, she was fortunate in finding Miss Eva Parslow, from an old Henley family, as nanny for the girls; she was kind and patient and unselfish and stayed for twelve years or so. In time Nanny Fleming, as she was known, found herself having to look after all manner of creatures as well as the children. In the early 1950s a young local boy, William Pound, came as gardener – a thankless job, as Peter, although passionate about forestry, did not care for flowers, while Celia was appreciative but vague about gardens. But in spite of having to contend with flinty ground and depredation by deer, rabbits and pheasants, Bill Pound stayed until he died in 1988, turning his hand to all manner of jobs in the house, including cooking breakfast, pressing trousers and finding Celia's lost possessions. He was not only saintly but quick and witty. Although Celia was very fond of him, she never realised how much she relied on him.

In the autumn of 1946, a few months after I was born, Celia accepted a part in *Call Home the Heart* by Clemence Dane with Sybil Thorndike. She took over, in fact, from Judy Campbell, who had to leave because she was expecting a baby (to be Jane Birkin). Celia toured in Peterborough, Sheffield and Manchester, until she too was obliged to pull out for the same reason. This caused her old friend Tim Nugent to ask, 'Sybil all right?' 'You *ruined* my play,' Sybil Thorndike boomed at us when we met her in later life.

Soon after Lucy was born, John Burrell invited Celia to join the Old Vic Company (then performing at the New Theatre as the Old Vic itself had been damaged by a bomb in 1941). She was free to choose any part within reason, so she asked Peter's advice. He suggested St Joan. Shaw was approached and raised no objection. It was the sort of challenge that, in theory, she needed in her career. Alec Guinness was to play the Dauphin.

Way back when she was still at school, Celia had seen Sybil Thorndike in her famous interpretation of the role; she had also seen Ludmilla Pitoeff who too had given a performance remembered by many. 'I am convinced,' she said in an interview in *Theatre World*, 'that Sybil Thorndike came nearer to Shaw's conception than any of her successors ... Hers was undoubtedly the right way to play Joan. I could never hope to play it that way, so there would be no use in trying. I work along different lines.'

Her performance, in the end, was quiet and sensitive, less militant, and, according to most people, did not quite come off. Although it had purity and clarity, it was lacking in strength. Her voice once more let her down; it did not have the power. There was no earthiness about her, nothing of the soldier. The other actors in the play, such as Alec Guinness and Peter Copley who played Brother Martin, found her performance moving, but more so in rehearsal than on the stage. Alec Guinness was superb as the Dauphin – but the production was dull, and the scenery drab – a 'quite deplorable revival' wrote T.C. Worsley in the *New Statesman*. Another review compared the production to the sun in spring: 'Its clarity is greater than its power, its beauty more notable than its authority. Its radiance illuminates Joan's face, but whether it would have driven the English out of France is another matter.' Noel Coward had attended the first night and had written in his diary on 3 December: 'Dined with Larry and Viv [Olivier] and went to the opening of *St Joan*. Very excited at the prospect of Celia playing that part but was a little disappointed. She was lacking in guts and rather like Peter Pan. Alec Guinness was wonderful; the production was artsy-craftsy and fairly bad.'

It cannot in fact have been the right moment to have tried this difficult and taxing role; the war was not long over and she had, at an advanced age, just given birth to the two girls. Her physical strength, so necessary for such a part, cannot have been at its greatest.

At home there was a discussion as to whether Nichol, now eight, should be allowed to go to the play. Was it sensible for him to see his mother burnt at the stake? Might it not be rather traumatic for a small boy? Nichol was thrilled when it was resolved that he could go, but bitterly disappointed when, after all the build up, the burning of his mother took place off-stage.

'At the moment I enjoy taking an active part in the upbringing of my three children, and as I only appear two or three times a week in *St Joan*, it means that I can devote a good deal of time to them in the country.' This would be the pattern while the girls were small; Celia would take on a few things that did not involve an enormous commitment – to the exasperation of Binkie Beaumont and other producers – but she felt, as she had during the war, that her place was at home. She was torn between home and work – a dilemma more common now than it was then – and racked with guilt. Work was more like a passionate hobby.

Home was so removed from the theatre. Although she liked her fellow actors ('I like them very much,' she said much later in an interview. 'They are generous, funny, warm and good company. I've only really not got on with 2 people – well 1½ really.') And she adored working with them. But on the whole their friends were not directly involved in the theatre. Now that all the little cousins had left Merrimoles, old friends would come and stay – the Nugents, Ronnie Shaw-Kennedy, a bachelor who came frequently, the Caccias. Mary Clive came less often; she had been widowed in the war and was now less inclined to leave her house in Herefordshire where she lived with her two children. Peter's mother would come and stay, driven by her chauffeur, who was called Vivaldi. Amaryllis, too, came, bringing her cello (she had become a most distinguished concert cellist). And Celia's mother, Ethel, stayed on other occasions; her penchant for reading out disasters from the papers always annoyed Celia.

With an increased petrol ration, their local network of friends widened. There were the Bretts at Watlington, the Troughtons at Hambleden (Dick Troughton was one of the few people who could bring Peter out of himself and make him cry with laughter), Lady Hambleden at Ewelme, the Osbert Lancasters in Henley (his famous cartoon character, Maudie Littlehampton, was thought by many to have something in common with Celia, both in appearance and pronouncements), Lord and Lady John Hope at Rotherfield Greys, and Michael and Lady Pamela Berry at Kidmore End.

Closer to hand was the actor Alastair Sim and his wife Naomi with whom Celia used to play tennis. She played cards and mah-jong with Carol Pakenham-Walsh, an old friend who was paralysed from the waist down and who lived in Nettlebed with her two children. Lt-Col Frankie Wilson, who had worked with Peter in India, and his wife Judy moved into Windmill Cottage in Nettlebed which belonged to Peter. Frankie Wilson was a brilliant draughtsman and illustrator, and every Christmas would design a special card for Merrimoles, usually poking fun at Peter's lack of a musical ear or his love

of shooting. The Hart-Davises and the Gambles and the Alexanders were still around, though the McCulloughs had moved.
A little later, Colin and Lady Anne Mackenzie and their small
children came to live in Nettlebed. Most of these families
had bulge babies too, so there was a lot of to-ing and fro-ing
of nannies and their charges – Nanny Ming (as Eva Parslow
was known), Nanny Berry, Nanny Hart-Davis, Nanny Brett,
Nanny Dennis (Pam's new name). Nannies were still called
by their employers' names, and would stay with a family until
the children had gone to boarding-school and often longer.

There was also Paula. Paula Long was a great beauty, an
early *Vogue* model. A little older than Celia (though never
entirely accurate about her age), she had been married three
times; her third husband, 'Boy' Long, had lived and farmed
in Kenya and they had been part of the now legendary wartime
Happy Valley set, Paula being one of the few people to emerge
with any credit from the stories of that time. Having left Kenya
with no money, she was lent a bungalow, about a quarter
of a mile from Merrimoles, by Colin and Gladdie Buist (Colin
Buist, a retired naval commander and old friend of the Duke
of Windsor, had a farm which abutted the estate), and there
she remained for thirty-odd years until Alzheimer's disease
meant that she could live on her own no longer. Paula was
warm and unaffected, with enormous style and excellent taste;
she adored children, having none of her own, and indeed had
many friends of all ages and milieux. (The grander ones tended
to have twenties' nicknames – Baba, Bobo, Cocky.) She combined great generosity with a certain self-centredness. She
always maintained that she was Russian – and she never learnt
to drive. She became a great friend of the family, almost part
of it, and Celia drove her everywhere. Although they often
infuriated each other, Paula was always welcome at Merrimoles, and the children spent a lot of time in her bungalow.

Celia really liked family best. She enjoyed doing things
with friends, bridge and tennis in particular, but she was not
one to gossip for hours, or unbutton herself at all. She would
get into a state about going to a party and always dreaded
them, and then to her surprise would have a good time. She
never curried favour. She could seem off-hand; this was partly

because she was extremely short-sighted. Her eyes, so expressive in her acting, were rarely seen in ordinary life, hidden
behind thick-lensed glasses. She still made little effort with
her appearance – a perm now and again, perhaps a suit from
Jaeger, an occasional expensive pair of shoes – though when
the occasion demanded, she would splash out on an evening
dress and look very good. She always had an excellent slim
figure, and to the end of her life was proud of the fact that
she could touch her toes. She did not like extravagance; the
economies of the war had become deeply ingrained in her.

Peter now looked forward to running the estate that his
uncle had so generously given him just before the war. He
also joined the Territorial Army, looking perhaps for the regimental life that he had never really had during the war. For
a while, on Tim Nugent's nomination, he was on the Advisory
Board of the Lord Chamberlain's office, the official censor.
He was happy to play the part of the landed gentleman, adding
to his small income with some journalism. He wrote a weekly
column, signed Strix, for the *Spectator*. (Many of these pieces
were later collected into slim volumes and published by Rupert
Hart-Davis – *My Aunt's Rhinoceros* (1956), *The Gower Street
Poltergeist* (1958), and *Goodbye to the Bombay Bowler* (1961)).
He also wrote brilliant if characteristic fourth leaders for *The
Times*. The following, entitled 'The Carriage Waits', is a typical
example on a domestic theme and carries a flavour of Merrimoles at the time:

Small children who go out to a party have to be fetched back from
it; so much, even in the worst-regulated households, is almost axio-
matic. Some fathers occasionally volunteer, some – perhaps less
rarely – are detailed for this duty. Few, until they have performed
it several times, realise in how many delicate social problems it is
liable to involve them. In order to fetch children from a party it
is first of all necessary to know where the party is taking place;
and many a father before now has discovered, on the very eve of
setting out on his errand of mercy, that he has been inadequately
briefed on this fundamental point. 'Ursula's birthday party' – that,
he knows, is the social function which his offspring are attending;
and Ursula he identifies with reasonable certainty as the pretty little
girl who had a sort of fit at the fireworks. But who are Ursula's

parents, and where do they live? His mind is a blank on the subject. He seems to remember being told that Ursula has a pony – or was it a Siamese cat? But that is not enough to go on, on a dark winter's night; and if his spouse is absent he is often obliged to make several anxious telephone calls to other parents of the younger set in the neighbourhood.

Less than half an hour later, having parked his car in a flower-bed, he has gained admittance to the scene of the revelry. The continuous din of tin-whistles, mouth-organs, and hooters is punctuated by the intermittent bursting of balloons, each explosion being followed by a wail of grief and rage. 'You've come', says Ursula's mother, advancing in a slightly distrait manner through all this pandemonium, 'for yours?' This is the moment when, if everyone's luck is in, the man's children make their appearance, thus enabling Ursula's mother to identify him and dispelling his own suspicions that he has come to the wrong house.

His children, after unloading on him a selection of paper hats and balloons and enjoining him to take the greatest care of them, are led away to be prepared for the homeward journey. The man finds himself becalmed in a group of ladies with whom his acquaintance, if any, is slight. He feels – needlessly no doubt – at a disadvantage. The only possible topic of conversation is, obviously, children, and these ladies know so much more than he does about (so to speak) the points of a child, are so infinitely better informed about which children belong to whom, that he cannot hope to say anything intelligent or even sensible. He feels out of place, and this feeling is not lessened by the calculated and rather pitying look with which the ladies assess him. 'I wonder,' each seems to be asking herself (and no doubt they will ask each other the moment he has gone), 'why his wife didn't come? He looks so lost and unhappy. I wonder . . .' But at last his children reappear, looking dissipated but cheerful. 'Say goodbye.' They do so, with infinite reluctance; and the man as he shepherds them out to the car feels that he has made unnecessary heavy weather of a really perfectly simple operation.

A month after Lucy was born, Peter had an accident. A horse he was riding fell on him, crushing his pelvis. Although only a short distance from Merrimoles he was unable to move. He was rescued by chance by a Pole from the former American camp in the woods. He was laid up for several months, though not for as many as his doctor advised, scolding him: 'Everybody's bones take the same time to heal, whoever you are.'

In August he went out shooting rabbits with Frankie Wilson. 'First shots fired since I broke my pelvis. I sat in a chair like a rajah and the gun felt very heavy.' The doctor would not have approved. But Peter was tough and he was obstinate. Some friends claimed that his spirit never quite recovered from this accident, though it is more likely that, like others, he had simply aged during the war and been disorientated by it.

This injury did, however, mean that Celia and Peter were able to take a short holiday together; they took Nichol by boat to Stavanger in Norway. There they stayed for a few days in a hotel where they were amazed and delighted by the quantity and variety of food available.

Peter's nomadic life was, however, largely over and his life as a country gentleman began. (On Lucy's birth certificate in 1947, he put 'landowner' as his occupation.) And although he loved the land and the woods, and was happy to have a settled life with his family, something he had never really known with his exotic mother, ultimately it bored him. Although he was patient in temperament, he was also restless. He was amused by the details of estate management and pain-staking about them, but they never really taxed his powerful mind – and the financial side of it always bored him, even though, contrary to what many thought, he did not have much money. Evelyn Waugh paid him a visit in 1946 when staying with Lady Pamela Berry:

I went to call on Peter Fleming who lives next door. Too extraordi-nary. He is very rich and has built himself the most hideous little Golders Green villa. He farms 2,000 acres and never has an egg or a pat of butter and lives on rations from the local Co-operative Stores. He dresses in khaki shorts and a military shirt. His wife has had to leave the stage because they have no cook.

Peter's journalism was as elegantly written as ever, but fiction eluded him. Before the war he had longed to write a play, but he never succeeded. After the war he began a novel called *The Sett*, but failed to finish it. He wrote no more short stories. Either he had no true creative imagination, or, more likely, he suppressed it; either way he felt it a failure – and once or twice, late at night, uncharacteristically, admitted as much to his younger sister, Amaryllis. When his brother Ian wrote *Casino Royale* in 1952 and James Bond came into the world, Peter was delighted for him; he was never jealous of the great success of the Bond novels, though he may have felt a little more keenly his own inability to write fiction.

After the war, Peter's interest in the theatre waned. He still occasionally reviewed plays, and he was a good judge of performance. He encouraged Celia and gave her advice, when she, ever indecisive, could not make up her mind about an offer, but, once she had accepted a part, he would not interfere. Some claim that he came to resent the theatre, but there was no suggestion of that at home. Always ill at ease at social events he was particularly uncomfortable in the exuberant company of actors. He felt strongly about family support on first nights and always lent his to Celia. But at the same time, he took it for granted that the household would be run – or, certainly, Celia thought that he assumed that. So, for the next ten years or so, while her daughters were little, she boxed and coxed with home, films and theatre, thinking that she enjoyed home, actually often enjoying work more. Her luck with her choice of work during the 1950s was mixed.

21

Films in the fifties

Celia followed Shaw with Shakespeare, playing Ophelia to John Gielgud's Hamlet in a BBC broadcast. Andrew Cruickshank was the King. It was transmitted on Boxing Day 1948 and repeated on New Year's Eve. It was seventeen years since she had played Ophelia in New York, and this time the text had not been massacred.

Early in 1949, while giving the little girls their bath one evening, the telephone rang, and on answering it with dripping hands, she found Noel Coward at the other end. He offered her a part in a film of one of the remaining small plays from 'Tonight at 8.30'. She was delighted. Although the part was in no way as interesting as that of Laura Jesson in *Brief Encounter*, she must nevertheless have felt that she was on reliable ground. The film was called *The Astonished Heart*. It was produced by Sydney Box and directed by Terence Fisher and Anthony Darnborough, Coward's 'little darlings' having gone their own way to film Dickens. The film is about a psychiatrist who after many years of marriage (to Celia) falls madly in love with a friend of hers (Margaret Leighton); his professional training fails to help him resolve his own emotional crisis and, after being sent by his wife on a holiday with his mistress, he returns and throws himself out of the window of their flat. Michael Redgrave was to play the psychiatrist, but, early in rehearsals, Noel Coward replaced him with himself. It was a piece of gross miscasting; Coward looked quite out of place as the passionate lover of the leggy Miss Leighton. She looks magnificent but her scenes with Coward are ridiculous. The psychology was dated and crude. Celia, back in her old role of the wronged wife, looks tired and depressed, and, indeed, Joyce Carey remembers her being irritable during the making of it that hot summer. Even Joyce Carey seems dull as the psychiatrist's assistant. The film opened first in New York (the first British film to do so), and then in London in March 1950. 'Seldom can expectation have wilted so quickly and so completely as it did in face of *The Astonished Heart*,' wrote C.A.Lejeune. 'The film's worst fault is that it fails to touch the emotions at any point.' Coward's flair seemed to have deserted him; it was a humiliating failure.

Celia put it behind her and that summer returned to the Old Vic company to join them for a tour of Italy in *Twelfth Night* (*Dodicesima Notte*). From 1944 to 1949 the Old Vic had enjoyed a glorious period under Laurence Olivier, Ralph Richardson and John Burrell until, in 1949, Olivier and Richardson were abruptly sacked by Lord Esher, the chairman of the Old Vic Theatre Company. Some say that those five years produced the finest theatre in the twentieth century. There had been, without question, some superb productions, such as *Peer Gynt*, *Richard III*, *Uncle Vanya*, *Oedipus the King*. The transition from the old triumvirate to Hugh Hunt, the newly appointed director, was not entirely happy. *Twelfth Night* was an early production under the new regime.

The cast for the tour of Italy included Roger Livesey as Sir Toby Belch, Ursula Jeans as Olivia, Celia as Viola, Robert Eddison as Sir Andrew Aguecheek and Ernest Milton as Malvolio. Ernest Milton was an old pre-war actor who had become rather sour and difficult; he was a baroque figure, a sort of genius, but paranoid. Celia had acted with him nearly twenty years earlier in *Death Takes a Holiday* where he, playing Death, had swooped around the stage in a long black cloak in Edwardian fashion. She had asked him before they set off on this tour, whether he spoke any Italian. 'No', he replied, 'but I have mastered the phrase, "*Dove la principessa?*" That will get me through, don't you think?' He adored Venice where, with his head held high, his aquiline nose, he was transported into the past. He became very annoyed with Celia. He told Alec Guinness (who related the story in his memoirs, *Blessings in Disguise*) while dining with him and his wife, Merula, shortly after their return, 'Celia Johnson is Beelzebub!' He meant it; so Alec Guinness said, rising to her defence: 'But Ernest, Celia is one of the most loved women in the profession and profoundly admired by us all, both as an actress and as a person. What right have you to say something so monstrous?'

'I have my reasons,' he replied. 'She went down the Grand
Canal in a gondola doing *The Times* crossword puzzle and
never once so much as glancing at Venetian palaces.' Alec
defended again: 'She's as blind as a bat and probably couldn't
even see the canal. And, anyway, why shouldn't she do *The
Times* crossword in a gondola? She has a passion for cross-
words.' 'I say she is an evil woman.' 'Oh come off it!' 'So
I am a liar?' – and he left the house, to return a little later
to finish his duck, but to speak not another word.

Their director, Norman Marshall, had jaundice, so, led by
Roger Livesey the actors directed themselves. Hugh Hunt,
the new director of the Old Vic, accompanied them to Italy.
They went via Paris on 10 June 1950 which was, as it happened,
Robert Eddison's birthday. Celia, having discovered that he
had never seen Paris, hailed a taxi and sent him off to see
the sights, telling him to see as much as he could before they
caught the train for Italy. He was very touched. That was
the sort of generous gesture, based on instant inspiration, that
she was rather good at; consistent good works she cared for
less.

They opened in Florence, as part of a festival, then went
to Rome, Venice, Milan, Trieste, ending in Turin. It was
hard work; it was also glorious. They had left post-war aus-
terity and the tail-end of rationing in England, with London
in rubble, and found themselves in beautiful cities in hot sun-
shine. There was food and there were new cars on the roads;
it was a huge contrast. Celia, as before, responded to the
Mediterranean sun, and enjoyed the beauty. She came to love
Italy and was always amused by the Italians. In Venice they
stayed in a lovely hotel on the Grand Canal, and she and
Ursula Jeans insisted on going by gondola (and no doubt she
occasionally lifted her eyes to the palaces) to the stage door
of the Fenice Theatre. Trieste was still under the triumvirate
after the war and there the company were entertained by
the British contingent who were based in a castle on the cliffs
overlooking the Adriatic. In Turin news came of further
trouble in Indo-China and a tremor passed through them all.

Many of the cast, soon after their return, went on into
the production of *Twelfth Night* that was to open the newly

restored Old Vic. It had been closed for a decade after having
been damaged by a bomb. Peggy Ashcroft played Viola for
the opening production. Before the grand opening in
November at the Old Vic, they tried it out in Oxford and
the company came over and lunched at Merrimoles.

The following year, one hundred years after the Great Exhi-
bition of 1851, and to restore morale after the ravages of the
war, the Festival of Britain was held. The theatre played its
part; Binkie Beaumont put on no fewer than eight plays. He
asked Celia to play Olga in *The Three Sisters* at the Aldwych.
It was, on the face of it, an excellent cast: Margaret Leighton
and Renée Asherson were Masha and Irina, and Ralph
Richardson played Vershinin. Diana Churchill and Harcourt
Williams were also in it and Peter Ashmore was the director.
Chekhov, with his nuance and sensitivity, pathos and humour,
should have been the ideal vehicle for Celia's talent but she
did not find the part easy.

I wonder how many people realise how difficult it is to play in one
of his [Chekhov's] plays. At least I find it so, on coming to him
fresh. At first sight one might think his characters were easy to
impersonate. They are so vividly drawn, so distinctive, so full of self-
expression in almost every line, that they might appear to play themselves. Yet there is something elusive, hard to catch. *Three Sisters*
is unlike most other plays. It is like a piece of subtle, impressionistic
orchestral music, where all the parts have to be welded skilfully
together. It is a play where the characters have a strong, almost
intense effect on one another, and yet this effect is an 'oblique' one,
felt and implied rather than directly expressed. To the actor or actress
this presents special difficulties, for you are not so much playing
scenes with people, as in other plays. You are contributing to a
delicate orchestration. In these circumstances you feel at first rather
in the dark, wondering whether the subtleties are making any impression at all. Finally, you find that they are, for the master's hand
has calculated every shade of effect.

To some, her performance was clearly too subtle: 'Miss Celia
Johnson made curiously little effect,' wrote T.C. Worsley in
the *New Statesman*; however, the *Spectator* was of the view
that 'Miss Celia Johnson's performance could scarcely be bet-
tered'.

It was generally agreed that the production was ponderous and never came alive; it failed to find the necessary magic – 'much of the play's essence, its haunting sadness and its pervading humour is lost'. For Celia it was the beginning of a rewarding professional relationship with Ralph Richardson.

Towards the end of that year she made two films. First, *I Believe in You*, for Ealing studios, a worthy if stilted piece in which Celia, uncharacteristically, played a schoolmarmish probation officer. Cecil Parker also played a probation officer, a new recruit coming to the profession late and fast learning the ways of petty criminals, and Sir Godfrey Tearle was a magistrate. None of it is very convincing, but like most Ealing films of that period it has its moments and is beautifully cast in the small parts (George Relph, Laurence Harvey, Ursula Howells, Gladys Henson, Katie Johnson, Sidney James). It is remembered now chiefly because it gave Joan Collins, as the delinquent girl on probation, her first part. She 'has a photogenic face, good voice, and might turn into an actress if she wants to learn and doesn't let quick praise unsettle her', wrote C. A. Lejeune. Celia thought her rather precocious. The camera was less kind to Celia, who was described as 'sad-eyed', but who, according to Lejeune, 'still reserves the magic trick of pulling out the extra stroke of emotion that catches one unawares'.

That particular trick was seen again in the second film, *The Holly and the Ivy*. A screen adaptation of a highly success-ful play of the same name by Wynyard Browne, it was about a garrulous and absent-minded vicar (Ralph Richardson) and his grown-up family – daughters (Celia and Margaret Leighton) and son on National Service (Denholm Elliott) – and their gathering for Christmas in the rectory in Norfolk. Directed by George More O'Ferrall and made at Shepperton, it is very much a filmed play with long static takes that has as its subject, like many plays of that time, family relationships thrashed out in the drawing-room. In fact it is in the kitchen, with Margaret Leighton, that Celia's old trick, noted above by Lejeune, is seen again. It is just a short scene in which Celia, chiefly through her eyes, shows great truth and feeling.

'There is certainly a natural magic about Miss Johnson's playing,' wrote *The Times* critic. The film was well received and occasionally appears at Christmas on television; it is very dated. She must have had quite fun as, in the cast, were her old friends, Hugh Williams and Roland Culver.

In her next film, made in 1953, *The Captain's Paradise*, directed by Anthony Kimmins, she at last had an opportunity to play comedy, something she had been longing to do. She also had another excellent scene of washing up – or rather of tipsily rinsing a sherry glass under a tap. There is many a cliché in the acting of drunkenness, but Celia avoided them. She made the very most of an ordinary part as the conventional home-loving wife of a ship's captain (Alec Guinness). The captain keeps a glamorous mistress (Yvonne de Carlo) in another port: he puts on his carpet slippers when with Celia, and goes out on the town with Yvonne, changing the photograph in his cabin half-way between the two ports. The story turns on the homebody longing to live it up, and the night-clubber longing to cook rissoles and darn socks, and the confusion that ensues. Alec Guinness is excellent and the film is very funny. Both he and Celia had difficulty with the dancing they had to do; he was taught the mamba by Yvonne de Carlo; Celia in a sort of liberated jitterbug left it to instinct and gave a wonderfully comic and impromptu performance, throwing a defiant glance at her horror-struck husband (Alec Guinness). This film was the first indication of her true potential as a comic actress. Only her voice lets her down with its over-refined vowels and a rather shrill tone.

Picturegoer published an article about her in 1952 entitled 'Why don't we see more of Celia?' It describes her as elusive. 'There has always been a battle going on inside her between her home and her career, and her home life has mostly been on the winning side.' Merrimoles is described, as usual, as informal and unaffected.

These films, though none of them very special, suited her well with their limited timetable of work. She had a horror of long runs in the West End, no doubt born of her two years in *The Wind and the Rain*, so much of which had been spent in great anxiety over Peter's whereabouts in Central

Asia. She also enjoyed small children and did not want to miss her daughters' early years. She was after all the product of a very conventional upbringing, the traditions of which said that your main purpose, as a woman, was to be a wife and mother. Did she also subconsciously rein herself in a bit and not take on too much for fear of jeopardising her marriage? In that rather dull period of theatre in the early fifties there was no shortage of offers. Even television was courting her. A memo from the head of television drama at the BBC went out in July 1954: 'For interest's sake – and without involving anyone in great expenditure of time – have we any means of ascertaining how many parts we have offered to Celia Johnson? I, for instance, wrote *Promise of Tomorrow* for her. I would be interested in the exercise.'

The reply came:

Celia Johnson was definitely approached for *Candida* (Royston Morley) in 1951, and for Caroline in *If This Be The Error* (Stephen Harrison) in 1953. She was also approached for the lead in *This Happy Breed* and *The Deep Blue Sea*. We have no definite notes but can say from memory that we have made her a firm offer for practically every play produced by Royston Morley in which there was a suitable part. Stephen Harrison has asked for her on more than the one occasion mentioned above and both Ian Atkins and George More O'Ferrall have asked for her in the past. We have not been asked to approach her for about a year now.

What conclusions the BBC drew from this exercise are not known – but they did not hook her until 1956, when she did a play called *The Letter* by Somerset Maugham. She was blithely unaware of her desirability. She was also, probably, like most actors of her generation, suspicious of television.

She made only two more films in the 1950s (and only two others during the rest of her life). Carol Reed, an old friend, must have persuaded her to be in his film, *A Kid for Two Farthings*, a sentimental story about an old East End tailor and a small boy who gets hold of a kid goat with a crumpled horn and pretends that it is a unicorn that can make wishes come true. It was based on a book by Wolf Mankowitz. Because of Carol Reed's reputation, it was respectfully received and indeed won second prize at the Cannes Film Festival in 1955, but really it is a mis-hit. Celia, as in *This Happy Breed*, was out of place in the East End, and again the camera did her no favours. 'Celia Johnson plays the mother without benefit of glamour.' The cast included Diana Dors, who was the most glamorous of the buxom, peroxide blonde actresses who were popular in the fifties. She surprised Celia by settling down, when she was not needed on the set, to do painting by numbers. The kid, Theodora, failed to co-operate, first by turning out to be male (and was thereafter known as Butch) and secondly, by growing far too quickly.

Lastly, in 1957, she was very good as Miss Trant ('a pleasant woman who has decided to seek adventure after a quiet country life') in a mediocre musical version of J.B.Priestley's novel *The Good Companions*, about a stranded provincial concert party. With that, at the age of fifty, her film career came to a halt for eleven years.

Sometime in the 1950s she wrote a piece called 'Film Star Manqué'. (She sent it to her brother John who was now an established literary agent.)

For a short while, some years ago, I was a sort of sub-film star. This was very surprising, and by the time I had got used to it I stopped being one. I was never very good, frankly, I was very bad at doing the sort of things that film stars are required to do by the publicity department. I remember, in Paris, being photographed shaking hands with the engine drivers at the Gare du Nord. I got the giggles and they must have thought me rather impolite but I wanted to tell them, as if they didn't know, that they were not shaking hands with a real film star but only with me, and that it was very nice of them to be so kind and pretend so well. Later on I used to try to do better by over-playing it more and giving great, goofy smiles and wearing long, smart French gloves, but it wasn't a part that suited me.

At a Berlin film festival that I attended, I managed to be so insignificant that the organisers omitted to invite me to the main celebrations in a vast open-air amphitheatre. This delighted me, but the kind director who was with me was so annoyed by the rebuff and slight to me and to the film that he planned a tremendous splash at the opening night of our film. He arranged to go on stage and make a speech in German building me up, and read telegrams and tributes from anyone he could think of, and then I was to come on in my most splendid dress and bow and smile in a scintillating manner and be snowed under with flowers and make a little halting speech in German ... the halting part was easy enough ... and everyone would see that I was a great and fine Film Star. As I waited in the wings to go on and do this I couldn't quite understand why the director's speech was taking so long, but when at last I heard my name and floated on, wreathed in smiles, I found a face of anguish greeting me. 'That was a near thing', he gasped in my ear, while heaving great wodges of flowers towards me, 'I had to spin out my speech for ages because I simply couldn't think of your name.'

So none of this do I regret, but sometimes I get a sort of nostalgia for the actual work of filming. I miss the strange, unmistakeable smell of size and paint that you find on all film sets and the hot powdery smell of the makeup rooms. I miss the curious sort of camera worship that goes on. It has its own devoted band of acolytes who feed it and polish it and push it gently about and shield it from harsh lights. They even fling blondes in front of it like tributes to a savage god. There is an organised confusion on a film set when nothing seems to happen for hours and then everything goes quiet for a few seconds, and in those few seconds you have to try and fit something consistent and true on to something that you probably did days before or have not yet done. There is a challenge in trying to act in a little cut-off bit of light, with no audience but the technicians and a fastidious director. Those technicians not concerned with the take are probably filling in their football pools and if you can make them look up and watch to the end of your shot you have probably achieved something.

I like the dedication that great directors have, when nothing matters except the film they are making and they cannot think that anything matters to anyone else either. I like being measured for focus by a tape from the end of one's nose to the camera and measured for light by the camera-man with his meter and I like to watch the skill of the technicians and I forget all the things I don't like. They were many. Mainly the waiting about, particularly on those depressing days when one had an early call, and that means dawn rising, and then, because of some hold-up, not be needed on the set until dusk. Rushes I never liked. That is when you see the shots of the day before and are horrified at your lack of subtlety or the size of your nose.

I used to be annoyed by what I thought was the waste, but at the same time impressed by the lordly way in which anything – however peculiar, rare or costly – could be produced at a moment's notice. I liked the machine that can make cobwebs, delicate threads of a rubbery solution shot from a spray in a twinkling and the detailed observation shown by the continuity girls, who can tell you the length of ash on your cigarette necessary to match for a close-up. I have always liked professionals and to watch professional film-making from the inside is a pleasure, though not, I think, from the outside, and I am glad that for a while I was able to do this. I never felt anything but surprise at being there, but I also think and hope that I became a professional at it on the set, though never on parade.

22

Wild animals

Binkie Beaumont of H.M.Tennent was a figure of enormous power and influence in the theatre from the late thirties to the 1970s. He was devious and slithery and hard-headed; he could not tell the truth and yet you could trust him, or at least if you were a star you could. He often did not bother with contracts. His power base was a little office above the Globe Theatre in Shaftesbury Avenue. From there he would put on ten or so plays a year and from there he would hire and fire. If, for one reason or another, an actor was out of favour with him, then a whole area of theatre was barred to him. Binkie's productions were not adventurous, though some of the dramatists he promoted who seem safe and established now were less so then (Rattigan, Christopher Fry, N.C.Hunter). He cast plays very effectively. The designers he employed included Motley (Elizabeth Montgomery, Sophia and Margaret Harris) and Roger Furse, all highly professional, and his lighting man was Joe Davis. No actor or actress of whatever calibre working in the West End through the war and beyond could ignore Binkie. His declining years in the late 1960s, when the theatre he knew was slipping away from him and his empire shrinking, were sad and pathetic.

Binkie simply didn't understand why actresses, such as Celia or Peggy Ashcroft, should have children whom they wished to spend time with, and not give themselves utterly to his plans. Celia, who loved work but was not dependent on it, could deal with him in a perfectly straightforward way. No doubt there were parts she missed through not kowtowing more, but she was – fortunately for her and although she did not fully realise it – in a strong position. He appreciated her talent – and her popularity, for Celia from early days had had a very loyal following of fans – but he despaired of her commitment. He would say, when discussing a play, 'Oh, Celia will only do it if she wants a pair of new curtains.'

In the 1950s he was a voice frequently to be heard on the telephone in the hall at Merrimoles. Celia and Binkie must have met in 1933, when Binkie had produced *The Wind and the Rain*. *Rebecca* was his production (he thought Celia excellent in it) as was *The Importance of Being Earnest* and *The Doctor's Dilemma* in the war. Well-made, well-cast plays under proscenium arches, with glittering first nights were his thing.

That was the theatre of the early fifties. *The Deep Blue Sea* put on by Tennent in 1952 epitomised it. Terence Rattigan, best known then for *French Without Tears* and *The Winslow Boy*, was very much in vogue. This play was the story of a vicar's daughter, the wife of a judge, who falls for a young pilot, one of those who had fitted so gallantly into the RAF only to find themselves misfits after the war. The young man, out of his emotional depth, fails to reciprocate fully her passion and causes her to contemplate suicide. It is, like several other Rattigan plays, a story of unequal love and had been based on the actual suicide of a lover of his, though shifted from homosexual into heterosexual terms. Peggy Ashcroft played the wife, Hester Collyer, to great acclaim, Roland Culver the judge and Kenneth More gave a well-judged performance as the pilot, who would flick his cigarette butt on to the floor to show his devil-may-care attitude. Hester was a strong part – implicitly about a middle-aged lady being struck by sex – and required a certain unveiling of the soul.

Although standard contracts were still for the length of the play, Binkie, no doubt realising that he might have difficulties otherwise, now let his stars have a six-month get-out clause. He allowed Peggy Ashcroft, who like Celia had small children, to have a long holiday and Celia took over for a while. Rattigan was thought lucky to have secured both of them for his play. Frith Banbury, who directed the play, says that they each took hold of the part in different ways. Peggy was the more tragic, and Celia the more pathetic. Whereas Celia brought tears to the eyes more readily, Peggy hit you in the stomach. Peggy's technique was the more assured. Celia 'added a sense of utter desolation which tore at one's heart'. It was a *succès d'estime* and a commercial success, and it must have been fun for Celia, who was seen in the theatre so little at this stage, to have had a satisfying part in a popular production. There is a world of difference in acting to a full house night after night, with friends pouring round to your dressing-room afterwards, to playing in a flop to dwindling houses when friends and relations turn up out of loyalty and try to find something encouraging to say afterwards.

In 1952 King George VI died, and Princess Elizabeth became Queen. As such, she attended the Royal Film Performance that autumn at the Odeon Leicester Square. Peter and Celia were invited and I, aged six, was asked to present a bouquet to the young Queen. We all stayed with Peter's brother, Richard, and Uncle Phil, in the Fleming house in Hyde Park Square, where various Fleming cousins who worked at Robert Fleming, the bank, stayed during the week. (At weekends most of them returned to their families in the Cotswolds to hunt with the Heythrop, and in August they all moved to Argyll to shoot and fish. They got on astonishingly well considering they worked, lived and played together.) There, Nanny brushed my hair a hundred times for the occasion. Celia thought the Queen wonderful.

Celia was a keen, though not a blinkered, monarchist, and the Coronation of the Queen in June 1953 gave her a lot of pleasure. Indeed, Merrimoles installed a television for the occasion; this was rather advanced for there were not many television sets in the neighbourhood (although the little Rubin girls who lived half-way down the hill to Henley and who were granddaughters of Sir Michael Sobell, the electronics manufacturer, had several sets, much to the envy and incredulity of the Fleming children). Family and friends crowded round to watch the ceremony and the Union Jack, as was the custom then, was hoisted up the flagpole in the garden.

Nichol had by now left his prep school, Sunningdale, and was at Eton. To his delight, Celia had bought a Humber Super Snipe, a handsome car, and, to Peter's dismay, she had acquired a poodle from Naomi Sim (Alastair Sim's wife). Peter always had gun dogs, about whom he affected not to be sentimental. He abhorred sentimentality over pets and animals, thinking they should either be wild or have a purpose, such as a gun dog or a hunter. In fact he ill concealed his soppiness and always became deeply attached to his labradors. Spoof the poodle however, having neither purpose nor being feral, was not the sort of pet he approved of. But the little dog – a mangy sort of poodle – turned out to be highly intelligent and a great character, and lived for many years. Lucy and I, however, were on the wild side; Lucy was a tomboy and was always at the top of a tree or racing about on a pony. I was very shy and shot upstairs whenever anyone visited the house. Neither of us would put on a dress if we could possibly help it. Our manners left a lot to be desired.

The informal and unaffected character of Merrimoles noted by journalists who occasionally came to interview Celia became even more so when Peter began to introduce wild animals into the household, which already boasted the labradors, the poodle, a cat, ponies and a horse or two. There were a couple of charming owls, one of which drowned in the swimming-pool (which had been built in 1950); the other was given Lucy's deceased pet dormouse to eat. There were two fox cubs, Satan and Sophie – Satan had only three legs, having lost one in a trap. They romped with the labradors, and after a while, until they met sticky ends, lived wild and came in only to be fed, 'leading a double life between the beechwoods and the drawing-room sofa', as Peter wrote in the *Spectator*. The kestrel, a great success, did the same, living in the woods and coming to the hand when whistled for. The raven (Countess Dracula) was considered rather dull, and was attacked by the dogs. The call of the wild was not for Nutto, the grey squirrel: 'Just like a little ornament,' said Nanny, when Nutto sat on the mantelpiece. She also ran along the pelmets, and would help herself to chocolates and leave them on top of bookshelves. She stole all Peter's best ties and chewed them up for her nest. Nutto was at her most boisterous at the time that Peter was High Sheriff of Oxfordshire, and as such had to entertain judges to lunch. The dignity of these occasions would be destroyed when Nutto leapt from the curtains to the dining-room table, and in the end she was banished from the house. Peter wrote:

A month later, Nutto still uses my house as a *pied à terre*, but apart from stripping the wisteria and on two consecutive mornings stealing the butter off the breakfast table she has not done us a great deal of harm. She seems however bent on establishing a reign of terror in the neighbourhood and has effected an entry into several cottages within a radius of a mile of us, to the consternation of their occupants. On paper it looks as if she must come to a sticky end before too long; but such is her resource and agility that it will not be easy to bring her to book. Last time I saw her she was sitting on top of a cupboard in the dining-room, eating a grape with a preoccupied air and spitting the pips venomously across the room. 'Nutto', I said, 'one of these days you will go too far.' She looked at me with contempt and went on guzzling.

Celia, struggling to run a household, and never mad about animals, had to contend with the wild menagerie. The animals, as might be imagined, although popular with the children, did not help to smooth relations with the cook or the daily cleaner. Nanny, however, took them entirely in her stride and mostly looked after them. Celia in her acting, especially of comedy, had a knack of depicting herself doing her best while at the mercy of events; it sometimes happened in life too.

Although there were a lot of jokes and a lot of fun at Merri-moles – it was a very relaxed place – it was about this time that there were also beginning to be strains, after nearly twenty years, in the marriage. Peter and Celia weathered these, but during the rockiest moments, both unquestionably suffered and there were times of unhappiness. Peter, fearful and clumsy before female tears, no doubt handled matters badly. As we have seen, neither was inclined to unburden himself or herself, and doubtless grievances were insufficiently aired. A combination of guilt and stiff upper-lip was not perhaps the right healer. Celia may have confided in somebody, but more likely she did not; as her father had noticed when she was a child, she kept her own counsel. During the war, Peter had written to her about his friends: 'I like my friends very much and also respect them; and I'm getting to be so rude in company and so uncommunicative out of it that I sometimes feel I shan't make any more.' Indeed, Peter, always prone to taciturnity, turned in further on himself. Both were in their late forties – not an easy age – but both were courageous and obstinate, and they had been through so much that they were not going to give up that easily. Peter had never been exactly a companionable husband; although kind and sensitive beneath his tough facade, he was always a loner, and with Celia's work, his travels and shooting, they had always led more separate lives than many couples. For holidays, Peter never came to Polzeath, and Celia did not always go to Scotland, though they still enjoyed skiing together. Their lives slowly became more independent. In spite of this, family life remained fun, and was enormously important to both of them.

23

The Reluctant Débutante

With a brief spell in a comedy by Felicity Douglas called *It's Never Too Late* at the Westminster Theatre in 1954, Celia was beginning to be drawn back to the theatre again. The critics welcomed her return in what was a pleasantly silly family entertainment. It was one of those plays that she carried effortlessly: 'the dramatist has some of the credit, but most of it is Miss Johnson's' – was a typical comment. The character that she portrayed was a mother who writes a novel, and who leaves her turbulent and selfish family to go to America to be honoured as a novelist, and to concentrate on her writing. However, she discovers that in trying to escape from her family for the benefit of her art, she is doing no good to either, and her muse deserts her. It was to some extent Celia's dilemma too.

By 1955, when Lucy and I were eight and nine and Nichol was in his last years at Eton, she was beginning to feel that she could let the brake off and devote more time to the theatre. The girls were settled at local schools, riding their ponies, playing with friends round the woods, in and out of Paula's bungalow. Celia, with Nanny's invaluable support, had seen them through their tiny years, keeping a delicate balance between work and home; it was an achievement to be proud of. She still wanted to be at home for the school holidays – much to Binkie's and other producers' exasperation – but from now on she would keep fairly regularly in work, especially during the winter months.

In 1955, Jack Minster, a producer whom Celia respected (and who was known as Jolly Jack, because of his pessimistic outlook on life), offered her the part of Sheila Broadbent in *The Reluctant Débutante*. This was a comedy by William Douglas-Home about the problems of getting a daughter fashionably married by way of the upper-class marriage market, 'the season'. Celia played the débutante's mother. When discussing who should play the young man, William Douglas-Home remembers that Celia suggested Jack Merivale. 'And is he a good actor?' asked the producer, Paul Clift. 'I wouldn't know about that,' answered Celia, 'but he can drop me every night on Henley Bridge on his way home.' Jack Merivale got the part, and very good he was too. Anna Massey, Raymond Massey's daughter, was chosen for the débutante; she was seventeen and very nervous; a little way into rehearsals she was not making much headway with the part and it looked as if she might have to be dropped. Celia, together with Ambrosine Philpotts, an actress of Celia's age with a throaty voice who was also in the play, pleaded for her retention and suggested a little encouragement. Anna made a great success of the part of the débutante and so began a distinguished career. Celia, as time went on, would quite often take an interest in a young actress in her play, perhaps remembering how Gerald du Maurier had given her encouragement (Rebecca Saire and Sylvestra le Touzel were two young actresses with whom she acted later and who she thought showed promise). The play was very much in the 1950s formula – wit in the drawing-room of the upper-classes (a line such as, 'I'm always in love with someone', followed by the retort, 'You must be oversexed', brought the house down) – but, and this some critics grudgingly agreed, *The Reluctant Débutante* was skilfully constructed and amusing. 'It is hardly an important play but it is a very funny one.' William Douglas-Home, a Scottish aristocrat, seldom found favour with the critics (although in the 1960s, Harold Hobson, for the *Sunday Times* began to sing his praises). J.C. Trewin wrote of this play: 'Mr Home has an ear for nonsense, and Miss Johnson (surprising to those who used to think of her as an emotional actress) the tongue to utter it.'

Celia handled the comedy beautifully, especially the first scene in which there is a complicated sequence of telephone calls

– harder than it sounds [wrote Trewin]. It is largely a matter of timing, of neither appearing to get incredibly rapid service nor letting aeons pass while, presumably, the voice at the other end says 'Yes' (or maybe 'No'). Celia dials her wrong numbers with an air; she addresses the wrong people with a flourish; and she is still in a state of telephonic rapture as the curtain flickers down for the last time.

Ivor Brown described her as

fibbing and prattling ... she was always the lady, serving us with a dry white wine, and never the gin queen. Earnestly bewildered, a darling bungler, she carried off by sheer virtuosity an opening scene of almost continuous telephoning which could easily be tedious. As I said, the stars shone on Mr Home, especially the bright particular star that is Miss Johnson.

It was an excellent vehicle for her gift for comedy, and her first real flaunting of it. Noel Coward wrote in his diary of Celia's 'curious distinction'. Her daughters were allowed to go to see it; they sat with their father in a box for the first night. When William Douglas-Home said to Peter how good Celia had been in the play, he agreed, saying with typical understatement that she was 'quite an adequate performer'.

'Except for playing light comedy to an enraptured audience,' Laurence Olivier has written, 'acting is not an enjoyable craft.' Celia enjoyed *The Reluctant Débutante* so much that, unusually, she agreed to extend her contract and played in it for nine months, even over the school holidays; coaxing the laughs from a full house was intoxicating. The play was a great success and was later made into a film, having clocked up seven hundred and fifty performances on the stage.

It was therefore still running in 1956, the year which is generally considered pivotal in the development of British theatre in the second half of the twentieth century. The production of *Look Back in Anger* by John Osborne at the Royal Court (following Brecht's *Mother Courage* and Beckett's *Waiting for Godot*, both put on in 1955) heralded a new naturalism and a different class base in plays. Out, in terms of fashion, went the brigadiers and the French windows (and the débutantes) and in came working-class protagonists, regional accents and, in the course of time, the open stage. At the same time a wide-ranging debate influenced by Brecht on the nature and purpose and structure of the theatre began.

Nothing was sacred any more: the curtain went; language slackened; the old structure of acts and scenes was rebuilt. There was no part of the theatre that did not undergo re-examination and experimentation – not, of course, all at once but through the late fifties and into the sixties.

Censorship of plays by the Lord Chamberlain's office was belatedly abolished in 1968. Much of the theatre of the early 1950s had harked back in spirit to the cosy but formal West End theatre of the 1930s. Rehearsals with actors in denim trained in the Method were a far cry from, say, the old Marie Tempest plays where woe betide you if you did not dress your best, with suits and polished shoes, for rehearsals. The changes were inevitable and salutary and beneficial, even if some of the new plays, greeted as masterpieces, have not lasted, but, as can be imagined, they hit the old guard badly. Some actors, the bolder ones (Olivier, Ashcroft), accepted the changes, recognising the value of some of them, and, albeit nervously, swam with the tide. Others deplored the new order and stuck to the sort of productions they understood, often laying themselves open to the critics' raillery. Kenneth Tynan of the *Sunday Times*, whose astuteness was rendered sarcastic by his arrogance, in particular was feared. The West End cavalry, he wrote, 'went out with a flourish, its banners resplendent in the last rays of the sun'.

Celia in the main belonged to the latter group, the reactionaries, though she was not as die-hard as some. But, naturally conservative, unacquainted with most of the new directors, suspicious of cant and forever associated in people's minds with quintessential English gentility, she stuck to the sort of plays and set-ups she knew. Even so, not all the plays she elected to do over the next few years were considered rearguard.

She would choose a play if she felt it was well written, it offered a good part and if it seemed likely that the cast would be sympathetic and good. There would always be a lot of jockeying of the 'I'll do it if you'll do it' variety, which Aubrey Blackburn, her loyal agent, probably handled with finesse. But acting to Celia, in some ways, was, like bridge or tennis, her favourite pastimes, much more fun if you were playing with people of the same standard as you. It was harder work if you were not. It was all a matter of timing – timing of the casting and timing in technique. It is timing quite often that sets apart the true professionals.

In 1957, Frith Banbury, who envisaged Celia and Ralph Richardson for a new first play by a schoolmaster that he had been asked by Binkie to direct, could not believe his luck when both agreed to do it. He had sent the play to Celia, who had liked it and when asked for suggestions for leading men had given a list with Sir Ralph at the top. Binkie, and indeed Sir Ralph, were not pleased when Celia said she could not rehearse until she had returned from Cornwall with the children at the end of the summer holidays. The play was called *The Flowering Cherry* and its author, the schoolmaster, was Robert Bolt. It was about a suburban insurance salesman, Jim Cherry, who has a perpetual fantasy about moving to Somerset and cultivating a little apple orchard, but when it becomes possible for his fantasy to become reality, he backs away. Sir Ralph was excellent as the empty braggart. As W. A. Darlington has said of him: 'Of all our actors, Richardson has most completely the faculty of standing still on stage, looking perfectly ordinary, and somehow conveying that he is not ordinary at all.' Celia was the long-suffering wife (Isobel Cherry) of the self-deluded salesman. Their children, played by Andrew Ray and Susan Burnett, were typical teenagers of the 1950s, the boy awaiting his call-up papers for National Service and the girl doing a course at college. It is a nicely observed play, centring on Richardson's man of straw.

Harold Hobson, on a second viewing, wrote in the *Sunday Times* that those who missed Richardson's performance 'will never fully know how magnificent the English stage can be at its best. It filled me with a joy which almost made me forget the hatred and the scorn which it is apparently the official policy of "drama" to pour on plays whose characters do not change for dinner or who eat fish with fish knives.' (He was lining up with the old guard). He also found on seeing it for the second time, 'a more intense poignancy in Celia Johnson's "No, no, no, no, no", when faced with the last and most pitiful of Jim Cherry's evasions.'

Ralph Richardson had a line towards the end which included the words 'little rat'. He did not care for this phrase and refused to say it. Robert Bolt was obliged to write him a four-page defence of the line, but still he would not say it. Celia, peering short-sightedly at her script in rehearsal, did not notice the omission first time round. Second time round she did and asked him about it. He explained that he thought that the words 'little rat' were not quite right; she simply said 'Oh', in a quizzical sort of way. Nothing more was said, but from then on he said the line – and Frith Banbury realised that the best way to get Sir Ralph, who was not always amenable to authority, to do something was through Celia. Andrew Ray, who played their son, had a slight speech defect which used to irritate Sir Ralph; there too Celia was able to pour oil on troubled waters.

So it happened before the first night. Sir Ralph, with a bit of adrenalin, had a tendency to overplay; he was better the evening after a matinée when some of that adrenalin had been used up. For that reason it was thought a good idea to have a full run-through if possible directly before the first night. Frith, using Celia as a pretext, put it to Sir Ralph. 'Oh well,' he said, 'I suppose if the dear girl wants it, we must keep her happy.' All went well and Sir Ralph was marvellous. He would also enjoy, as a play went on, embroidering here and there. In this one he made a great play with a keyhole, so much so that they thought of renaming the play 'The Keyhole'. Celia, if anything, underplayed; she was never a show-off. While they were on tour Frith had to try and bring her up a little and bring Sir Ralph down – but once in tune they were captivating. Celia was rather annoyed by the set – there was a wall which petered out symbolically half-way across the stage, and she could not understand why it could not continue right across. The play was a little bit of naturalism with a layer of poetry supplied by Sir Ralph. It marked the end of Robert Bolt's career as a schoolmaster and his beginning as a dramatist. He won an award for most promising new playwright and went on to write *A Man for All Seasons* and many successful screenplays, several for David Lean.

Before opening at the Haymarket, they had played at the Royal Court Theatre in Liverpool (always one of Celia's favourite cities; she liked the Adelphi Hotel, much of the city's architecture and the excellent little antique shops in the back streets). One evening in her dressing-room before they opened, she said to Frith: 'What a relief to be doing something I know how to do.' He was astonished and told her that he had always thought, like everyone else in the theatre, that home was what she enjoyed. She replied, 'No, I am hopeless domestically.' And away from home, on tour, she had great fun; she had a ball.

Home and profession came together in the making of family home-movies. Nichol had an 8 mm cine-camera, so he was camera-man and director. The stars were Celia, Peter and their old friend Ronnie Shaw-Kennedy. The girls, some of their friends, their ponies and their pets all had parts and Peter wrote the script. The first film (silent) was about a peppery colonel and trespassing children. The second was about buried treasure and a pair of international crooks (Celia and Ronnie) and the third (science fiction) about an invasion by Martians. They were much enjoyed and – to the family – hysterically funny. Peter described the process in the *Spectator*.

There are several important differences between the country-house theatricals of my youth and the Swiss Family Robinson type of film production which in the school holidays bedevils my middle age. The former all took place indoors and in roughly the same place. It was not unknown for an actor and an actress, when not required upon the stage at rehearsals, to withdraw to the billiard-room with the declared intention of running through a scene which neither of them felt quite happy about; but the whole cast were not continually being transported, together with all their stage properties, from the chalk pit at A to the ruined church at B. The logistics were much simpler.

In our film the whole of the action has to take place out of doors, as there is never (according to the director) enough light indoors. The nearest we have got to an interior shot shows one of the actors leaning out of a window and talking to somebody on the lawn . . .

The fact that as a unit – an exceptionally misleading term – we are permanently on location makes us dependent on the weather. What you wanted in amateur theatricals was bad weather, to stop the less dedicated Thespians going to point-to-points instead of attending rehearsals. We, of course, want the opposite ...

Looking back on the stupendous epic which we made last holidays I cannot help wondering whether, in venturing into the realm of space fiction, we did not overtax our resources. The question is really an academic one, for whatever theme we chose would overtax them; and in many ways Martians, being readily recognisable as something of the sort, are easier to project than human beings, for they do not have to waste time explaining who they are.

The business of putting the audience in the picture is a problem which the script-writer has inherited from the dramatist. The old Enter-two-gentlemen-meeting formula on which Shakespeare so often and so indolently relied is, like the butler-footman colloquy in vogue three hundred years later, far too leisurely for use in a film which, though packed with incident, lasts only ten minutes. Moreover all our dialogue has to be recorded on tape and tacked on to the film after it has been developed; experience has taught us that this leaves little scope for beating about the bush or indeed for verbal niceties of any kind.

The players find it difficult enough to keep a straight face when actually being filmed; they find it virtually impossible when 'dubbing'. We have learnt that dialogue cannot be too laconic. We know now that, while Metro-Goldwyn-Mayer, with their greatly superior resources, can easily afford 'My God, you unutterable swine!' it pays us hands down to stick to 'Swine!'

A year ago we might easily have embarked on some such sequence as this:

SIR MARMADUKE (with a sneer): And who might you be?
DETECTIVE-INSPECTOR WUTHERING-HEATHCLIFFE: I am Detective-Inspector Wuthering-Heathcliffe, Sir Marmaduke. Scotland Yard felt it essential that an officer of the Special Branch should investigate the dastardly attempt upon the life of your daughter.

Today this would be boiled down to:

SIR JOHN (speaking slowly, as though to a foreigner): Are you from Scotland Yard?
INSPECTOR JONES (nodding vehemently): Yes.

In country-house theatricals there was always a tendency for members of the cast to infiltrate into the production items of an exotic, picturesque or facetious nature which happened to be available and which had caught their fancy; it went back, I suppose, to charades.

Nowadays they would be called gimmicks – those swordsticks, fans, sjamboks, lorgnettes, scimitars, snuff-boxes, fancy waistcoats, feather boas, pomanders, poshteens and Astrakhan hats on whose incorporation in the *mise en scène* the actors and actresses, with or without the approval of the producer, insisted.

In a family film the same tendency is noticeable, but on a far grander scale. In even the worst-organised amateur theatricals the plot of the play was a constant factor; but in our films the plot remains throughout the subject of controversy and disputation, everybody having his or her own idea about what ought to happen next. In these circumstances there is almost unlimited scope for gimmickry, and cries of 'But we simply *must* bring the cat in!', 'Can't I wear my new chaps?' and 'Couldn't somebody get their head cut off on the circular saw?' are heard on all sides ...

Though it would be premature to give a final judgement (for the sound-track remains to be added) I incline to the view that last holidays it was a mistake to allot, in a drama primarily concerned with the invasion of our planet by Martians, quite so prominent a part to a piebald pony.

Celia's performance, as usual, was exquisite.

24

Chin Chin at fifty

In the birthday honours in June 1958 Celia was awarded the CBE 'for services to the theatre'. It was her second medal; she had received one after the war for her work as an auxiliary policewoman. On 18 December that year she celebrated her fiftieth birthday, a fortnight after opening in a play by her old friend Tam Williams.

Hugh Williams, together with his wife Margaret, wrote several successful light comedies in the 1950s (*Plaintiff in a Pretty Hat*, *The Irregular Verb To Love*). *The Grass is Greener*, in which Celia played Hilary, was about the wife of a peer who falls for an American tourist, an oil millionaire (played by Edward Underdown) who, during a tour of her stately home, had wandered into the private apartments. The play ends with a rather melodramatic duel. Joan Greenwood, whose voice was described as 'thin charcoal toast spread with new honey', and Moray Watson and Tam himself were also in the cast. It was very much in the French-window style, a throwback to the thirties. The *Daily Telegraph* described it as an 'evening off' from heavier social concerns. Another newspaper said that it was a refuge for the Tired Business Man, for whom there was now nowhere to go, whereas before the theatre used to be entirely for him. Kenneth Tynan, in the *Observer*, thought it a 'vulgar and tasteless play', but conceded that 'the audience loved it'. It was very successful and, like *The Reluctant Débutante*, was subsequently made into a film.

Like many of her colleagues, Celia thought she would like to try her hand at directing. She chose for her début *Special Providence*, one of the plays in a double bill called *Double Yolk*, also by Hugh and Margaret Williams. Jack Minster directed the other, *A Sparrow Falls*. The two plays had an ingenious connection which brought a gasp from the audience. It was not a happy experience for Celia, although Anna Massey, who was in *Special Providence*, thought that she directed well.

She remembers her recommending getting the walk of a character right before anything else. After a not very encouraging try-out in Brighton, they changed the order of the two plays, but to no avail. On coming to London, to the Phoenix, after a slamming by the critics on the lines of 'bad eggs', it closed after ten days. Celia had been so nervous before the first night that she had been physically sick. She never tried directing again.

After a summer at Polzeath and Black Mount, where she avoided the slog on the hill, but instead fished the river for salmon or took the children fishing for trout on the lochs, she started rehearsals, with some trepidation, for the part of Pamela Puffy-Picq in a French play by François Billetdoux called *Chin Chin* (so called because the author thought it was what the British uttered every time they drank a glass of sherry). It was an intense play in which some detected an underlying religious theme. A man and a woman are thrown together after their respective spouses have run away with each other. They drink together and then become destitute. Peter Daubeny and Michael White, the producers, had persuaded Orson Welles to play the man, Cesareo Grimaldi. He signed a contract, and later accepted an invitation to lunch at Merrimoles to discuss the play with Celia and the producers. Peter and Celia, uneasy hosts at the best of times, waited and waited. He never turned up. No one saw him for several months, but, as Michael White said: 'You do not sue Orson Welles.' Anthony Quayle played the part instead, extraordinarily well. The theme was rather depressing, yet the play was entertaining – 'an offbeat moony little inconsequence'. Many people found it bizarre, too bizarre; others thought it memorable and affecting. Harold Hobson, in particular, was wildly enthusiastic about it, and it was his recommendation that kept it running. With heavy architectural sets by Sean Kenny, and a most peculiar hat for Celia, it was a change for her from a light French-window comedy. She thought it a daring choice for herself but unsuitable for her daughters and forbade them to see it.

The girls were now at boarding school. Celia had not been able to decide where to send them, so after inspecting various reputable schools, asked Peter to go and look at the next on her list, Cranborne Chase in Dorset. He, never having any trouble with decisions, thought it looked fine and so there we were sent, I in 1959 and Lucy a year later. 'The patter of your tiny feet is sadly missed,' Peter would write.

The girls were becoming bulky, obstinate teenagers; Nichol was making his own life working first in publishing, then in television. The theatre was changing, the influence of television was growing; that heady decade, the 1960s, was beginning; at fifty-plus Celia must have wondered what her future in the theatre held – just as her domestic obligations were diminishing. Perhaps that was why she had tried her hand at directing. There are parts for middle-aged and elderly actresses, but there are no King Lears, no Othellos, only perhaps Lady Macbeth, but that never came her way. She had yet to plunge into television.

She was therefore glad when at the end of 1961 her old friends, Virginia and Anthony Thesiger, suggested that she accompany them on a trip round the world. She was always an enthusiastic traveller, and this would be a complete break. She was to fly with Virginia to Beirut, go on to India, join Anthony, who was on business, in Rangoon and continue on to the Far East and California, circling the globe – a two-month trip, from January to March 1962. Such a trip was still uncommon then. She enjoyed it all, the sights and smells of India, the junks in Hong Kong, Hawaii where she amazed the Thesigers by malibu boarding (her training on the Cornish surf standing her in good stead) and the comfortable sunny life of Los Angeles. Celia was always entirely natural, sincere in her enthusiasms. She was less at ease on the formal occasions, the grand dinners with strangers which a trip such as this inevitably entails. From Virginia, the most loyal of friends, it had been an inspired invitation.

The following winter, the very cold one of 1962–63, Celia was back on the boards at the Haymarket in *The Tulip Tree* by N.C. Hunter. This was a play about a failing middle-aged marriage in which a successful publisher leaves his dowdy wife who mourns her dead son; the conclusion, which is neat and predictable, brings them together again. It was smoothly

directed by Glen Byam Shaw, a much-loved director, and
the designs by Motley featured a tree whose leaves turned
with the seasons. After touring in the North, it opened in
smog just before Christmas, and was then in effect killed off
by the severe weather of the new year.

When in a play in the West End Celia liked to leave Merrimoles at tea-time, drive the two hours (in the days before
motorways) to London, and then drive back again after the
performance. A bowl of tomato soup would have been left
on the Aga and, when she returned at midnight, she would
crouch on the floor before the fire in the old nursery and
drink the soup with a slice of bread and a glass of wine. That
was all she wanted. She might have had a cup of tea and
a little patum pepperium on toast before leaving for the
theatre, but nothing else. On days when she had a matinée
as well as an evening performance, she would stay in London
the night before, with Virginia, or with Pam (who had a flat
opposite Harrods), or with the Nugents, or with the Flemings
at Hyde Park Square. As she grew older, and her eyes, always
poor, became worse, that tiring nightly drive (after a powerful
performance – often draining both physically and emotionally)
would worry her family. Although she, like Peter, was seldom
open to persuasion or suggestion, this time she did listen to
advice. Stan Nowak, who had been in the Polish camp in
the woods at the end of the war and had stayed on to marry
a Nettlebed girl, Brenda, ran the grocer's shop in the village.
He delivered fruit and vegetables to the house and also had
a small car-hire business. Mrs Patterson, the then cook,
suggested that he might be able to do some driving. The
management of *The Tulip Tree* agreed to pay and, with Celia
complaining and protesting, he began to chauffeur her to the
theatre. The first day he drove too slowly, but by the end
of the first week it was clear that the arrangement was a success.
Stan's steady driving and his patient and agreeable
temperament were perfect for the job. He drove her to and
from the West End for the rest of her theatrical career, and
she adored him.

Apart from Sundays, the theatre recognises only Christmas
Day as a holiday so, after the performance on Christmas Eve,

Celia would drive back to the country and fill the children's stockings. Christmas was always spent at Merrimoles; family service was attended in the village and cousin Nona (a Fleming relation of masculine mien who ran a pack of beagles) would come to lunch. It was always fun, with quizzes and games. Celia would return to the theatre on Boxing Day and Peter would often take the children to Scotland to stay with the Keswicks in Dumfries.

Intimations of mortality began that icy winter of 1963. A cancerous lump was found on Peter's neck. Although the cancer, contrary to diagnosis, was to spread no further, and although Peter was angry at the secrecy and the humbug over cancer (and wrote an effective article on the subject), he was undoubtedly rattled. His brother, Ian, was also unwell. James Bond was ten years old and the first movie, *Dr No*, had appeared. But as Bond's popularity and earnings grew, so, sadly, Ian looked less and less well, and was less able to enjoy them. It upset Peter very much. As Celia said later, when asked about the relationship between those two brothers: 'They had a way of making each other laugh uncontrollably and half the time the rest of us hadn't the vaguest idea what was so funny.'

In the late summer Celia began rehearsing for a comedy, *Out of the Crocodile*, by Giles Cooper, a new writer with a somewhat surreal sense of humour. As John Mortimer wrote in the *Evening Standard*:

When the curtain rose, it seemed as if what was cheerfully known as theatrical revolution was at last an end. Here, in a play by an important new writer, was something that looked suspiciously like a French window, there was the table with the tray of drinks, the telephone, and the rattle of applause for Miss Celia Johnson. In fact what took place turned out to be a sporadically hilarious, intelligent parody of the middle-class play and a comment on the ludicrousness and irresponsibility of middle-class life.

A couple (Celia and Cyril Raymond, her husband in *Brief Encounter*) leave London for Brighton every weekend, where-upon a stranger (Kenneth More) unknown to them uses their

London flat to entertain his girlfriends; when the couple happen upon this clandestine arrangement, they end up acting as servants for Mr More. The whole thing, though funny in parts, did not quite come off, despite acting that was highly praised. Celia 'sharply conveys the anarchy which lurks behind every nervous face in Harrods'.

Soon after it opened, President Kennedy was assassinated.

25

Ibsen, Coward and Chekhov

Life imitated art in 1964 when Celia found herself the mother of a reluctant débutante, or more likely the reluctant mother of a débutante. Although girls were no longer presented at Court, as had been the custom, 'the season' persisted, starting with tea parties at the beginning of the year, cocktail parties in the spring and dances in the summer. I 'came out'. Celia, though social life was never important to her, entered into it all in fairly good heart, and, on Peter's instigation, a dance at Merrimoles was planned for the end of May. ('Mum,' he wrote to me, 'is coping splendidly – behind a cascade of complaint – with the Ball.') Lucy, who had gone to New Zealand as an auxiliary lady-in-waiting to the governor-general, Sir Bernard Fergusson, an old family friend, returned in time for it, and Nichol invited a lot of his friends. Confrey Phillips, a popular band-leader, provided the dance music. In spite of Celia's misgivings (she was always an extremely anxious hostess), it was great fun; indeed the whole summer was. Young friends of the children began to fill the house at weekends.

Two weeks before the dreaded ball, Sir Laurence Olivier rang Celia to invite her to play Mrs Solness in *The Master Builder* by Ibsen at the National Theatre. Diana Wynyard, whom he had first cast for the part, had had to pull out because of illness (she never recovered and died on the 13 May). Celia was asked, in these rather sad circumstances, to take her place. She felt it an honour. The history of the National Theatre in Britain is long and complicated. First suggested in 1848, it eventually, after many false starts over the years, came into being in 1963 with Olivier as its first director. It did not enter its permanent home on the South Bank in London until 1976, but for the first thirteen years, it used that congenial theatre in Waterloo Road, the Old Vic. They were brilliant years.

The Master Builder, in the second year, was the twelfth production. Sir Michael Redgrave was to play Solness, Maggie
Smith Hilde Wangel, and Peter Wood was to direct. Laurence
Olivier, a fine judge of actors, had a high opinion of Maggie
Smith's talent, especially in comedy. 'Watching Maggie's brilliant work in light comedy,' he wrote in his *Confessions of
an Actor*, 'I felt compelled to offer her a change of climate.'
Perhaps he thought Celia too should extend her range. Celia
was ridiculously anxious. She saw it all as a sort of promotion
and wasn't sure that she was up to it. She wanted to widen
her classical experience, but her various attempts so far had
not been altogether successful.

The play, set amid Rudolf Heinrich's sets of rusting iron
and cracked timber, was in many ways ill starred: Diana
Wynyard had died; Michael Redgrave turned out to be on
the verge of a nervous breakdown, the symptoms of which
he later put down to the onset of Parkinson's disease, and
gave a very artificial performance; and Maggie Smith, to start
with, played it for laughs. The critics were not wholly
impressed. Celia got off lightly; *The Times* thought that hers
was the only performance to convey the play's spirit – 'a black-
costumed ghost hovering in the shadows and turning her enormous panic-stricken eyes on everything that interrupts the
household's deathly routine'. Bernard Levin, who reviewed
for the *Daily Mail*, thought she had one moving passage, 'but
for the rest all we see are those bush baby eyes and the put-
upon suburban wife that they subtend'.

After five months Laurence Olivier took over from Michael
Redgrave, and the great and the good turned out for his opening night. The critics returned and were impressed. Olivier
simply took hold of the part of Solness in his bold and dynamic
way and portrayed him as a thrusting vulgarian – and the
whole play came together. Maggie Smith's performance had
developed almost beyond recognition. Bernard Levin no
longer saw the suburban housewife in Celia, but spoke of
her 'genuine tragic depth'. The *Telegraph* thought her Aline
Solness 'as perfectly played a small part as we are ever likely
to see'. Once again, Celia had underestimated her own capa-
bilities. 'I needn't have worried,' she said to us. For Olivier,

despite his success in the part, it had been a nightmare; for the first time he had suffered genuine stage fright, and had only just muddled through, speaking the words with teeth clenched. '*The Master Builder* remained, for as long as I was in it,' he wrote, 'a source of much anxiety.'

As Nicholas de Jongh wrote many years later in his obituary of Celia in the *Guardian*: 'Her parched, wrenching performance of the woman was akin to an announcement of her unused powers. She had arrived again.' It pitched her into a new field of possibilities. It gave her a new interest and a new challenge just when it was needed, just as the nest had emptied: Lucy, who, ever since sitting in the wings of the Haymarket during *Flowering Cherry* as a small girl, had only thought of being an actress, left home to start work at Farnham repertory company, and I went to Oxford.

There had been highs and lows that summer. Mrs Val, after generously paying for the dance, died in July, and at her funeral in Nettlebed, the family had been struck by how ill Ian looked. He died a fortnight later on 12 August – his son Caspar's twelfth birthday, 'the glorious twelfth'. Peter was shooting, as he always did on the 12th, with the Keswicks in Dumfries, and Celia was there too, when the news came. Ian was only fifty-six. Ian and his mother had been in different nursing homes in Brighton that summer, and although both had seemed unlikely to recover, Peter, Amaryllis noted when they went together to visit them there, had been unable to contemplate their deaths. It seems that the death of his father in the First World War, when he was nine, had affected him very deeply. In the snippet of autobiography that he began to write fifty years later, he was never able to get beyond that point of May 1917.

Noel Coward, by the mid-sixties, had been out in the cold for some time; he had been eclipsed and derided. The prevailing image of him in silk dressing-gown smoking through a cigarette holder was at odds with the current more plebeian trend, and his sharp light plays of bright young things were out of date. He remained, however, to many within the profession, the Master. The National Theatre, on the recommendation of their literary adviser, Kenneth Tynan, decided to do a revival of Coward's *Hay Fever*. Tynan excused the choice thus: 'To test the stamina of plays that were praised in the fairly recent past is part of National Theatre policy – hence the decision to revive *Hay Fever*, directed by that author.' Tynan, for all his scorn of the old West End, knew good theatre when he saw it and had always been an admirer of Coward. Coward remarked: 'I'm thrilled and flattered and frankly a little flabbergasted that the National Theatre should have had the curious perceptiveness to choose a very early play of mine, and to give it a cast that could play the Albanian telephone directory.' And *The Times* wrote a leader on the turning of *Hay Fever* into a classic.

Coward had written it in three days in 1924 specifically for Marie Tempest, i.e. for a famous prima donna oblivious of her artificialities. Although described as 'flippant' and 'trivial', it had been a success. There is a view that those plays of Coward that were designed for a particular actress (*Hay Fever* for Marie Tempest and *Private Lives* for Gertrude Lawrence) never fully come alive in the hands of a successor. Dame Edith Evans, then seventy-six, took the part of Judith Bliss this time; incomparable, with her jowled appearance and resonant vibrato voice, she wobbled gloriously through the part, albeit a little forgetful and a little out of place. She was simply too old. When she left the cast in 1965, Celia took over.

Here was comedy she could really get her teeth into. The cast 'that could play the Albanian telephone directory' included Maggie Smith, Robert Stephens, Lynn Redgrave, Robert Lang, Derek Jacobi, Anthony Nicholls and Louise Purnell – and they were indeed excellent. Under Coward's direction, their timing was meticulous. The story, light as a feather, is about a weekend in Judith Bliss's house near Marlow, for which she, her husband, a writer, and her two grown-up children, have each asked an admirer. Art once again imitated life in a small way; the Bliss household was not unlike Merrimoles – the children turning up with different friends, bedrooms at the top of the house which could well be described as a 'little hell', as one is in the play, manners a little off-beat, party games dominated by the home team, and an intractable housekeeper. Celia knew where she was with Coward and she enjoyed the whole thing enormously. She was a far cry from Marie Tempest, but Coward wrote in his diary, 'Celia was quite enchanting and very very funny.' Look for witty lines in the play and you will not find them; the humour lies entirely in the timing, the juxtaposition of dialogue. Coward wrote:

To me the essence of good comedy writing is that perfectly ordinary phrases such as 'Just fancy!' should, by virtue of their context, achieve greater laughs than the most literate epigrams. Some of the biggest laughs in *Hay Fever* occur on such lines as 'Go on', 'No, there isn't, is there?' and 'This haddock's disgusting' ... I would add that the sort of lines above-mentioned have to be impeccably delivered and that in the current performance they certainly are.

He was thrilled with the enthusiastic reception given to this production. 'Such (almost) unanimous praise has not been lavished upon me for many a long year and to pretend that I am not delighted by it would be the height of affectation.'

Those two excellent parts at the National gave Celia, too, a terrific boost of confidence. She had turned that middle-aged corner with success, and she was now able to recognise and enjoy the fact that she was an actress. While the children were small it was as if she was half-pretending that she was not. She had not aged well, her round face had gone very gaunt and her thin English skin lined easily; her face in repose looked rather sad but it lit up with laughter and smiles. She now knew that her acting transcended her looks, and she continued to eschew any cosmetic artificiality, just occasionally treating herself to a facial and an infrequent perm in Henley.

Actors and actresses of her generation had, at first, looked down their noses at television and held themselves back from it. Gradually they came to realise that it held all manner of new challenges and opportunities. Celia first succumbed to modern television in 1956 – although her very first television part had been Desdemona in an early transmission of *Othello* from the Alexandra Palace in 1937 – when she acted in a play called *The Letter* by Somerset Maugham, an experience she found terrifying. She wrote afterwards to someone at the BBC:

'The critics all seemed a bit carping but odd and different
sorts of people who saw it seemed to enjoy it so I hope some
of the 8 million were entertained. I don't think I've ever been
in quite such a frenzy of nerves and panic but, except for
Sunday, I enjoyed it all tremendously, and Sunday after 9.30
was fun.'

In those days, complete scenes were done at once for television and the process was alarming; it was not like films
when you just did one take at a time. Celia, to start with,
was fractionally stagey on television, but, always a fast learner,
she soon developed the natural technique necessary for the
small screen, and, as she took on more television during the
1960s, she became, not surprisingly, extremely good at it.

In 1964 she played Lady Nelson in *Bequest to the Nation*
by Terence Rattigan, directed by Stuart Burge for ATV. This
was Lady Nelson's view of Nelson as related to his nephew,
and showed the hero from the other side. Lady Nelson had
a pronounced limp, and Celia worked hard at her gait. She
became fascinated by Nelson and began to collect little plaster
busts of him. Rattigan took an interest in the production and
would turn up at Elstree in his Rolls-Royce which contained
a cocktail cabinet. The play was later put on in the West
End.

She began to look forward to doing television – she knew
she could do it, the work was limited in time, and it was
very popular. The West End became more and more alien,
not least because there was nowhere to park; she was getting
older and with six evening performances and two matinées
a week, it was tiring.

But it was not for that reason that she regretted agreeing
to be in a play at the Royal Court Theatre – *The Cresta Run*
by N.F.Simpson – in the winter of 1965. The Royal Court
had been the cradle of the theatrical revolution in the 1950s;
all the plays by Osborne and Wesker and others which broke
new ground had been put on on its stage; avant-garde directors
congregated there to try their hand. Although by the mid-
sixties their influence had pervaded the old West End and
older actors had dared to tread upon a new sort of stage,
the Royal Court, and the English Stage Company which

resided there, were still seen as progressive. Too much so for Celia – after two weeks of improvisation and games during the rehearsals of *The Cresta Run*, she walked out. 'I've never done it before, but I couldn't go on,' she said. She felt very guilty.

It was therefore with some trepidation, shortly after this incident, that she went to meet Lindsay Anderson, a leading director of the Royal Court school, who had been invited to direct *The Cherry Orchard* at the Chichester Festival Theatre, to discuss playing Madame Ranevskaya. Each regarded the other with some suspicion. When Lindsay Anderson said that he didn't like to plan moves beforehand, Celia said: 'I do think the director should do a little bit of preparation.' The discussion then turned to how characters should talk in a Chekhov play, and Celia suggested that perhaps Ranevskaya should talk in an actressy way, as she had been an actress – confusing her with Arkadina in *The Seagull*. After that, they got on well, though Lindsay Anderson would be irritated by her habit of doing *The Times* crossword in any spare moments; as she always did her work superbly, when called on to rehearse or perform, he felt he could not remonstrate.

The summer of 1966 that Celia spent at Chichester was a happy one. Her old friend Tam Williams played her brother, Gayev, Tom Courtenay played Trofimov and became a friend of Celia's and of Lucy's, and Ray McAnally, John Standing, John Laurie and Sarah Badel also took part. Celia's Ranevskaya was not wholly admired; she showed the humour, the sensitivity and the wilfulness of the impoverished gentlewoman, but when it came to the selling of *The Cherry Orchard*, she failed to unleash the required Russian emotion, so strong was her natural control and restraint. Her Englishness was her undoing. In the middle of the last performance of the play that summer, a huge cheer was heard off stage – as England won the World Cup.

Celia's thorough Englishness sat perfectly well with Ayckbourn. In 1967, Alan Ayckbourn was not a name that anyone had heard of. Celia was sent a script of a play of his called *Relatively Speaking*. She found that her first reading of it made her laugh out loud, and was immediately keen to do it. It is a neat and clever play, bordering on farce, about confused identities between a middle-aged couple, the man's former secretary and her boyfriend. The dialogue is quick and sharp, the timing all, and therefore, as with Coward, Ayckbourn is greatly enhanced by first-class acting. Michael Hordern played Philip, Celia's husband, Richard Briers and Jennifer Hillary the young couple, Greg and Virginia. Nigel Patrick directed it.

Untried comedy by an unproven playwright is one of the riskiest businesses; there is no telling whether it will work or not before an audience. (Celia always dreaded the very first night before an audience more than the official opening night, and would pray before reaching the theatre in Brighton or wherever, that it had burnt down.) They set off for a long tour of Newcastle, Edinburgh, Sheffield and Leeds, before coming in to London. From Newcastle she sent a postcard: 'N'castle is quite friendly to our little piece – it seems to make them laugh but we are still in a frenzy every night because it is so difficult to do.' And from Edinburgh she sent another: 'We were a tiny little smash hit in N'castle but who knows what lies in store.' All, however, went very well and only London was left to conquer. Success on tour does not necessarily ensure success in the West End, but the company was beginning to sense that they were on to a good thing, and when they opened in September at the Duke of York's Theatre, J.C. Trewin wrote that, 'During the final half hour at the premiere I have never known a house so weak with laughter.' Celia was thought to have given one of the best comic performances of her career. The *Sunday Times* said that it didn't realise that she could be so funny. Irving Wardle, one of the younger critics then, wrote: 'I am compelled to admit the existence of a good play that has practically nothing to express.'

It was Ayckbourn's seventh play but his first in the West End; his name was assured. From then on, if Celia was ever asked who her favourite playwrights were, she would always include Ayckbourn. If he has a weakness as a playwright, it is his endings. *Relatively Speaking* ends with Philip (Michael Hordern) holding up a pair of men's slippers, and asking Sheila

(Celia) about them. Celia supplied the line, 'Wouldn't you like to know?' with a roll of her eyes, and it remained.

She came out as usual after six months and immediately took a large family party – the children, Pam, Pam's daughter Detta and others – to a house in Elba. She was in good spirits, swimming and playing tennis in the late summer sun.

26

Headmistress, *Hamlet* and a pension

Celia's two lives, the one as Mrs Fleming, the other as Miss Johnson, continued to run in tandem. Her life as Mrs Fleming, at Merrimoles, was very full. She played bridge whenever she could with her friends in Nettlebed, the Armitages, Nancy van Duzer, Paula (who played badly but always, to Celia's fury, held good cards). She played tennis. Competitive always, she liked to win. On Sundays she would be absorbed by Ximenes, an exceptionally difficult crossword in the *Observer* (and, later, its successor, Azed). She adored watching racing on television, with favourites among the jockeys and trainers, such as Fred Winter, and she was passionate about the test match. Peter gathered friends for an annual cricket match against the Nettlebed XI, the lunch for which always caused Celia much anxiety though in the end she would enjoy the occasion. Shooting lunches in the winter she dreaded as much and enjoyed less. She was a familiar figure pottering short-sightedly round the shops in Henley. She and Peter dined with their old friends and neighbours; others came to stay. In February 1966 they joined Tony and Mary Keswick for an amusing trip to Istanbul. At home the children refused to abandon the nest and one or other returned most weekends bringing friends. The billiard-room (that Edwardian fantasy of Peter's when he used to write from Delhi during the war) came into its own. Celia's old mother, Ethel, died at last at the age of ninety-one after a rather querulous old age, the latter part of which was spent in various nursing homes; her death, in senility, was a relief.

Perhaps the person Celia became closest to at this time was Lucy Moorehead, wife of Alan Moorehead, the former war correspondent and writer. They had probably met through Osbert and Karen Lancaster, who lived in Henley and who were great friends of the Mooreheads. Lucy, clever, perceptive and unconnected with most of Celia's life, became a very

good friend. The Mooreheads lived in Porto Ercole in Italy
and Celia was always welcome there. She would fly over for
a week or ten days after doing some television or other piece
of work, and relax in the sun with lively chatter, a lot of
laughter and some bridge.

Increasingly there were calls on her, as Miss Johnson, to
do this or that, judge this or open that. Some she accepted,
taking them more in her stride than she used to. The charity
she was most firmly attached to was that for multiple sclerosis,
and the meetings she attended most regularly were those of
King George's Pension Fund for Actors, of which her old
friends, Tim and Rosalie Nugent, were pillars. However, it
cannot be said that she was a tireless worker for charity. There
was always a stream of fan letters. They would pile up on
her untidy desk and every day she would say, 'I must do
my fan letters today,' and put it off. One devoted fan, known
as 'The Fan' from first seeing her in *Pride and Prejudice* in
1936, sent her, and in due course her children as well, handsome presents every Christmas and birthday. They finally
met after about thirty years, but the impression was that The
Fan preferred the more distant relationship.

Celia was very pleased that her younger daughter Lucy
had decided to go on the stage. It meant, too, that for Celia
there was someone in the family who knew and understood
what she was doing. Peter had distanced himself from the
theatre and Celia had kept family and work so separate that
she rarely talked about it at home. Lucy becoming an actress
and being keen on the whole theatrical world meant that
theatre spilt over into home much more. Celia took on a flat
in Chelsea, which both made her life easier in that she didn't
always have to do that tiring night drive back to the country
after a performance and also provided a base for Lucy.

In the winter of 1967 she and Lucy began rehearsing together
for another revival of *Hay Fever*. Celia's spell in the play
at the National Theatre had been all too short and it was
thought that her performance as Judith Bliss could be brought
to a wider public. Peter Bridge put on a new production,
the cast of which included Roland Culver, an old friend who
lived near Henley, Richard Vernon, Prunella Scales, Lucy,

and Simon Williams, Tam Williams' son. After playing at
the O'Keefe Centre in Toronto, where the timing was very
difficult because the laughs got lost in the recesses of the
huge auditorium, they came to London for a ten-week run
at the Duke of York's. The production was, inevitably, compared unfavourably to that of the National Theatre, but it
was still very funny and highly popular. Michael Billington
wrote of Celia that her great virtue

has always been her total lack of artifice: she is usually at her best
in parts (like Mrs Solness in *The Master Builder*) which require a
quiet, barely concealed desperation. And even in a comedy like *Relatively Speaking*, she is ideal mainly because she is so unactressy.
Ironically, the only quality in which she is deficient is the only one
that is absolutely essential for Judith Bliss: panache.

He goes on to say she almost makes up for it in sheer craft,

and her performance is crammed with excellent detail: before settling
down to play the piano she removes her rings with a suitably artful
flourish; she elbows her offspring out of the way whenever they
threaten to steal the limelight, and when her husband commends
her fortitude there's a slight stiffening of the back and a histrionic
lifting of the shoulders.

Celia had very much liked Maggie Smith who had been in
the National *Hay Fever*; both had the same no-nonsense
approach to acting and both relished comedy. When Maggie
Smith, in conversation with her dresser at the National
Theatre, said that she was making a film of Muriel Spark's
book, *The Prime of Miss Jean Brodie*, and that the part of
the headmistress had yet to be cast, her dresser suggested
'Miss Johnson' – and so it came to be. Celia returned to filming
after ten years. The director, coincidentally, was Ronnie
Neame, who had been the camera-man on David Lean's wartime films. The story is about a teacher of great influence
and independence of mind in a conventional girls' secondary
school (Marcia Blaine) in Edinburgh. Celia was never
comfortable with accents, but she worked hard to achieve the
prim Morningside accent necessary for Miss Mackay. Without
question, memories of Miss Gray, her impressive headmistress

at St Paul's, informed her performance, though Celia was
in no way physically like her. The story is set a little after
the time when Celia was at St Paul's, but it reminded her
of her school days.

Peter and the girls attended the premiere in February 1969,
while Celia was on a rare trip to New York doing a television
play about a heart transplant. While in New York, she dined
with Alistair Cooke, an old acquaintance, whose mother had
been at school in Manchester with Celia's mother. She also
met Lauren Bacall there, who said to Celia how pleased she
was to meet her, as 'Bogie and I were at your feet.' Celia
was enormously chuffed.

While there, she also missed her television performance
of *Relatively Speaking*. For the four years from 1967 to 1971
she was seen regularly on British television in 'Play of the
Month', as the BBC's main drama offering was called. As well
as *Relatively Speaking*, she was to be seen in *Ghosts* (a much-
praised production with Tom Courtenay as Oswald Alving),
Hay Fever (less successful), *The Marquise* also by Noel Coward,
The Cherry Orchard and a Wednesday Play, *The Cellar and
the Almond Tree* by David Mercer about a batty aristocrat
living out her days at the top of her former castle in Eastern
Europe. She let herself go as this eccentric lady in a somewhat
atmospheric production. She clearly enjoyed working in television more and more.

Soon after the television showing of *Relatively Speaking*
in 1969, I contracted glandular fever and became rather thin
and run down. While the doctor suggested eating some buns
and cream cakes, Celia thought it a good idea to get away.
Feeling guilty about the extravagance, she booked the two
of us on a Swan's Hellenic cruise to Greece and Turkey.
We joined the SS *Ankara* in Venice and sailed round some
of the Greek islands to Istanbul, down the Turkish coast and
back to Athens. We were spoonfed history, archaeology and
culture in the pleasantest possible way, and looked after with
great efficiency by Miss Goodrich who ran the cruises. At
Aspendos, Celia was asked to declaim, to demonstrate the
acoustics of those Greek theatres. In the sun and comfort
I perked up, and Celia, ever the eager traveller striding out

with her glasses on the end of her nose, acquired a taste for Swan's cruises round the Greek islands.

The following winter, 1970, she accompanied the Mooreheads to Africa. In 1966, Alan Moorehead, though not at all old, had had a stroke which had left him partly paralysed down one side and unable to communicate except by means of a very limited vocabulary: 'absolutely', 'fantastic', 'bloody awful', 'do that thing', were his main expressions. He wanted to revisit the places he had been to in Africa when writing his most successful books, *The Blue Nile* and *The White Nile*. Celia accompanied him and Lucy; she was very good with Alan and particularly adept, with her crossword mind, at guessing what he was trying to say, and she made it more fun for Lucy, for whom looking after Alan could be a considerable strain. She returned with many indifferent photographs of lions in the distance, having loved every minute. Celia was not a fussy or complaining traveller, merely enthusiastic. Tristram Powell, who directed her in *A House and its Head*, a dramatised documentary about Ivy Compton-Burnett for BBC television, remembers that, during discussions about where they should stay in Hungerford for the filming, when there was a certain dissatisfaction with the noisiness of the chosen hotel, Celia said: 'I don't mind where I stay, as long as I can watch Mastermind.' The only trouble with her lack of airs was that very occasionally she would be ignored or treated with less than respect, and then she would, rightly, bridle quietly.

Celia, now over sixty, was beginning to regret that she had not done more Shakespeare. In an interview a few years later when asked why she would have liked to have done more, she said: 'Because he's the best, you know, and it's good to have played the best.' Therefore when the director Anthony Page called in at Merrimoles one day and offered her the part of Gertrude in a production of *Hamlet* at the Nottingham Playhouse, at that time run by Stuart Burge, she accepted. Alan Bates was to play Hamlet. Anthony Page was a modern director of the Royal Court school and at that time much influenced by Iranian culture. He talked of stripping the play of naturalistic illusion. Following such a guideline, the design by William Dudley consisted of a stainless steel box, variously described by the critics as a 'biscuit tin' and a 'remote controlled mousetrap', and Celia, as Gertrude, had to lie down on a couple of rectangular blocks. It was generally agreed that the sets did nothing for the play. Alan Bates gave a creditable performance as Hamlet, though he stood and moved badly. 'I suppose it would be thought anti-egalitarian to expect a *princely* manner?' carped one critic. Celia presented Gertrude 'as a dainty, queenly woman of a most dismaying frivolity'. She was, according to Michael Billington, 'not the usual wilting voluptuary but a distraught, untidy, maternal figure caught up in events beyond her comprehension'. It was a clear and decent performance in, for her, a somewhat uncomfortable milieu. She enjoyed it, for it was more of an intellectual challenge than many of her roles; total concentration on acting was what absorbed her. She also revelled in Shakespeare's language; it gave her the same, almost physical pleasure that poetry did, and she was always amused by the little extra details that you could find in the text when paying close attention to it. Although she had done so little Shakespeare, she knew many of the plays intimately.

Peter and the girls set off for Nottingham for the first night, as was the old custom. Peter's pipes and his labradors left their fragrance in his cars, but having no sense of smell himself, he never noticed. Being a zealous believer in fresh air, he always drove with both front windows open whatever the season; this mitigated the smell, but didn't make for a very comfortable journey.

27

Widow and grandmother

Shortly after Celia finished in *Hamlet*, which came to London for a short run at the Cambridge, the last rather unstable housekeeper, nicknamed 'The Bat', left, and Celia began to learn to cook. The process caused her a lot of torment, but slowly she mastered it and became a good cook, although she didn't have the necessary appetite or interest in food to become brilliant. As long as food was piping hot and covered in pepper, Peter, who had also no sense of taste, was happy. She was to be seen, standing at the Aga, peering nervously into a boiling pan, getting rather irritated with the stream of advice coming from the children and their friends. It may seem odd that she had avoided cooking for so long, but many of her friends – Paula for instance – never learned to cook.

Lucy was making a name for herself at the Royal Court. Having a mother (or father) in the profession works both ways; it gets you the helpful introductions in the first place, but then you have to prove yourself twice over and suffer the comparisons. Lucy was succeeding on her own account. She had met and decided to marry Joe Laycock (not an actor), the son of a distinguished soldier, Sir Robert Laycock. The Laycocks were acquaintances of the Flemings, and very old friends of Paula (throwing her into a quandary as to which side of the church she would sit at the wedding). Joe's grand-mother, Freda Dudley Ward (remembered now for her long liaison with the Duke of Windsor when he was Prince of Wales), had married Paula's first husband, Bobby Casa Maury, but all three had remained great friends. Freda's elder daughter, Angie, had married Bob Laycock, who had died in 1968, and her younger daughter, Pempie, was married to Carol Reed. Everyone thought well of the match between Joe and Lucy, and the wedding was planned for the end of July 1971 at Merrimoles. Celia, with Peter's help, started planning the occasion at the same time as grappling with cookery books and rehearsing *The Cherry Orchard* for television.

Spirits were high. *The Cherry Orchard*, produced by Cedric Messina, had been fun. She and Peter spent a summer weekend they much enjoyed with the Queen Mother at Royal Lodge. Celia planned to leave with Pam for another Swan's cruise soon after the wedding. The day was hot and sunny, a brass band played, and friends from way back (Mary Clive, Ronnie Shaw-Kennedy), neighbours (Robert Morley, Gladys Cooper), Nanny, members of the estate staff, Fleming, Johnson and Laycock cousins (Paula placed herself in the Laycock pews) attended. Lucy and Joe left by helicopter to spend their honeymoon travelling by jeep through southern Turkey.

A couple of days after the wedding, Peter and Celia were invited to lunch at Royal Lodge again. Then after a very jolly gathering of Flemings for Peter's cousin, Lorna Schuster's daughter, Joanna's wedding the following weekend, Celia left with Pam for the Swan's cruise in Greece and Peter for Glenkiln (the Keswicks' house in Dumfries) and Black Mount, as was his habit in August.

Again Celia enjoyed the Greek islands and had a lot of fun with Pam; increasingly they made each other laugh. But, a fortnight later on their return flight to London, Celia was summoned to the front of the aeroplane and handed this message: 'Dear Celia, Bad news I fear. Poor Peter dropped dead out shooting today. Absolutely no pain. Making all arrangements. All our love, Richard.'

He had died at Black Mount the day before. As he had done since he was a boy, he had set out with his brother Richard and many of his cousins to walk up grouse on one of the steeper beats. They had not gone far when a covey flew up in front of Peter; he shot a right and left, his dog retrieved them and moments after he had handed them over to Ian Macrae, the stalker walking next in the line to him, he fell to the ground. He was found to be dead, of a sudden heart attack. He was sixty-four. He was carried back to the Lodge, accompanied by his aunt, Joan Fleming (old Uncle Phil's wife), Richard, and one or two others. The rest went on with their day on the hill. Some have found this odd, but that is to misunderstand the Flemings and how well they understood Peter. It was unquestionably what he would have wished; in any case there was little to be gained from everybody moping in the house, better to walk and mourn outside.

Nichol and I met Celia at Gatwick, thronged with summer passengers, and returned to Merrimoles. Richard drove down from Scotland with Peter's dog and his belongings. Richard was then, and continued to be until his death six years later (also untimely of heart, also in August in Argyll), an enormous support and a valued adviser to Celia. (The bond between the Fleming brothers was very strong; after Peter's and Ian's deaths, Richard, although chairman of Robert Flemings and with eight children of his own, would always find time to help Nichol or to visit Ian's son, Caspar, when he was ill in hospital.) Paula had us to meals for the next few days and provided a comforting diversion. Lucy was on her honeymoon somewhere in southern Turkey but no one knew where.

Celia was stunned – but went about the various funeral arrangements. Peter had already made many of them himself; he had planned it in 1967, four years earlier; he wanted the service to include the hymn 'The day thou gavest Lord is ended', his coffin to be made of beech or oak from the estate, he wanted his dogs to attend, and, he added, 'I have never been keen on flowers.' He also said that if there were to be a memorial service it should be in the Guards' Chapel in London, where 'the parking facilities are unrivalled'. This had been thought out by someone at the age of sixty who was never ill.

He had been low over the last few years, drinking more than he should have (and he was one of those people whom alcohol made maudlin rather than merry), but recently he had been more his old self and he and Celia had been enjoying things together. He had eventually, after several years' struggle with the finer bureaucracy of the Civil Service (about which he was both patient and funny), got clearance to write a book about deception in the Second World War and had just begun it. Since the war he had continued with his rather urbane journalism in the *Spectator* and *The Times*, but the more he grew out of tune with the times, the more emphatically he wrote about his gamekeeper or Eton, dirty words at that time; Strix became blimpishly and wilfully old-fashioned. In 1959, he had written to the editor, Brian Inglis: 'For some time I've had a feeling, latterly reinforced by some rather drastic sub-editing, that Strix rather clashes with the rest of the paper, like a stuffed stoat in the bar of an airliner.' He had also written a small number of excellent books on odd historical events. *Invasion 1940*, written in 1956, was a first-rate account of Hitler's plans for invasion and England's schemes to counter it. Described by himself at the time as an 'interim report', it still reads well and conveys the atmosphere of summer 1940. He wrote *Bayonets to Lhasa*, an account of the Younghusband Mission to Tibet in 1903–4, an odd little episode of British Imperial history, *The Siege at Peking* about the Boxer rebellion of 1900, and *The Fate of Admiral Kolchak*, a book about the White Russian leader who, for a year in 1919, was styled Supreme Ruler of Russia. They were all excellent books of historical journalism about events which had taken place in lands through which he had travelled in the 1930s. Occasionally he would travel for an article or research. Just before he left on one of these sallies, Rupert Hart-Davis wrote to George Lyttelton (in their published correspondence): 'He [Peter] sets off on Friday for Outer Mongolia, and I can't say I envy him. He is rather like an old charger sniffing the air of the battle-field.'

He loved the estate and, in the 1960s, when taxation was at its direst and inflation had begun to rise, in order to try and make it profitable, he built an advanced dairy unit. He became very knowledgeable about forestry, and was most conscientious about all manner of committees and trusteeships. He shot as often as he could, taking great pride in what to him was his dogs' prowess but what to others was their wildness. It is quite possible that for the last two or three years of his life, he really had not been well. He would never have admitted it or gone to see a doctor. Two days before he died, returning from a day's shooting, Chips Keswick, who was with him, suggested that they should try for a snipe in a bog on the way back. 'I've never in my life refused that kind of suggestion,' he said to Chips, 'but I just don't think I can go on.'

No one could deny that it was the death he would have wished – doing what he enjoyed best, in a place he loved, in preferred company, after a couple of spectacular shots.

Celia treasured the letters of condolence – and she looked, for a moment squatting in front of the fire that autumn, very young. Perhaps, as happens when people die, she remembered the old days. They had been married for thirty-five years, many of which had not been easy, but, recently, they had seemed set for an almost companionable old age. Some years after his death, Celia received a letter from an Australian living in Papua, New Guinea, asking about Peter and *Brazilian Adventure*, a book he much admired. She answered his questions and added, 'One of the things that most pleased me in my life was the dedication in the book.' This was a confidence that she would only have made to someone she didn't know, living on the other side of the world.

Peter – strong, fearless, funny, reliable, kind, but stubborn and selfish perhaps – was possibly never fully true to himself. A cool and ironic detachment masked deep and sensitive feeling; by the end of his life the mask was a little too firmly in place.

Friends rallied round Celia that winter; she went to stay with the Keswicks, with the Mooreheads; she called in on Rupert now living in Yorkshire (his son, Duff, having taken over his old house, Bromsden). Richard Fleming gave her and Nichol advice about the estate. Amaryllis came to stay quite often with her cello and was always a most welcome visitor. Celia took on Peter's labradors, helped organise the shoot that winter, as he would have wished, and rehearsed *Separate Tables* by Terence Rattigan with Deborah Kerr for an evening in celebration of Rattigan in January 1972. Those who saw her performance that night thought it one of the best things she had ever done. Bill Pound, the gardener, cooked the breakfast, fed the dogs, and saw to it that the house ran smoothly.

Merrimoles, not a warm house, must have been dark, cold and lonely. Celia had never been entirely on her own there before; it must have been strange and doubtless she was glad of the company of the labradors. She began to play a lot more bridge; it certainly helped her through the first months. Nichol became engaged to Sarah Ponsonby, but in the end, after much anxiety, which was agonising for all concerned, the wedding never took place. At a time like this she missed Peter's clear-cut decisive advice, shaky as it could be on matters of the heart.

Peter had been quite sure – and had complained to us about it – that he would never have any grandchildren. In fact Lucy was already expecting a baby when he died (life and death, as so often, going hand in hand) and Flora was born on 16 March 1972. Celia was on tour in a new Ayckbourn play, *Me Times Me*, in Birmingham and Brighton, but between those two places she managed to get home to see her granddaughter – a most perfect baby. *Me Times Me* to everyone's surprise, as Ayckbourn now had considerable renown, and to most people's disappointment, did not come into London; it was funny, predictably, but a very confused third act lost the audience. Celia was almost relieved at its failure; she really wanted to get home and see Flora. The Laycocks lived at Merrimoles that summer, and Celia was overjoyed to see a pram sitting out in the garden; it reminded her of the early days of Merrimoles. She struck a close bond with Flora; new life began.

28

Lloyd George

Not only was Merrimoles the Laycocks' home for the time being, it was also used as such by Nichol and by me at weekends. Paula, too, was in and out, though the first signs of Alzheimer's disease were beginning to make her a little scatty. People came and went and Celia took it all with remarkable equanimity, though she was often very tired. Once more she set off on a Swan's cruise, taking both Pam and Ralph this time, and as it had done before, it did her a power of good, and they all enjoyed it.

William Douglas-Home had a new play on at the Savoy, *Lloyd George Knew my Father*; in it Lady Boothroyd, the wife of General Sir William Boothroyd, resolves to sacrifice her life to prevent a bypass being built through the park of her stately home. Ralph Richardson and Peggy Ashcroft played the General and his wife. When Peggy Ashcroft came out after six months, Celia was asked to take over as Lady Boothroyd, and in October 1972 she opened in it with Sir Ralph. She was brilliant. Peggy Ashcroft had, as always, been excellent, but whereas she had given the play overtones of tragedy, Celia emphasised the comedy, raising laughs in all sorts of places. As so often with William Douglas-Home, the upper-class setting and the lightweight theme of the play disguised its craftsmanship. Of no great weight, it was a success and very jolly. 'They will have to run a bulldozer through the Savoy to get rid of this one,' remarked the *Evening News*. How did it pass muster, this tale of the aristocracy, with the more fervent critic? Irving Wardle wrote in *The Times*: 'As agit-prop shows are judged on theatrical skill, so it is the lot of entertainment plays to be scrutinised for social content.' He decided that *Lloyd George* 'just about scrapes through the liberal censorship ... For once here is a copper-bottomed West End comedy that takes its stand on the virtues of the over-sixties, and rounds on the usually dominant middle-aged squares with a derision hitherto reserved for greasy anarchist boyfriends. Hurrah!' In the seventies a fierce debate was conducted in the theatre about how political the content of a play should be.

Celia took a little time to pick up the rhythm of Sir Ralph's cadences – she was naturally faster than him – but once synchronised, their two performances were magically complementary. Prepared to lay down her life to prevent the bypass being built, Lady Boothroyd chooses the wood for her coffin. Celia held up and compared the samples of wood for her coffin, as if picking a chintz for curtains, with an off-hand seriousness that was masterly. Her husband, General Sir William Boothroyd, puts on full regimental dress for her proposed demise and orders his butler and former batman to sound the last post for her ladyship. Sir Ralph, in this somewhat anachronistic setting, captured brilliantly the inattention, the absent-mindedness, the habit, the irritation, the odd deep wound of a fifty-year marriage.

For Celia, the theatre, in this case, provided just the occupation, the companionship, the success for her revival after a difficult year following Peter's death. She enjoyed working with Sir Ralph, and William and Rachel Douglas-Home were old friends whose company she greatly enjoyed; with her full make-up on between matinée and evening performance she would play bridge in her dressing-room with William and friends of Nichol's, Christopher Balfour and Ian Dunlop. (Celia's children resisted learning bridge as they knew that, had they been able to play, their lives would not have been their own.) She made a new friend of a young actor of twenty-two, Simon Cadell, and sometimes dined with him after the show. He helped her clear the London flat when the lease came to an end, and occasionally escorted her to award ceremonies. Lots of others came to see her in the play. She continued to drive back with Stan Nowak to Merrimoles most nights after the play. Stan would wait until she was into the house and had turned on a light before going home.

On 22 March 1973 Binkie Beaumont died in London, and four days later Noel Coward died in Jamaica. Mark Amory, a friend of Nichol's and devotee of the theatre, who was staying at Merrimoles at the time, remembers noticing that Celia seemed rather upset, and was surprised, thinking both of these old men of the theatre rather old hat. When he asked Celia about them, she said: 'There are only about five people who understand what I am trying to do and those were two of them.'

She was still in *Lloyd George* in May when Johnny Grimond and I were married at Merrimoles. She coped heroically with the wedding and later left, driven by Nichol, for the evening performance. So matter of fact was she about her work, so callous were we, that it didn't occur to us to postpone the wedding until after she had finished her play. A month after the wedding, Lucy had her second child, Robert.

Celia, now sixty-five, took a dive, professionally, into old age. She was asked to play on television a very old lady living, as some gentlewomen used to, in a hotel in South Kensington. The story, called *Mrs Palfrey at the Claremont*, by Elizabeth Taylor, was about the loneliness of an old lady who is befriended by a young man (Joe Blatchley); she persuades him to pretend to be her nephew and asks him to lunch at her hotel. Directed by Michael Lindsay-Hogg, it was an excellent and poignant piece of television. Celia, again, as she had done here and there over the years, touched the emotions. That year she was nominated best actress for her performance in it at the BAFTA awards. She was flattered and took no notice and wasn't going to go to the ceremony (she tended to avoid those large show-business gatherings) until they rang up and whispered that it would be in her interest to go. So off she went, after much fuss about what to wear, and indeed received the award. She was genuinely surprised and honoured. It was another boost to her always fragile self-confidence – and she embraced television with greater enthusiasm.

She was still Mrs Fleming locally, and as such, she much enjoyed collecting her pension from Stan who now ran the village post office – but slowly Miss Johnson was coming more and more into her own. Indeed a view began to be expressed that she had been seriously underestimated as an actress – though never in fact by fellow-actors; she had always been an actor's actress of superb technique. The old order was passing; she and her generation, now approaching seventy, were to be seen less in the theatre. Sybil Thorndike celebrated her ninetieth birthday in 1972. Others, Gladys Cooper for instance, passed on. Many a time Celia read a sonnet or some such at a memorial service in St Paul's, the actors' church in Covent Garden.

Odd people sought her out. Bette Davis, on a trip to London, rang up, expressed her admiration and was invited to lunch, thereby causing panic about the cooking. Celia was becoming, in her way, a grand old lady, and rather enjoying it. She was free now to do what she wished, where she wished, how she wished.

Pam and Ralph had moved to a farmhouse on the estate and this ensured that she would not be lonely. Paula, too, elegant as ever, though madder by the day, was much in evidence. The bridge cronies gathered regularly in a little room at Merrimoles, known by the gardener, Bill Pound, who used to bring them tea, as the Casino, and she kept in touch with old friends. She was also happy in the company of the young who came to stay for weekends – Teresa Keswick, Christopher Balfour, Janet Lyle, Mary McDougall and many others. She returned to Polzeath taking the grandchildren, and often her niece Emma, her brother John's daughter, of whom she was very fond, and loved it more than ever, surfing enthusiastically. She accompanied the Mooreheads, once back to Kenya and once to the Caribbean.

In August of 1975 she went to Black Mount for a service conducted by a Highland minister to dedicate a cairn erected in Peter's memory. Celia valued the occasion and had fun with the Flemings. After that she returned to Black Mount most summers, enjoying the company and hospitality of Uncle Phil's son, Robin Fleming, his wife Vicky, and his sister Sylvie Rittson-Thomas. Pam and Ralph, with some difficulty, persuaded her to join them on a cookery course in Dieppe; they were as interested in food as she was uninterested. She returned in triumph with a medallion in the shape of a frying pan on a ribbon, having mastered Crêpes Suzette. Her moods were always up and down, and she did get tired, but her innate gaiety came out more. Two more grandchildren were born: Lucy had Diggory in 1975 and I had Jessie a year later.

She was an excellent, if not exactly hands on, grandmother. She had a knack of getting through to children and making them laugh and she was always amused by them; in the same way that she observed and laughed at odd snatches of human behaviour, so she found children's remarks funny. But she also always took children seriously. Flora, in particular, she was very fond of. She began to write verses, sort of glorified nursery rhymes, for them. Having inherited her father's facility for verse and not having used it much since she won a nursery rhyme competition at St Paul's, she now began to scribble little poems. She also started a children's story in the style of E. Nesbit, her favourite children's author.

She loved the seasons in the Chilterns, the cherry blossom in spring, the early leaves on the beech trees, the bluebells below and the rich autumn colours, and, looking after the labradors, she walked much more – over towards Greys Court (the house that Mrs Val had sold in pique when Celia had married Peter) or up round Joyce Grove. (After Peter's old dogs died, she bought a young brown labrador from William Douglas-Home's son; she called him Oscar because, she said, she had always wanted to have an Oscar.) She seldom went to the theatre, only occasionally to see a friend's performance or something that had been particularly recommended, although she came to love the ballet. The performances of Fonteyn and Nureyev that she had been lucky enough to see in the 1960s had given her as much pleasure as anything. She preferred television to the theatre and watched it avidly – usually sitting on the floor, very close to the set – not plays so much as series like 'Z Cars' or 'Softly Softly', 'Dad's Army' – straightforward well-made television. She worshipped Morecambe and Wise, thinking their timing superb. Many an afternoon she would watch the racing, though she was too cautious about money ever to venture more than the smallest bet. At night she listened to the insomniac's friend, the BBC World Service, accumulating odd snatches of information which she would impart at breakfast.

Like most people as they get older, she became very set in her ways and her views. Although she was never difficult, she was not exactly easy, and although she was really very game and not on the whole backward-looking, her children considered her stuck-in-the-mud. She would, for instance, claim that the recently introduced satsuma compared poorly with the old-fashioned tangerine, that they didn't have the same flavour; 'satsuma' therefore became a term within the family to indicate something which she criticised merely because it was new. She would start to complain about some change or innovation, most likely in a shop in Henley: 'Satsuma, satsuma' her children would cry. In the late 1960s and early 1970s when flower power and hippiedom produced all manner of fashion, if she passed someone in the street dressed in an unorthodox way, she would say, turning her head as they passed and fractionally too loud, 'What has he come as?' Her politics were straightforward Tory of a fairly unreflective though not dogmatic kind. For many years after the war she would not, if she could help it, buy anything German. She continued to smoke, but never before lunch. She was teased mercilessly – and she prevailed on Nichol, who didn't have the family commitments that Lucy or I had, to fetch and carry; he was endlessly patient and always funny.

In the autumn of 1974, she was inveigled briefly back into the West End in *The Dame of Sark*, another play by William Douglas-Home. This was based on the German occupation of the Channel Islands during the war, and the relationship between the German commandant and the Dame of Sark, the hereditary ruler of that island. There was not much comedy here, but a touching little piece of tragic history. The play was not in fact intended for the West End, but had been put on as part of the Oxford Festival at the Oxford Playhouse. It went so well there that the producers wanted to bring it into London. First they had to persuade Celia. She wrote to me, at that time living in America, after it opened in Oxford: 'It seemed to go quite well but I was exhausted – we'd had a long dress rehearsal in the middle of the day. The thought of doing it again tonight appals me. I can foresee pressure

to make me go to London with it, but I shall try to resist.'
She was unable to, as she wrote a week later:

Well, we seem to be a smash hit, with rave notices in the S. Times
from old barking H. Hobson and everyone is extremely pleased and
over excited and now, of course, talked me into going to London
with it. It really seemed too mean for them all not to, but I ought
to have remembered how that always gets one down. One can be
tough with management and things but not so easily with one's
fellow-actors.

So she agreed to do twelve weeks with just one matinée a
week.

Tony Britton, whom Celia didn't know before, played the
German commandant. After a little nervousness at the outset,
they soon realised that they both simply wanted to get on
with the job, and they got on well together. Celia liked Tony
very much, thought very highly of him professionally, and
found him cosy, kind and sympathetic. After the play finished
they carried on a bantering correspondence by post-card, and
Tony kindly helped her out with poetry readings at a festival
in Nettlebed church.

Having been persuaded to go to London (probably her liking
for Tony tipped the balance), she first had to have her wisdom
teeth out. They had made her feel not at all well and had
reduced her appetite from tiny to almost non-existent. A week
before opening at the Duke of York's she was operated on.

The play, when it opened in London, split the critics down
the generations. Those who could remember the war found
it very moving: B.A.Young – 'I have not often been so moved
as by Miss Johnson's Dame'; Milton Shulman – 'I found this
play a most credible and touching experience'; those who were
too young to remember the war found it risible, full of clichés
and wartime stereotypes. 'Frail but indomitable,' wrote one.
'Miss Celia Johnson exercises her familiar routine of fighting
back tears, thus making them flow the more copiously from
her adoring public.' Another considered her a sort of dinosaur,
saying the play was 'of interest if you want to see the last
stiff upper-lip and one of the last of our old pros – Celia
Johnson.'

The play did good business; though during the height of the IRA bombings in London that winter, it dropped off considerably. She wrote to me then:

The play is a bit less packed on account of the bombings. The Police keep issuing us with new orders. Go out at once. No, stay where you are. Do nothing. Report everything – and so on. I've been staying a couple of nights with Ginny [Virginia Thesiger] in Lap of L and trying to do some Christmas shopping ... I went to lunch with Patricia Hambleden and sat next to lovely David Cecil and the Sunday before ditto with the Glendevons next to equally lovely H. Macmillan so I am moving in classy intellectual circles. Otherwise little to report. I seem to spend my time on the M4 or on the stage.

(She was sad when the Glendevons decided to move from the neighbourhood later that year: 'A pity – they are really so kind and nice – and very good friends.')

Later Celia and Tony Britton played *The Dame of Sark*, directed by Alvin Rakoff, very successfully on television for Anglia; indeed, it got the highest ratings for independent television for the week it was on, beating all manner of popular shows. 'I say,' she wrote to Tony, 'what about us being Top of the Pops.'

29

Fifty years on the stage

On 1 January 1975, while still in *The Dame of Sark*, she wrote to me about how Christmas had been at Merrimoles:

Here it was a question of trying to control the young – Robert [her elder grandson] is a menace of strength, ingenuity and volatility with a strongly developed exploring instinct ... and calm down the old: Paula was not in good form and very sort of fussed about everything and furious with Colin [Buist – their neighbour]. I think her back was hurting and Birdie [a friend of Paula's] kept taking me on one side and saying how difficult she was and I could see that. Meanwhile Colin was, naturally, talking about shooting to me, with Nichol and Lucy giggling behind his back.

We plough on in the theatre. Our business went down with a wallop before Xmas, owing I suppose to the bombings (it was the same with all the theatres) and since then we've gone up a bit, but it remains to be seen how we do during Jan. I leave, if we last that long, on the 15th Feb, and that will be quite enough. Today, to my surprise, is a Bank Holiday, and Nichol and Janet [Lyle] and Christopher [Balfour] and the Nelson girls are all riding over to Watlington and I (guess what) am about to Play Bridge. Nichol has written to you about the farm problems. I hope it works out. Richard [Fleming], as usual, has been marvellous. Lucy is busy with her telly series and, woe, woe, woe, Joe has lost his licence for 3 months for speeding ... After not having written for ages this could hardly be a more boring letter, but there have been a lot of interruptions including one from Roy Plomley. I'm doing 'Desert Island Discs' and find to my consternation it's almost at once and, of course, I've done nothing about it. Oh dear. What shall I take as a luxury?

She took, on this occasion, a Rolls-Royce. 'I could drive it along the beach while there was some petrol in it. I could use its headlights until the battery ran out. And after that I could live in it.' An edition of Trollope was her chosen book for the island. It was, in fact, the third time that she had been Roy Plomley's castaway on 'Desert Island Discs', that radio programme of enduring popularity. The first time

had been in 1945, the second in 1954, and the last 1975. On
the first occasion she had chosen Elgar (the *Cockaigne* overture), Coward, Yvonne Printemps, Joyce Grenfell, a song
called 'My Guy's Come Home' (no doubt appropriate for 1945)
and finished with Beethoven's *Pastoral* symphony. For her
second choice nine years later, she included a Bach cantata,
'My Resistance is Low' by Hoagy Carmichael, Handel's *Water
Music*, Offenbach's *La Belle Hélène* (as 'something really smell-
ing of the theatre'), Kathleen Ferrier singing 'What is life
to me without thee', a carol, Yvonne Printemps again, and
Mendelssohn's *Midsummer Night's Dream* overture. She took
a book on astronomy and a rose cutting. This last time her
choice was entirely classical – Bach, Haydn, Mozart, Prokofiev
(to remind her of the ballet), Beethoven, – but for one Coward
('I must have Noel because he was wonderful to me') and
one carol ('Oh, Come All Ye Faithful'). In none of the programmes did she give very much away about herself.

To younger people in the theatre or to people in television
who had not met her, she could seem rather intimidating.
Though she was not entirely aware of it, she had a formidable
reputation as a distinguished actress and, although friendly,
she was not effusive. They expected her to be rather grand,
which she wasn't, though she could sometimes ride roughshod
over people. When the television director, Alvin Rakoff, came
to direct her in a play for Anglia Television by William Trevor,
called *The Nicest Man in the World*, they started off very much
on 'Miss Johnson', 'Mr Rakoff' terms. Celia played the widow
of 'the nicest man', and one of her main scenes took place
in a cemetery at her husband's funeral. Shooting took place
in a large cemetery in South London during a very cold spell
in November; there was a biting wind and a penetrating damp-
ness – the most unpleasant of all British weather. There was
one take in which the vicar was to make a funeral oration
by the graveside, and while he is speaking Celia stops thinking
of the funeral and remembers her wedding; her expression
was to change accordingly. John Shaw, a former silent film
star, played the vicar. He was called from a little chapel some
way away where he was sheltering to come and do the scene.
But Celia interrupted and said: 'Don't call him, it's much

too cold for him, he's very old.' Alvin Rakoff said that they had to have him there to feed her the lines. Celia insisted they shouldn't get him, but that if Alvin were to stand in his place by the graveside, and simply say 'funeral, funeral, funeral', and then at the appropriate moment change to 'wedding, wedding, wedding', she could manage perfectly well. So they played it like that, and Celia performed brilliantly to the director as vicar. Alvin was on his knees afterwards and said: 'Please may I call you Celia?' 'Yes, Alvin.' It was to be a rewarding relationship which led on to the televising of *The Dame of Sark*, and later to Shakespeare, and might, had she lived, have brought her together with Olivier on television.

In 1977, the year of the Queen's Jubilee, she undertook one more play by William Douglas-Home, *The Kingfisher*. Following her husband's funeral – again – Evelyn (Celia) calls on an old flame, Cecil (Ralph Richardson), who had proposed to her many years ago. He suggests marriage again much to the annoyance of his devoted manservant (Alan Webb) who would like to keep Cecil to himself. The rekindling of an old romance at an advanced age and the jealousy of the old servant was an opportunity for Sir Ralph, Celia and Alan Webb to act to their heart's delight with the benefit of all their years of experience. Lindsay Anderson, the director, had looked forward to directing the three of them (he had recently directed Richardson and Gielgud most successfully in David Storey's play, *Home*), but this time found both Celia and Ralph pretty well impervious to suggestion. Sir Ralph had never been all that amenable, but even Celia now went her own way. Peering at them from behind the back of the stage at a preview, he muttered to Joe Davis, Binkie's old lighting man: 'They've got me licked.'

The play was lightweight – but a well-made vehicle for the three old pros. 'The play is so much a celebration of the actors, that what happens hardly seems to be the matter of the play,' said *The Times*. 'At curtain-fall, Home's evening of civilised banter leaves us pondering ... whether dreams can ever be brought to reality, whether love is one thing and marriage quite another . . . and whether we shall ever see these peerless artists in more rewarding roles,' said the *Telegraph*.

The Kingfisher had originally been intended for the National Theatre, but owing to a fuss about successful National productions transferring to the West End – a move thought probable for this play – it was put on instead at the Lyric. Half an hour before it was due to open there, the lights in the West End went out, and remained out for a couple of hours. The first-night audience, which included Nichol, Lucy and me, took to the local pubs. Lucy nipped round to Celia's dressing-room and found her very calm, playing patience. Sir Ralph was reading a book by candle-light. Lindsay Anderson was impressed by the steadiness of their nerves. The curtain finally rose at nine o'clock. Celia and Sir Ralph, and indeed Alan Webb, now represented a fast disappearing generation of actors and they were, in whatever vehicle, an enormous draw to a theatregoer of a certain age. The fans came. Celia was very fond of Sir Ralph, very much in awe of him; she enjoyed his eccentricities such as his turning up to rehearsals on his latest BMW motorcycle, his nodding head, his clever eye for an antique. He, like her, was quite shy, and when she invited him to lunch at Merrimoles she got into a terrible state of nerves about how the occasion would pass off.

In 1978, her seventieth year, on 19 March, the Gallery First-nighters (a long-established association of theatre fans) celebrated Celia's fifty years on the stage by giving a dinner in her honour at the Europa Hotel. She was, as usual, dismissive ('Isn't it silly; apparently I've been fifty years on the stage and they want to give me a dinner') but very flattered. Old friends and colleagues like Joyce Grenfell, Ralph Richardson and Richard Vernon attended, and the pudding was called Surprise Celia.

Hers had been the sort of career, schooled entirely in the theatre, that can no longer be. It had covered fifty years of great change, encompassed the war and passed through some of the most brilliant periods of British theatre. Celia's career had started – officially – in 1928 with the part of Sarah in *Major Barbara* at the Theatre Royal in Huddersfield. That was the year that the first sound film to be shown in Britain

– *The Jazz Singer* – arrived. Broadcasting was in its infancy; television still a dream. Fifty years later, six days before her celebratory dinner, she had recorded the BBC Television Shakespeare series. It had been an extraordinary half century to have been an actress.

As a child she had seen Fred Terry in *The Scarlet Pimpernel*; as a girl she had seen Sybil Thorndike play *St Joan*; as a student she had been watched by Shaw, and as a newly fledged actress in the West End, she had played with du Maurier and with Nigel Playfair, and that doyenne of Edwardian theatre, Marie Tempest, whose heyday had been at the turn of the century and who, as a child, had been taken by her mother to Downing Street to ask Mr Gladstone to persuade her to desist from the stage.

The West End, when Celia started out, was a plush and cosy world. An orchestra played music before the curtain went up and during the intervals. Rehearsals were short and you dressed formally for them. The 'first night' was genuinely the first night, so the production was often ragged. *The Wind and the Rain* which played for a week at the Opera House in Manchester in 1933 was one of the first plays to have a try-out outside London. After the war, a provincial tour before opening became the custom. Lighting in the old days was unsophisticated, technology non-existent. Actors stood in frozen poses for production photographs. The director – often the leading man – had less power. In an interview in 1981, Celia said: 'Nowadays there's such an over-reliance on the director that sometimes the actors get squished.'

Celia did her first work for radio in 1934, as Portia in *The Merchant of Venice* (for which she was paid 21 guineas). Radio had from the beginning an enormous audience (two million licensees in 1927). In 1932 transmissions began from Broadcasting House, where proper studios enabled radio acting to become more professional. Acting by voice alone is not easy, but Celia became very good at it. She did many broadcasts before the war, many readings during the war, and stories, more readings, poetry, quiz shows after the war. Radio broadcasting is the most ephemeral of all performances, but requires no less professionalism and concentration. Celia could read

most movingly and, especially during the war years, she did
so to great effect. However, her most cherished notice was
that for Juliet, which she played on radio at a tender age:
'Old Juliet spoils play.' She first acted on television in 1937
at the Alexandra Palace as Desdemona – a production indeed
that was a far cry from the BBC Shakespeare series of the
1970s and 1980s.

Indeed she played in many more classics on the radio and
on television than she ever did on the stage. Perhaps she should
have taken James Agate's advice in 1930 and gone out and
played every part she could ('Celia and Hero and Nerissa
and Sweet Lavender') and stretched her range. She didn't.
Before the war she moved with ease from one long-forgotten
lightweight play to another. Forgotten they may be, but most
of their authors were fashionable playwrights of the time –
John van Druten (talked of in the same terms as Coward),
Keith Winter (compared with Chekhov), Warren Chetham-
Strode. Her career was most typical of its time. She was fortunate in having an ability to make the very best of poor material,
to shine through rubbish; as Peter wrote to her in 1944: 'It's
rather nice the way you have only to appear, in however
fiddling a production, for everyone to say you stick out a mile
and are a lovely genius.' Indeed, she carried some plays that
didn't deserve their luck. Or was it the playwrights who were
fortunate? So often her talent was greater than the play, but
sometimes the play was greater than her talent (*St Joan*, argu-
ably, *The Cherry Orchard* and *The Three Sisters* surprisingly);
there were all too few occasions when there was a perfect
match between her qualities and the play – *Pride and Prejudice*,
The Master Builder and *Relatively Speaking* are possible
examples. She was always happier in modern dress. Her odd
large-featured gamine looks and slim figure were unsuited
to most costume (except for Rex Whistler's beautiful and flat-
tering dresses for *Pride and Prejudice*), and she did not like
dressing up; it wasn't part of the appeal of the theatre for
her.

The war brought those circumscribed, upper-class theatre
days to an end. Not that the theatre did not enjoy great popularity during the war, but it relied on old favourites to divert

and entertain. The playwrights of the thirties, with their light social touch, had had their day. Shaw and Wilde, tried and tested, were required, with the odd new apposite play, such as Rattigan's *Flare Path*, striking a chord. The courteous old gentlemanly actors were disappearing. Young actors were called up, and some never returned to the stage after the war. Apart from the brief period in *Rebecca* in 1940, Celia barely trod the boards (except on two occasions to stand in, once for Peggy Ashcroft and once for Vivien Leigh) for six years. She felt unable to commit herself to a run. It was really quite by chance that she began to act in films then, but again the films that she made during the war, written by Noel Coward, directed by David Lean (*In Which We Serve*, *This Happy Breed* and *Brief Encounter*), could not be more truly typical of those years. She was never ahead of her time, never behind the times (except in certain respects in old age, and who is not); she always seemed to be exactly with the times. It was quite unconscious, and it may account for why she had such a very loyal following among people of her generation.

After the war, after a brief and not wholly successful sortie into classical theatre – *St Joan*, *Twelfth Night*, *The Three Sisters* – she held herself back from the stage and made a few mediocre British films. Not until Jack Minster coaxed out her gift for comedy in *The Reluctant Débutante* did she really begin to find her feet again and, in particular, to relish comedy. But good comedy is hard to come by and it is exceedingly difficult to spot in a raw script. That was why she was so taken with Ayckbourn's *Relatively Speaking*; although she knew nothing of the author, his script had made her laugh out loud at her first reading.

It was in the late sixties that she really began to enjoy doing television, and for the last fifteen years of her life, she would do one or two plays a year, and as her face, never photogenic, became more and more lined, so she became more accomplished at it. 'I do enjoy this, you know,' she said in America in 1981, 'working for the telly. I think I like it because it's all rehearsal and then you do it and are done with it. Rehearsing,' she went on, 'is the great joy of acting, at least to me. Building a character, bringing it to life. It's like a painter.

He's interested in the painting, in doing it – not in the picture hanging in some gallery. That's the way I feel about acting.' This accorded with Joyce Grenfell's observation at RADA in 1927, that Celia was interested in acting, not in being an actress.

In 1955 (the time of *The Reluctant Débutante*) she gave a talk on 'Woman's Hour' about acting, which described her approach to that most mysterious and elusive art:

Acting is odd. Sometimes I think there is nothing to it, and I wonder why I get in such a frenzy over it; and then, at other times, I think it's so clever and wonderful and soul-stirring, that I can't imagine how I ever had the nerve to try it. After I've seen Sir Laurence Olivier play a great Shakespearian part, I think I have heard the tongues of angels. There is acting, and there is great acting – and there is the wide world between.

But this is about my sort of acting, and just about the bones of how it works in a practical sort of way.

It starts, I suppose, when I get sent a script of a play with a note from the management asking me whether I am free to play in it. Then I read it, and I believe one's first impression of the play is most important and revealing. The first reading is like the audience's first sight of the play. As it unfolds to me, so it will to them, and though the producer will probe and worry and fuss during rehearsals, the main impact of the play when it finally goes on will be as fresh to the audience as my first reading of it is to me.

So I look, first of all, for a play that holds me – one that I want to know the end of, one that has dramatic quality, quality of the theatre – suspense – a leading-on-ness, and about people in whom one is interested. Actors are always supposed to be bad play-readers, they tend to look at the play from the actor's point of view, and the danger is they get carried away as a whole. There is certainly some truth in this, and one has to try and see the thing completely, and not to be entranced by the prospect of going mad and biting the curtains in a spell-binding manner in the last scene, or dying in convulsions at the final curtain.

I like a play, if it is a comedy, to make me feel silly and ebullient, and slightly mad, like a semi-controlled goon. I like a tragedy to make me cry – really cry – though probably not at the bits that will make the audience cry.

I can usually tell what effect the play has had on me by my behaviour at tea with the children. I seem to read plays, very often, before they come home from school, and being an actress I have tea with them very much in the character of the play I've been reading. Staring into the middle distance with a brave smile on my face, with my thoughts far away, after a not very good drama; or giggling and tossing my head after a not very good comedy; and I have been known to try to gather the children to me with loving gestures, after a play with a maternal plot – only they, very reasonably, won't have it! People always send me plays about being a mother, and I can't think why. I'm a most inferior one, compared with the people I hear about on Woman's Hour, who are clearly the rock, stay, adviser and everything else to their children, whereas mine are usually that to me.

Well, anyway, when all that is over, and the die, so to speak, not to mention the play, is cast, the company assembles for the first rehearsal. I never start to learn anything before rehearsals, because one learns as one works out the moves, and a lot of things affect the development of the play as rehearsals go on. Personally I love rehearsing. It is a gloriously carefree time. With no audience to worry over, one can experiment and invent. I suppose it is the nearest moment to being creative, if one admits that acting is creative. In fact I should like to do almost nothing but rehearse, with just occasionally a performance in secret. I don't really like audiences – they frighten me. I never like to know that some person by name is in front. I prefer to think of them as THEM – a lot of faintly nebulous blobs who laugh, clap, cough or just sit, but who are not actually persons in hats, coats and gloves.

I never think there's anyone *real* there watching, just as I don't think, really, that there's anyone listening to me now.

But that's just me. And as a matter of fact I was trying to make up my mind about what I think is important in acting. I believe the most vital thing of all is to make an audience listen. I think that the basis of the whole art of the theatre is suspense, what's going to happen next, whether in its crudest form as in a thriller, or its highest when the beauty and unexpectedness and perfection of Shakespeare's words, a sudden single word – can make one determined not to miss the next one. And that is the actor's job, to have the audience completely aware.

Then I believe one should say each line as if it had just come into one's head, not so easy when you've said them a hundred times. To balance that I believe one should listen to the other actors with apparent complete unawareness of what they are going to say. Obvious I suppose but sometimes very important.

Then I think one must never cheat, never go outside the author's intentions, to prove oneself clever or funny or lyrical or anything else. One must play fair with the author and fulfil his conception of the part with one's own personality and only add to that within fair limits. Anything else can unbalance the play. I hate acting that shows. I don't like acting that says 'Look at me being clever at acting.' I like it to come out from inside, not put on top, if you see what I mean. But I don't really know anything about the theory of it all. I just try to play a part by doing what I think that person would do at that moment and adding a little spice or flavour or something that indeed people have in reality. They seldom do the expected thing, do they?

People are odd, and so, as I said before, is acting, and so it should be.

So what was the nature of her talent? According to Frith Banbury, whose career as actor and director began before hers, she had a gift such as is only given to a few in each generation. Other actors (Alec Guinness, Robert Eddison, Robert Harris) agree. She had her limitations, her voice in particular had no sonority, and was weak in the lower register; she was no mimic and she was never to be a heroic dramatic actress, but she had an elusive and all important ability to express emotion with truth and without sentimentality. Occasionally it would misfire, but seldom. Her timing was superb, her restraint admirable, and she would always bring an intelligent approach to a part. She was unsentimental. She did not show off. She could not tell a lie in her acting (nor was she very good at lying in ordinary life). She was proud of her professionalism and her ability to switch on and off was legendary. Many are the stories of her finishing a tragic scene, when not only the audience but hard-bitten stage hands as well were affected by her performance, and coming straight off, saying, 'I think 12 across must be rabbit', as she picked up *The Times* and her pen. During the making of *This Happy Breed*, David Lean got very ratty with Celia and John Mills one day, while they were preparing for a harrowing scene in which Ethel Gibbons (Celia) receives the news of the death of one of her children. The two were laughing so that tears

ran down their cheeks. David Lean told them to pull themselves together and called for their make-up to be repaired.
Then he said, 'Let's go – action!' To his amazement, within
moments he was crying at their performances.

When rehearsing for *The Deep Blue Sea*, there was a scene
when Celia had to open up more than she was accustomed
to; she did it very well, but when Frith, the director, suggested
doing it again, she said, 'I don't think we need, do you?' It
was if she had revealed too much.

Kenneth Barnes, the former principal of RADA, wrote in
his memoirs about the motivation for taking up acting:

Was it a personal urge for dramatic self-expression – or a wish
to become like someone seen and admired on the stage – or a vain
search for admiration through publicity? It may partake superficially
of all these, but the dominant motive – whether deep and self-giving
or trivial and self-centred – will be seen in the eyes.

He also said that the twin elements of memory and imagination
were vital and that absolute concentration in acting was imper-
ative. 'Eyes,' he wrote, 'are the keypoint of facial expression.'
Celia acted through voice, movement and gesture but above
all through her eyes, those hazel-green, very short-sighted
eyes. The lenses of her glasses were so strong towards the
end of her life to enable her to see any distance at all that
she couldn't see things close to, and so in order to do the
crossword or to sew, she had to push her glasses up on top
of her head to see the clues or the stitches. She would kneel
on the floor, newspaper or canvas two inches from her nose,
glasses on her head, packet of cigarettes nearby. It was one
of the few times in ordinary life that you saw her eyes. Friends
suggested that she try contact lenses, but she wasn't interested.
Her eyes were so expressive that perhaps she found it easier
in ordinary life to conceal them behind those unflattering
glasses.

The tragedy was that in spite of fifty years of largely rave
notices – critics always appreciated her – not until the very
end did she gain true confidence. She never lost her nervousness before a performance. Tristram Powell, who directed
her in television, was surprised when, on having to be propped

up in bed for one scene, she was found to be quivering. 'It never gets any better,' she said. In what must have been about her fifty-second year in the theatre, she suddenly said to me one day: 'You know, I really think I can do it now.' To Nichol, too, on another occasion at about the same time after a couple of glasses of sherry, she said, 'I think I've at last got the hang of it.' Critics, actors, directors, producers, stage managers, playwrights had all always known that she could do it, but it had taken her that long to stop putting herself down. There was always an iota of false modesty about her, but only an iota.

She once said in an interview with the *Radio Times*, when asked about her career:

Well I've always been very lucky. I started from RADA – I think I won a prize there. But all the same I couldn't get a job to start with – like most young actresses. And then I got what was a very big role for a young hopeful in a play called *Debonair* ... And I went on from there. I think luck plays a great part, and you've got to have a little talent as well. The luck's the most important thing, but it's no good having luck without talent.

Olivier said much the same in his *Confessions of an Actor*: the qualities which helped make an actor a successful actor were: 'Talent: this must develop into skill; luck: ... you must see that it has provided you with the right opportunities at the right times.' He added a third: 'Stamina: a gift seemingly not affected by disease, unless worn down by constant draughts.'

In Celia's fifty-third year on the stage, in an interview she gave during a visit to Los Angeles, she was asked whether she had any regrets: 'I do wish I'd done more Shakespeare, which always gives me my greatest satisfaction.' Anything else? 'Well,' she said, 'I'd have liked to have leant against walls in thrillers.'

30

Family tragedy

Although Celia had always said that she had wished that she had done more Shakespeare, she was nevertheless rather staggered when Alvin Rakoff came to her and said: 'Can I consider you for the nurse in *Romeo and Juliet*?' She asked for time to think about it, and walked through the woods around Merrimoles going over the lines. She agreed to do it, but felt that it was so much outside her range that she insisted on a get-out clause if either side was unhappy after a week or so. Of course the clause was never put into effect, and so, fifty years into her career, she returned to Shakespeare.

This production was the second in the ambitious BBC Shakespeare series (though the first to be shown). The plan was to televise every Shakespeare play for posterity ('The First Folio of Television', as the American sponsors called it). The producer of the first ones was Cedric Messina, and the producer of the later ones was Jonathan Miller. The plays were in the end a mixed bag with few outstanding.

Celia, once settled, threw herself into *Romeo and Juliet* and loved it. It had been adventurous casting, and some thought it worked; others did not. The memory of Edith Evans, in an indelible performance, was still strong. Celia's nurse was not a round earthy comforter, more a humorous, spirited peasant, with arms flapping; she developed an effective rolling broad-legged walk. Her accent was less happy – a mixture of Cornish, South Oxfordshire and Yorkshire – but in spite of it she nevertheless wrested the feeling out of the part and brought it forth. It was a bold performance which could have slipped up; some thought it quite wrong. But she made the part her own – and did we catch glimpses of dear Nanny, observed at close quarters over so many years, in her interpretation? Patrick Ryecart played Romeo and Rebecca Saire, who was fourteen, Juliet, and as usual Celia took an interest in the younger players.

In the same Shakespeare series she played the Countess
of Roussillon in *All's Well That Ends Well*, directed by Elijah
Moshinsky, normally a director of opera. It was beautifully
designed, like a Vermeer painting, and most effectively lit,
and was one of the more successful of the whole canon. Celia
and Michael Hordern were given a joint award for their performances. Celia was very glad to have played both those
parts, and when representatives of the BBC and some actors
went to America to promote the series, she was persuaded,
by dint of an offer to travel by Concorde about which she
was wildly excited, to accompany the group. They met Rosa-
lynn Carter in the White House and attended a number of
gruelling formal dinners.

A suggestion came in 1979 that she should join Trevor Howard in a television adaptation of *Staying On*, the novel by
Paul Scott about an elderly couple, the Smalleys, who 'stay
on' in India after Independence, in straitened circumstances,
their lives a compromise between the old raj and modern
India. Both she and Trevor Howard were tempted: Tusker
and Lucy Smalley were marvellous parts, and the bringing
together of the two of them thirty-five years after *Brief
Encounter* was an attractive idea. It was a Granada production.
Celia made her plans. Then Independent Television went
on strike and the whole plan had to be postponed.

In September 1979, a fourth grandchild, my second
daughter, Rose, was born, and that winter a small dinner party
was held at Merrimoles for what was thought, probably erroneously, to be Paula's eightieth birthday. Celia also attended
Joyce and Reggie Grenfell's golden wedding; at their request
she had written a poem for the occasion, which her niece
Emma Johnson had written out in elegant script. She had
been saddened to see how ill her old friend Joyce was (she
died a few days later at the end of November). Then, not
long before Christmas, she was invited by other old friends
the Glendevons (the former Lord and Lady John Hope, who
had lived for many years in Rotherfield Greys a few miles
from Nettlebed) to a small dinner party in London which
the Queen Mother was to attend. While Celia was standing
chatting before dinner with a drink in her hand, she suddenly

felt something go snap within her and instantly felt quite awful. She went and lay down in a bedroom, felt no better, so excusing herself called a car to take her back to Virginia Thesiger's flat where she was staying the night. On the way she told the driver to take her to a hospital and notify Virginia. So she found herself in the casualty ward at the Westminster Hospital and was extremely ill for about ten days. Perhaps it had been a stroke; no one would commit themselves to a diagnosis. Although she was very weak and rather alarmed, the doctors sent her home for Christmas, whereupon on arriving at Merrimoles, much to everyone's surprise and delight, she recovered with extraordinary speed.

Meanwhile, it looked as if *Staying On* was able to go ahead after all. The plan was to film it in India, in Simla. But in view of Celia's strange and violent illness there was much discussion, particularly in the family, about whether she should go or not. Celia, however, knew a good part when she saw one, and nothing or nobody was going to stop her going. Her main concerns were that all her scenes should be lumped together, so that she need not be there too long and could get back to see her grandchildren, and that she would be able to get the World Service on the radio. She suggested to Amaryllis that she accompany her and Amaryllis would have liked to but couldn't because of her concert commitments. Off Celia went in March 1980 and settled into the Woodville Palace, a stone-built house with pre-war furnishings, just outside Simla; there she enjoyed the clear hill air, the glorious views to the snow-topped Himalayas, and was fascinated by the whole thing.

Staying On had won the Booker Prize in 1977. It took up the story of the Smalleys who had figured in a very minor way in the now famous series of novels, 'The Raj Quartet'. This television production, of which Irene Shubik was the producer, was intended as a pilot for 'The Raj Quartet'; she also wanted to see whether it was possible to film for television on this scale entirely in India; it had never been done before. They were an odd lot – a large Granada crew from the North of England, Celia and Trevor Howard, and the Indian actors,

Saeed Jaffrey, Zia Mohyeddin and Pearl Padamsee, Irene Shubik, the director Silvio Narizzano, and others, in an Indian
hilltop town, a former British hill station. Given the age of
Celia and Trevor and the camera-man Wolfgang Sushitzky,
who was older than both of them, it was agreed that a doctor
should accompany the group. In the event, apart from a couple
of mishaps to Celia, they were the only three who never had
need of his services.

Celia abhorred the union practices of the Granada technicians whereby, when they were filming up a mountain, and
delicious food was provided for a meal, the union complained
that there was not the choice to which they were entitled;
whereby Kashmiri market workers were hired for a pittance
to move the heavy lights while the well-paid British, whose
job it was, stood by; whereby, on arrival, extra money was
demanded for oxygen deficiency. The juxtaposition of their
quibbles and demands to the startling poverty which is always
evident in India was striking. Some of the crew, indeed, had
to be flown home because they were unable to withstand the
cultural impact of India.

Celia's first mishap was in the bathroom at the Woodville
Palace; she slipped and banged her cheek on a soap holder.
It was not a serious injury, but in due course it gave rise
to a black eye, which obliged the camera-man to photograph
her from one side only. Next, she short-sightedly tripped over
a little chain and cut her shin, which bled copiously. Uncharacteristically, she fell out with the director, Silvio Narizzano.
They all did. 'We work quite hard,' she wrote on a postcard
to Tony Britton, 'amidst a good deal of disharmony which
doesn't assist one's dwindling dramatic powers.' In the peaceful moments between working and the rows, she played
billiards and badminton, she read in the garden which was
filled with honeysuckle and wisteria, and she sometimes got
a game of bridge together with Zia Mohyeddin, who played
Ibrahim, the Smalleys' servant. With Trevor, she had a good
professional relationship, but no more than that. She always
liked him, but he was never a friend. She thought well of
his work and in the fragmented journal that she kept of the
trip, she wrote several times after a day's work: 'Trevor v.

good'. When asked later about their working together again after so long, Celia said opaquely: 'You pick up where you left off; it's a family thing.' In her journal she noted: 'No difference in filming now than 35 years ago except size of camera and easier sound.' She returned home after six weeks, much set up though a little tired. The eager traveller and the practised performer for once had come together. *Staying On* was scheduled to be shown that Christmas, of 1980.

Lucy, having lived in Herefordshire for some years, had returned to live in a house at Nettlebed. Celia was glad to have her and the three children, Flora, Robert and Diggory, nearby, but was concerned for them. Joe, Lucy's husband, was living part of the time on a boat which he kept on the Thames in London, and had taken up Buddhism. Two of the children, Flora and Diggory, spent the weekend of 13 December with their father on the boat. On the Sunday evening, a wild night, Flora, Joe and a friend of Joe's made to go ashore in the little dinghy attached to the boat. As a fourth person climbed down from the boat to get into the dinghy, it tipped up and Joe, Flora and the friend were thrown into the river. Joe yelled to Flora to hang on to the boat, but the rough winds and strong tide of the Thames meant that none of them had a hope. Those aboard took a little while to realise what had happened, and by the time the river police were alerted and searched the water, there was no sign of any of them.

It was a tragedy of the first order. It was a crushing blow for Lucy. It deeply affected Angie (Joe's mother) and his brother and sisters – and Celia. Flora, who was eight, had been a special child – fearless like Peter and Lucy, funny and talented and full of charm. The family, ashen faced, spent Christmas at Merrimoles, the rest of the grandchildren providing a point and a diversion.

On 28 December *Staying On* was shown on television – another diversion. It was well received and Celia was commended in particular for the nostalgic dance she does alone in their bungalow to the tune of 'I like coffee, I like tea'.

A month or so later a service of thanksgiving for Joe and Flora was held in Chelsea Old Church by the river (the site of the church where Peter and Celia had been married) and Celia read one of her poems, which began:

> Flora and Robert and Diggory
> Went for a walk in a wood.

For this occasion, she later admitted, she had had to call on all her professionalism to be able to go through with it.

31

Death of a Dame

A bleak winter followed. Lucy, together with Simon Williams (whom she later married), worked for Derek Nimmo's world touring company, travelling to many countries. The two boys stayed with Valerie Brett at Watlington and then went out to join Lucy in Hong Kong for the Easter holidays. Celia left for America for a second television promotional tour. After her duties were finished she went on to Los Angeles, and particularly enjoyed going to the races. There she received the following letter, forwarded by Nichol:

The Prime Minister has asked me to inform you, in strict confidence, that she has it in mind on the occasion of the forthcoming list of Birthday Honours, to submit your name to The Queen with a recommendation that Her Majesty be graciously pleased to approve that you be appointed a Dame Commander of the Order of the British Empire.

She was the ninth theatrical Dame to be created since the war. It was well deserved, and some considered it overdue. That and the Royal Wedding in July of Prince Charles and Lady Diana Spencer which she thought simply marvellous (though the flagpole had long since collapsed) kept her going that summer.

She was very frail. Her eyes were so poor that she was beginning to be a danger on the roads in her Mini Metro. Of her own accord she had given up driving at night. It seemed clear that neither was she going to be able to live on her own at Merrimoles, in its isolated position, much longer, nor was there any prospect of shifting her. Most ingeniously, through Lucy's and Pam's efforts, Linda Vintcent was spirited into the house. Linda had been married to Pam's son, Charles Vintcent, and was now without a home. She could drive, she could cook, she also loved horses and could help with those that Lucy kept at Merrimoles, and she was generally extremely resourceful. When it was put as an idea to Celia, she refused to countenance it – but somehow, in the teeth of opposition, Linda was got into the house and, against the odds, the plan worked. Celia liked her and allowed her to drive her and do some cooking.

She was again nominated by BAFTA for best actress for her performance in *Staying On*. This time she accepted the invitation to the award ceremony. She believed in *Staying On* and had enjoyed it, and she thought that she was in with a chance. But she was pipped at the post by Peggy Ashcroft (for *Caught on a Train* and *Cream in my Coffee*). 'I thought that she was just the tiniest bit hammy,' Celia said under her breath, competitive to the last. It was the only such occasion that she was disappointed.

That summer, Alvin Rakoff was filming *Voyage Round My Father* by John Mortimer near Henley. He brought the company, which included Laurence Olivier, over to Merrimoles, and they all had a sunny, gossipy lunch. Plans were hatched then by Alvin to bring Olivier and Celia together on television and he began to look into a Jeffrey Archer play that he thought appropriate for them.

The investiture later that year at Buckingham Palace was a great occasion. Celia made a friend of a diplomat who was in the line next to her, and Lucy, Nichol, Johnny and I took her out to lunch at the Savoy, which we all enjoyed. So buoyed up was she by the honour that she gave a lunch party at Merrimoles to celebrate. She invited some neighbours, some old friends, some actors, some Flemings, some Johnsons and the Queen Mother. For the first time she was almost relaxed about it, and the occasion went rather well.

She was still in demand. She starred with Paul Scofield in the second part of a television adaptation of Graham Greene's *The Potting Shed*, the first part having been made two years earlier before the production was brought to a halt by the technicians' strike. Anna Massey who was also in it thought that this time Celia had some difficulty with her lines, and that this upset her. She played Mrs Gladstone in an indifferent play in a series about prime ministers. With Robert Hardy, she recorded a commentary for a history of the Thames depicted by an imaginative pageant on the river – a sort of *son et lumière sur l'eau*. She thought it most effective and liked the fact that it was local.

Also locally, in the Kenton Theatre in Henley, early in 1982, she recorded 'With Great Pleasure' for BBC radio. This was an anthology of prose and poetry of her own choosing. She had always loved poetry; some poems gave her 'a sort of inward delight and glow' she once wrote. She kept common-place books of her favourite poems and odd bits of prose, and she sometimes gave poetry readings when invited to do so, so she had no difficulty in making her choice. She included Kipling, Betjeman, Fleur Adcock, Dylan Thomas, Ruth Pitter, Robert Graves, Walter de la Mare, James Elroy Flecker, a poem by herself, a bit of Peter's writing, something from Alan Moorehead, an extract from Jane Austen's letters and some anonymous little pieces. Some were read by her, some by Rosalind Shanks, and the rest by David Davis, an old broad-caster, whom she particularly requested remembering his clear, soft voice from 'Children's Hour'. The combination of their reading and her selection was very effective, and many who listened to the programme when it was broadcast in May 1982 were moved and entertained.

The publishers Andre Deutsch said they would publish the children's book that she had been writing after a little more work on it; she was terribly pleased. It had an old-fashioned E. Nesbit sort of flavour and a somewhat muddled conclusion. She had called it *The Lamppost Marauders* and had read it with success on the radio.

All the while, Sir Ralph Richardson and others were nagging her to accept a part in a play called *The Understanding* by Angela Huth. Celia liked the play but not enough to embark on something that might entail a West End run. However, persuaded in the end by Sir Ralph, who was very keen to do the play and was adamant that she should play the other main part, she agreed. Off she went to rehearse in early 1982 in a church hall near Paddington. Sir Ralph, aged seventy-nine, continued to arrive on his motorcycle. The play was about an old man and his long unspoken love for his sister-in-law. Its young designer, Jenny Tiramani, who had recently

designed a successful play called *Steaming* about a group of
women who meet in a Turkish bath, had no idea about English
gentility of a certain age. The clothes she produced – canary-
yellow polyester for Celia – were quite wrong. When Sir Ralph
saw Celia, Georgine Anderson and Margaretta Scott in them,
he said: 'Go and take those clothes off; you look like a bunch
of cooks on their day out.' Celia, after a fruitless shopping
expedition with the young designer, went to Henley and
bought what she wanted on her own. The director, too, was
a little out of his depth, so Celia and Ralph, as was their
wont, more or less directed themselves. Angela Huth, the
playwright, attended many of the rehearsals and remembers
Celia disdaining any textual analysis, and simply wanting to
get on with it. In slack moments, as had always been her
habit, she took the crossword out of her basket, or discussed
what vegetables she should buy for the weekend. Slowly the
play was cobbled together. It ran for two weeks in Richmond,
one in Brighton, and then had a week of previews in the
Strand Theatre in Shaftesbury Avenue. It was due to open
officially on Tuesday 27 April.

Celia had never performed before at the pretty Theatre
Royal on Richmond Green, although it was there that at the
age of six she had seen Fred Terry as *The Scarlet Pimpernel*.
In Brighton she stayed with Ben and Verena Hanbury. Verena,
daughter of the director, Anthony Kimmins, had been stage
manager on *The Grass is Greener* and had remained a friend.
The Hanburys and their children found Celia in exceptionally
good spirits; she played badminton, went to their son's school,
wanted to join in everything and sat up for hours. One night
she came back from the theatre, rather high, and said: 'Ralph
said he thought I was rather good.'

It was the April of the Falklands War – not a propitious
moment to open a play. The week of previews at the Strand
Theatre went quite well, though the theatre was too big for
this slight piece. But towards the end of the week she and
Sir Ralph received standing ovations. She let this drop in
the usual off-hand way: 'I didn't know they did that in the
theatre,' she said. She also admitted one evening when staying
the night in my house: 'I know this play is a mistake,' and

elaborated no further. I took it to mean that she knew that she hadn't the physical strength to do it. Her understudy, Eirene Beck, thought that she was under great strain, chiefly because Sir Ralph's acting was all over the place.

On the Friday night at the end of that week of previews, because she had a matinée the next day, she again stayed with us in London. In the morning we went to visit Paula, now living at The Priory, a nursing home in Roehampton, her mind gone. Beside Paula, who looked beautiful even in dementia, Celia looked very young, almost girlish. Then she went off to do the matinée. After the evening performance, Stan Nowak and Brenda his wife, who at Celia's suggestion had accompanied him this time, drove her back to Merrimoles. She was very talkative, and when they dropped her off at the house, she turned and waved goodbye.

The next day, Sunday, her day off, she had arranged a game of bridge and that afternoon she settled down in the Casino with her neighbours, Nancy van Duzer, Audrey Armitage and Philip Mitford. Celia played with Nancy and Philip Mitford was on her left. Celia was playing the hand and had reached a stage where it was a matter of her finessing the Queen of Diamonds, which Philip Mitford held. 'Now, just wait a minute . . .' she said – and moments later she slumped unconscious in her chair. It took the others a little time to notice what had happened.

The doctor was called, declared that she had had a stroke, described her as 'very poorly' and said that there was nothing to be done. Lucy was nearby; she came and managed to get Celia to bed and summoned Nichol and me. Two hours later, lying peacefully in her own bed, Celia died.

We all – Nichol, Lucy, Simon, Johnny and I – sat round the kitchen table for a while, numb, before making the necessary telephone calls. For once the show could not go on. (It did later with Joan Greenwood playing Celia's part, but the heart had gone out of it.) Like Peter, Celia had died doing what she liked best – playing a good game of bridge, at home at Merrimoles, after a week of undoubted triumph in the theatre.

The obituaries were generous. Jean Rook wrote in the *Daily Express*: 'We can get back the Falklands. We can never replace Celia Johnson.' She went on to compare her to a cucumber sandwich and a home-knitted jumper. That was her image; but, as we have seen, any form of preparation of food unnerved her, and her knitting was littered with dropped stitches. She would have been amused. The *Telegraph* wrote a leader: 'Quite simply, she was an exquisite actress with the sort of skill possessed only by the greatest of her craft – that of making a part her own so that it was never possible to see the role played by anyone else without thinking of her. Why should this have been?'

That was the enigma. From where did her dramatic imagination come? What was the mainspring of her talent? Her childhood was happy and unexceptional; even before she had left her sheltered home, her ability had shown itself. No wild experiences had informed her performances; no domestic instability or suffering had made her want to escape into other roles. It was all very ordinary. Later on, she was content with a small and constant group of friends, a local life and a single – if at times difficult – marriage. It was not the stuff of inspiration. Although she observed all around her, she was not over-curious about people and seldom pried. In dealing with others in life she showed no particular intuition into human behaviour. And yet, in a part, she could call on a deep core of human truth.

Agile on stage, clumsy off; calm and self-confident when working, flustered and doubtful about things the rest of the time; a courageous actress – for leading roles require far more courage than is evident – but a faint-hearted hostess; there were many contradictions in Celia. Beneath it all there was an underlying single-mindedness: she was passionate about the theatre. She had a gift (that 'curious distinction', as Noel Coward had called it) and she enjoyed it. At the end of the day she managed, with considerable success and in an age when it was not easy, to be an extraordinary actress, a steadfast wife and an endearing mother – to combine all three was an accomplishment.

Chronologies

1930 (cont'd)	Loveday Trevelyan in *Debonair* by G.B.Stern and F.Vosper, at the Lyric.
	Doris Lea in *Cynara* by H.M.Harwood and R.Gore-Browne, at the Playhouse.
1931	Elizabeth in *The Circle* by W.Somerset Maugham, at the Vaudeville.
	Grezia in *Death Takes a Holiday* by Walter Ferris, at the Savoy.
	Phyl in *After All* by John van Druten, at the Criterion.
	Ophelia in *Hamlet*, at the Walnut Street Theatre, Philadelphia *and* the Broadhurst, New York.
1932	Judy in *Punchinello* by John Hastings Turner, at the Globe.
	Elsa in *The Man I Killed* by Maurice Rostand, at the Apollo.
	Leone Merrick in *The Vinegar Tree* by Paul Osborn, at the St James's.
	Anne Hargreaves in *As It Was in the Beginning* by Merton Hodge, at the Arts Theatre Club.
	The Hon. Cynthia Lynne in *Tomorrow Will Be Friday* by Phillip Leaver, at the Haymarket.
1933	Betty Findon in *Ten Minute Alibi* by Anthony Armstrong, at the Embassy *and* the Haymarket.
	Stella Hallam in *Another Language* by Rose Franken, at the Lyric.
	Sheila Gray in *Sometimes Even Now* by W.Chetham-Strode, at the Embassy.
	Janet Carr in *The Key* by R.Gore-Browne and J.L.Hardy, at the St Martin's.
1933–5	Anne Hargreaves in *The Wind and the Rain* by Merton Hodge, at the St Martin's, Queen's *and* the Savoy.

1936	Elizabeth Bennet in *Pride and Prejudice* by Jane Austen, adapted by Helen Jerome, at the St James's.
1937	Judith in *Old Music* by Keith Winter, at the St James's.
1939	Jacqueline Hochepot in *Sixth Floor* by Alfred Gehri, adapted by Rodney Ackland, at the St James's.
	Cecily Cardew in *The Importance of Being Earnest* by Oscar Wilde, in Glasgow.
1940	Mrs de Winter in *Rebecca* by Daphne du Maurier, at the Queen's.
1942	Jennifer Dubedat in *The Doctor's Dilemma* by G.B.Shaw, at the Haymarket.
1947	Joan in *St Joan*, by G.B.Shaw, at the New (Old Vic Company).
1950	Viola in *Twelfth Night*, in Italy (touring with the Old Vic Company).
1951	Olga in *The Three Sisters* by Anton Chekhov, at the Aldwych.
1952	Hester Collyer in *The Deep Blue Sea* by Terence Rattigan, at the Duchess.
1954	Laura Hammond in *It's Never Too Late* by Felicity Douglas, at the Westminster.
1955	Sheila Broadbent in *The Reluctant Débutante* by William Douglas-Home, at the Cambridge.
1957	Isobel Cherry in *Flowering Cherry* by Robert Bolt, at the Haymarket.
1958–9	Hilary in *The Grass is Greener* by Hugh and Margaret Williams, at the St Martin's.
1960	Directed one play in double bill, *Double Yolk*, by Hugh and Margaret Williams, at the St Martin's.
	Pamela Puffy-Picq in *Chin Chin* by François Billetdoux at Wyndham's.
1962–3	Clare Elliot in *The Tulip Tree* by N.C.Hunter, at the Haymarket.

1963	Helen Hampster in *Out of the Crocodile* by Giles Cooper, at the Phoenix.
1964	Mrs Solness in *The Master Builder* by Henrik Ibsen, at the Old Vic (National Theatre Company).
1965	Judith Bliss in *Hay Fever* by Noel Coward, at the Old Vic (National Theatre Company).
1966	Madame Ranevskaya in *The Cherry Orchard* by Anton Chekhov, at the Chichester Festival Theatre.
1967	Sheila in *Relatively Speaking* by Alan Ayckbourn, at the Duke of York's.
1968	Judith Bliss in *Hay Fever* by Noel Coward, in Canada, *and* at the Duke of York's.
1970	Gertrude in *Hamlet*, at the Nottingham Playhouse.
1971	Gertrude in *Hamlet*, at the Cambridge.
1972–3	Lady Boothroyd in *Lloyd George Knew My Father* by William Douglas-Home, at the Savoy.
1973–4	Sybil Hathaway in *The Dame of Sark* by William Douglas-Home, at the Oxford Playhouse *and* Wyndham's.
1977	Evelyn in *The Kingfisher* by William Douglas-Home, at the Lyric.
1982	Acton in *The Understanding* by Angela Huth, at the Richmond Theatre *and* the Theatre Royal, Brighton.

FILM PERFORMANCES

1941	*A Letter from Home*, dir. Carol Reed for Ministry of Information.
1942	Mrs Kinross in *In Which We Serve*, dir. Noel Coward and David Lean.
	ATS officer in *We Serve*, dir. Carol Reed (for training).

1943	Cynthia in *Dear Octopus* dir. Harold French.
	Ethel Gibbons in *This Happy Breed*, dir. David Lean.
1945	Laura Jesson in *Brief Encounter*, dir. David Lean.
1949	Mrs Faber in *The Astonished Heart*, dir. Terence Fisher and Anthony Darnborough.
1951	Matty in *I Believe in You*, dir. Michael Relph and Basil Dearden.
1952	Jenny Gregory in *The Holly and the Ivy*, dir. George More O'Ferrall.
1953	Maud St James in *The Captain's Paradise*, dir. Anthony Kimmins.
1956	Joanna in *A Kid for Two Farthings*, dir. Carol Reed.
1957	Miss Trant in *The Good Companions*, dir. J.Lee-Thompson.
1968	Miss Mackay in *The Prime of Miss Jean Brodie*, dir. Ronald Neame.
1980	Mrs Wheeler in *The Hostage Tower*, dir. Claudio Guzman.

PRINCIPAL TELEVISION
PERFORMANCES

1937	*Othello*, BBC
1956	*The Letter* by W.Somerset Maugham, BBC
1965	*Helen and Edward and Henry*, ATV
1966	*Bequest to the Nation* by Terence Rattigan, ATV
1967	*Ghosts* by Henrik Ibsen, BBC
1968	*Hay Fever* by Noel Coward, BBC
1969	*Relatively Speaking* by Alan Ayckbourn, BBC
	The Cellar and the Almond Tree by David Mercer, BBC

1969 (cont'd)	*The Marquise* by Noel Coward, BBC
1971	*The Cherry Orchard* by Anton Chekhov, BBC
1973	*Mrs Palfrey at the Claremont* by Elizabeth Taylor, BBC
1974	*The Love Affair* by William Trevor, Anglia
1975	*Lloyd George Knew My Father* by William Douglas-Home, ITV
	A House and its Head by Ivy Compton-Burnett, BBC
	Jane Austen, BBC
1976	*The Nicest Man in the World* by William Trevor, Anglia
	The Emperor's New Hat by Angela Huth, BBC
	The Dame of Sark by William Douglas-Home, Anglia
1978	*Romeo and Juliet*, BBC
	Matilda's England by William Trevor, BBC
1980	*Staying On* by Paul Scott, Granada
	All's Well That Ends Well, BBC
1982	*Number Ten* by Terence Feely, BBC

RADIO BROADCASTS INCLUDE:

1932	*A Hundred Years Old*
1934	*The Merchant of Venice*
1935	*Henry V*
1937	*Othello*
1938	*I Have Been Here Before*
1939	*She Stoops to Conquer*
1940	*Liebelei*
	Johnson over Jordan
	Hamlet
	Pride and Prejudice
1941	*Finished Symphony*
	Sun Moon and Stars

1941 (cont'd)	*The Story of Margaret Catchpole*
	RUR
	The Gentle Aspect
	The Silver Cord
1942	'Country Magazine'
	Fanny Burney
	Alfred Lord Tennyson
	'Poetry Programme'
1943	*War and Peace*
	The Wind and the Rain
	The Lover
1944	'Atlantic Spotlight'
	Sense and Sensibility
	Gray's 'Elegy'
	The Romantic Ruin
	The Prisoner of Zenda
	'How to Woo'
	Rupert of Hentzau
1945	'How to be Good at Music'
	'Desert Island Discs'
	'How to Make Friends'
	'How to Face Christmas'
1946	*The Way to the Stars*
1947	'How to Appreciate Shakespeare'
1948	*Troilus and Criseyde*
	Rebecca
	Hamlet
1949	*Romeo and Juliet*
	The Undefeated
1950	*The Lady from the Sea*
1953	'English Journey'
	Madonna and Child
1954	*We Beg to Differ*
	The Enchanted April
	'Desert Island Discs'
1956	*Candida*
	African Queen
1957	*The Tortoise and the Hare*
1959	*The Vet's Daughter*

1961	'My Guests the Animals'
1962	*Mrs Dalloway*
1966	*Ellen Terry's Memoirs*
1967	'Jackanory. *Babar*'
	'Jackanory. *Babushka*'
1969	'Noel Coward at 70'
1975	'Desert Island Discs'
1978	*Middlemarch*
1981	*Mrs Earle's Surrey Garden*
	The Lamppost Marauders
1982	'With Great Pleasure'

Index

NOTE: *Plays and films appear under title; books under authors' names*